VEGAS BREWS

Vegas Brews

Craft Beer and the Birth of a Local Scene

Michael Ian Borer

NEW YORK UNIVERSITY PRESS

New York

NEW YORK UNIVERSITY PRESS
New York
www.nyupress.org

ISBN: 978-1-4798-8525-1 (hardback)
ISBN: 978-1-4798-7961-8 (paperback)

For Library of Congress Cataloging-in-Publication data, please contact the Library of Congress.

New York University Press books are printed on acid-free paper, and their binding materials are chosen for strength and durability. We strive to use environmentally responsible suppliers and materials to the greatest extent possible in publishing our books.

Manufactured in the United States of America

10 9 8 7 6 5 4 3 2 1

Also available as an ebook

CONTENTS

Introduction

Brewing Local Culture

The line stretches a hundred deep along the sidewalk, with the stray meanderer drifting into the parking lot. July afternoons in Las Vegas are not ideal for standing on pavement and asphalt on the west-facing side of an industrial park. But this is no ordinary industrial park. It's the soon-to-be-anointed Artisan Booze District. And this is no ordinary day. It's the grand opening of Bad Beat Brewing.

Sweat gathers underneath and saturates the assorted hats emblazoned with logos of nationally recognized and well-regarded pioneering craft breweries like Stone, Russian River, and Bell's. Though their hats are from elsewhere, these people are locals, or at least they're transplanted locals, as is the norm in the notoriously transient Las Vegas. The license plates on the cars that parallel the line suggest as much. Regardless of how long these individuals have lived in Las Vegas, it is home now, and today is their first chance to sip beers at a new brewery's taproom in their relatively new city. Even for those born in Las Vegas, the city itself is still relatively young compared to others across the American urban landscape, a fact that leads to the types of growing pains and identity struggles that more established urban areas have learned to deal with, or at least recognize as issues to address one way or another.

Individuals shift their weight from one foot to the next, giddy with anticipation; they're here to experience and help birth the second new brewery in the valley in the last year. Most seem to know there are a few more breweries planning to open over the course of the remaining months of 2014, and more on the horizon. Las Vegas locals looking for a sense of community, a sense of local identity, or merely a broadening of aesthetic offerings are eager to tap into the rising desire and supposed promise of craft beer. The patiently waiting thirsty sun-battlers feel like they're taking part in something new and important, something that *feels* different from the typical and clichéd experiences routinely offered in Las Vegas.

Sure. They could just be impatient. Or maybe the sun is getting to them. But heat be damned, there's craft beer here. And it's craft beer *from* here.

Two stacks of empty kegs serve as a gateway to the entrance. A ribbon of dangling kings, queens, jacks, and jokers hangs between the keg towers. Former professional poker player and founding owner Nathan Hall steps forward, says a few words, and cuts the cards, literally.

The doors open.

One by one, each person heads into Bad Beat's tasting room. Two long oak tables, surrounded by stools, stand between them and the bar where taps flow with freshly kegged beer from the hidden brewhouse behind it. The walls are minimally decorated, making the wooden sign with the Bad Beat logo—a poker chip with crisscrossing cards, a seven and a two to represent the local 702 area code—that adorns the far wall pop out to greet the eager crowd as they line up for some of Bad Beat's first public pours.

The chalkboard behind the bar lists each beer by name, style, ABV (alcohol by volume), and IBUs (a gauge of beer's bitterness). The man and woman in front of me receive their beers and quickly sniff and then sip the liquid in their glasses. Their heads rise and they look at each other, nod approvingly, and make their way through the growing crowd. I order and then quench my thirst with their most unusual offering, Ace in the Hole, a pale ale brewed with basil. It's kind of like pizza in a glass without the cheese. Each beer sports pun-infused names that come with cartooned labels depicting poker terms and roused gamblers. Their wheat-based German hefeweizen is called Bluffing Isn't Weiss. Ante Up Amber shows a woman pointing her finger, demanding the drinker to get in the game or get out. A successful gambler hugging his day's winnings adorns the bottles and cans of Hoppy Times, a typically citrusy and floral West Coast IPA.

Bad Beat's brews can be sipped while sitting on a bean bag next to an old Nintendo system that is the only electronic gaming system in the brewery's taproom, unlike most drinking establishments in Las Vegas. There's no video poker here, just some classic Duck Hunt. And there aren't any playing cards either, just a stack of Cards Against Humanity open to anyone who wants to test their moral compass while sipping on a few locally crafted elixirs.

I met Nathan and his pal Mike Dominiak when they were serving their homebrews at a local beer festival less than a year earlier. In fact, that particular festival convinced me that the burgeoning craft beer scene in Las Vegas deserved a full book-length treatment to delve into its "interactional potential" for constructing and maintaining local urban culture.[1] From behind the booth that belongs to the local homebrewers club SNAFU (Southern Nevada Ale Fermentation Union), they poured beer into my tasting glass. More importantly, they poured out for me their plans about opening a brewery.

Though the beer I had at the festival was theirs and, for all intents and purposes, tasted "good," they hired Weston Barkley, a former award-winning homebrewer and shift brewer at relative local stalwart Joseph James Brewing, to guide Bad Beat's brews. Weston is a versatile brewer with the ability to brew across the style spectrum. According to Mike, Bad Beat's "director of imbibing operations," their goal was to "nail a few particular styles out of the gate and then experiment and put out some really fun and innovative stuff." He also recognized the challenge ahead of them of trying to appeal to a population with a relatively low craft beer IQ.

> We don't just want to be the place that people go because we're local, because we're convenient. We want people to come because we make good high-quality beer that is brewed here and appeals to local tastes.

> The more and more craft beer is available and makes it into the normal everyday lives of people in Las Vegas, the more and more people will accept craft beer.

Across cities, suburbs, and towns in the United States and elsewhere, both "local" and "craft" have garnered increased valorization and are often treated as synonymous. As Mike's comment implies, they are not the same despite the common misuse of the two terms by local beer drinkers and local tourism boards alike. As we will see throughout this book, the meanings given to these terms and what they are supposed to represent are not straightforward and, in turn, are subjects of much debate.

"Local" has become a buzzword across many spheres of social life and is almost universally accepted as good and valuable, while "craft"—as both a verb and noun—paradoxically denotes a process and an outcome. And, as sociologist Richard Sennett argues, craft is also an ethic that connects the head and the heart through mindful interactions with material culture.[2]

Honing in on the presumed virtues of both local and craft, Bad Beat was now open for business and its owner's biggest gamble was under way. The poker theme was a deliberate and calculated move, to be expected from a guy who moved to Las Vegas from Virginia to make it in the poker world.

"'Bad beat' is a poker term where you're the underdog and you go all in with your money and you end up on top with a hand that shouldn't have won," Nathan explains. "It describes us perfectly. We went all in with our money, we didn't have as much experience, but by the end of the hand, we'll come out on top."

Labeling themselves as underdogs is common among craft beer brewers fighting a two-front battle. They fight for acceptance from the growing ranks of craft beer enthusiasts, affectionately *and* pejoratively referred to as beer geeks, nerds, and snobs. And they fight for shelf space, tap handles, and market share against the Big Beer giants,

FIGURE I.1. The Bad Beat crew celebrates after a long opening day. (Photo courtesy of Amber Barkley)

namely Anheuser-Busch InBev (Budweiser) and MillerCoors. Though their market share has slightly receded a bit more each of the past few years, Big Beer still dominates, accounting for about 90 percent of all beer sales.[3] Big Beer continues to have the necessary resources to buy craft breweries and put them under their own umbrella, morphing their offerings from "craft" to "crafty." Big Beer is also able to give bars, restaurants, and stores promotional materials like shirts, glasses, or coasters, to keep their beverages on tap or on the shelf. And they can also offer them extra money or build them new draft systems. Though that type of behavior—known as "pay to play"—in other cities can and has led to heavy fines and license revocation, it is commonplace in Las Vegas, a city where Big Beer has Big Contracts with Big Casinos.[4]

Playing with the dominant imagery of Las Vegas by using creative labeling and word play for their quality beers simultaneously provides

Bad Beat with an entry point into the flavor profiles of craft beer for locals and into local culture for visiting craft beer hunters. By adopting the images and terms of gambling, they pay homage to the industry that continues to support much of the Southern Nevada economy and continues to dominate many people's ideas about what happens in Las Vegas. In this way, Bad Beat is very much in line with craft breweries throughout the United States who seek to foster connections between people and the places where they live, work, and drink. The yearning for those types of connections is evident in the recent and continued success of craft breweries throughout the United States.

Yet Bad Beat's use of poker and gambling as a means for connection is risky. The move embraces a part of Las Vegas that is antithetical to the construction and maintenance of an organic local culture separate and distinct from the corporate-driven neon spectacle that most people outside of Las Vegas associate with the city. Perhaps Bad Beat's savvy appropriation of the city's dominant imagery is exactly the way to build a local culture in one of the world's most (in)famous tourist cities. Perhaps it's a way to tame the unruly narratives of the "desert of desire."[5]

Poker, like most table games, is about outmaneuvering and outfoxing the others around the table. While some games are about beating the house, poker is about beating one's opponents. Is this the message Bad Beat is sending to the other local breweries? Some people certainly think so. By most accounts, the local craft beer scene in Las Vegas and elsewhere is defined by collaboration rather than conflict. Tempers can run high, however, with the collective pressure put on craft-centric brewers to stand out and up against the city and its comfy relationship with Big Beer. Sometimes the closest of neighbors can become the fiercest of rivals.

For example, CraftHaus Brewery opened a few months after Bad Beat in the same office park. Yet there are squabbles over trivia nights and beer release parties, and one beer is suggestive of the ongoing tiff. Instead of a full lineup of varied beers, CraftHaus opened with a hop-forward IPA and a dry saison as their staples. In the spring of 2015, Bad

Beat produced a dry-hopped saison, naming it Frenemy. The label shows a clean-shaven man wearing a ball cap sitting across the table from a dark-bearded man; one held a dagger behind his back while the other hid a medieval mace behind his. It doesn't take too great of a stretch of the imagination to see these frenemies as Dave Forrest, the co-owner of CraftHaus and avid hat wearer, and Steve Brockman, CraftHaus's co–head brewer and bushy beard grower.[6]

The bickering between the breweries is mostly playful, though. Both have played important roles in the local scene, successfully making their beers available for sale at local liquor stores and convenience marts and on draft at an increasing amount of bars and restaurants. Their squabbles are minor compared to the larger conflict they're fighting against Big Beer and the Big City. Though this type of resistance isn't nearly as present in the craft scenes of New York or those throughout New England, or in other cities more open to the ethos espoused by craft producers and consumers, the Las Vegas beer scene is, at least in part, defined by resistance to a dominant and dominating Other.[7]

The Other in Las Vegas, paradoxically, is the dominant physical and symbolic force of the city. Though only four miles long, the Strip boasts a symbolic reach that stretches much farther. The Strip is pure synecdoche; for many tourists, commentators, and even some locals, it stands—incorrectly mind you—for the entirety of the city and the valley it's nestled within. Most large cities have a key feature or features like revered places and storied events that serve as "coded, shorthand expression[s]," write historian R. Richard Wohl and sociologist Anselm Strauss.[8] They serve "as masks . . . and impose the limitations which come from looking at a façade. They blot out what lies behind . . . in favor of the interpretation presented by the façade itself."[9] The embodied sensuous lived experience of urban life is much more dynamic and fluid than any one representation can encompass. There is, then, almost an inherent conflict between the way a city is represented and interpreted from *inside* the city versus from *outside* of it. Such a discrepancy has been documented through the rise of faux ethnic restaurants in the rapidly gentrifying Brooklyn borough of New York City, the tourism-fueled declaration of Chicago as the home of the blues, and the continued yet disputed reliance on public spectacles like Mardi Gras and the Jazz & Heritage Festival in post-Katrina New Orleans.[10]

This conflict—between how the city is perceived and how locals live in it—is a prominent feature of any "tourist city" aimed at producing "the extraordinary and unusual" for consumers away from home.[11] This is perhaps nowhere more evident and harmful than in and about Las Vegas, a city that started life as a tourist resort but transformed into a formidable metropolis.[12] Both belle of the ball and redheaded stepchild, Las Vegas has been revered as "the last honest place in America"[13] and reviled as "the grandest current enclave of non-reality."[14] Yes, the Strip might be the pinnacle of postmodern simulation or post-cinematic hyperreality.[15] But to assume that style trumps substance runs the risk of seeing the city as devoid of anything substantial.

Those who attended Bad Beat's grand opening and its subsequent releases and anniversary parties, as well as similar and related events at the other dozen or so local breweries, are doing something substantial. They move their bodies in and out of places to be with others who subscribe to a particular aesthetic disposition. Sociability is substantial unto itself, and becomes even more robust when it involves pushing against the dominant logic of a city that caters toward tourists rather than locals. Craft beer brewers and drinkers have a penchant for the new, the strange, and the "authentic" as part of a larger "interpretive community" loosely connected to other "locavore" and "do-it-yourself" initiatives that support creativity and an "ethos of craft" in opposition to mass production and "conspicuous consumption."[16] Such desires stand in opposition to the disenchanting homogenization that fuels the Strip and slithers its way out to the suburban strip malls in the form of Applebee's restaurants and so-called locals' casinos.

Made up of brewers, distributors, restauranteurs, bartenders, and consumers of varying intensities, the local craft beer scene has emerged in recent years as a catalyst for brewing something substantial in Las

Vegas. Or at least that's the idea. And that idea is intoxicating. Add beer to it, especially powerfully strong barrel-aged stouts and palate-wrecking IPAs, and it's easy to get drunk on the idea of cultural change and re-enchantment. By following the trends that have taken hold and fermented elsewhere, a practice not entirely inconsistent with the city's dominant logic, local Las Vegans have used craft beer to brew their own culture beneath and beyond the Strip's pervasive neon glow. *How* that change happens is what this book tries to tap, pop open, and let breathe.

This book is about Las Vegas, but even Las Vegas isn't *only* about what happens in Las Vegas. Nor is that true for any contemporary city, for that matter. Still, local identities, characters, and *social* actors are embedded in and emanate from local contexts through the complex and varied interactions of persons with each other and with the things around them. As anthropologist Clifford Geertz once quipped, "No one lives in the world in general," meaning that action and interaction within local contexts where people are embodied and emplaced are of the utmost importance for understanding the human condition.[17] The ways that local Las Vegas craft beer enthusiasts have consciously sought to build a local culture *for* themselves, though not solely *by* themselves, have broader implications for urban cultural practices, experiences, and forms of association.

This case study can teach us something about the dual forces of alienation and solidarity that affect the ways people practice local culture within specific urban contexts. We can learn something about scenes as the dominant social form of urban life, more so than archaic communities or minute subcultures. And we can learn how scenes are mechanisms for changing the taste and aesthetic demeanor of cities. To study urban culture is to study the existential and material crossroads of humanity. Cities are the wellspring of civilization. Their varied places and the varieties of experiences they foster, their diverse populations and the varieties of beliefs they hold dear, and their untethered paradox of prosperity and poverty make cities fascinating environs to explore. Many scholars are drawn to the continual challenge faced by both those who build them and those who live in them. As such, cities possess the firmest grasp on the contemporary human condition, and the struggle to further it, providing us with the widest stage to view social actors contending with and negotiating a social order continually threatened by difference, otherness, and the unanticipated.

A Craft *Coup de Taste*

Whether out of necessity or as a luxury, Americans have flocked to urban areas for new taste experiences. This is a historical trend with a recent uptick. Either as a response to the "smothering homogeneity of popular national culture"[18] or as a desire to connect mental and manual labor within a newly emerging "artisan economy,"[19] or likely some combination of both, new worlds of craft-based production and consumption have arisen as part and parcel of contemporary American urban cultures and environments.[20] As tastes were changing across the United States in the 2000s, outside of a few notable exceptions discussed later, Las Vegas mostly sat on the sidelines. After multiple iterations of both Downtown's Glitter Gulch and the world's most infamous four-mile street, the Strip, where pink flamingos have given way to white dolphins, the city's "tradition of invention" continued with a bit of lag time behind other urban epicenters.[21] As *the* "All-American City,"[22] Las Vegas is a consistently morphing amalgamation of current cultural trends. Yet it tends to follow rather than lead. Yes. The celebrity chefs came. The mixologists came. But craft beer, for the most part, wasn't a part of the city's evolving *tastescape* until its most recent national boom post-2010.[23]

With its first surge in the late 1990s and then again over a decade later, the social world of beer brewing and consumption increased in complexity as brewers challenged the traditional boundaries of styles and ingredients. All beers—from the lightest yellowy fizz of a light lager to the darkest brown sludge of an imperial stout—are brewed with some combination of water, fermentable sugars, hops, and yeast. The quality, variety, and amount of those ingredients lead to vast differences in style, taste, and appeal. Add to that the assortment of experimental ingredients that today's brewers are putting into their fermenting and fermented concoctions, from all sorts of herbs, flowers, and fruits to bizarre additions like dust from lunar meteorites and Rocky Mountain oysters, and it's easy to conclude that we are witnessing a veritable revolution in taste or tastelessness, depending upon, well, your taste.

Though revolution might be overstating what has happened and is happening in the world of beer, we are certainly in the midst of a craft beer *coup de taste*.[24] The past decade has seen a meteoric rise in craft beer brewing as both a home-based hobby and local business venture.[25] The turn toward craft beer signals a fundamental shift in both production and consumption away from the corporate control of popular culture. Though still presenting themselves in opposition to the macrobrewing Big Beer corporations, instead of fighting *against* the logic of late capitalism, craft brewers have worked *with* it in order to reorient the market. That is, they augment the market with more and, they hope, *better* products. This is a strategy that, according to communications scholar Christine Harold, recognizes "consuming publics" as having "agency and creative potential, rather than as an anemic body at the mercy of constrictive corporate forces."[26] Craft brewers and affiliates collectively believe that individuals' "creative potential" and their sense of taste can be awakened by providing publics with the "right" goods at the "right" price in the "right" place.

In 1996 there were about one thousand breweries in the United States. Two decades later, at the beginning of 2018, over six thousand breweries were in operation, with more planned for future openings.[27] Add to those numbers over one million American homebrewers and the widespread phenomenon takes on even grander social significance. Moreover, the (r)evolution of craft beer can be seen in hundreds of offshoot secondary markets. Craft beer drinkers can now easily find "proper glassware," books on food pairings, craft-beer-centric vacations, and, for bearded men, hop-infused oils to enable them to smell like the aromas of IPAs even when they're not drinking them. Parents who have read *Goodnight Moon* to their children before bedtime can read *Goodnight*

Brew to themselves. The book mimics the look of the children's classic but tells the tale of a brewery's workings and provides a fairly accurate depiction of the brewing process. And enthusiasts can cover their walls with posters and prints of their favorite beer labels or even hang up a wooden cutout of the United States with spaces for bottle caps to demark beers consumed from each state.

As Andy Warhol and others made clear decades ago, the boundary between art and craft is often ambiguous and spurious, and sometimes downright dubious. Yet the practices that produce them are often quite similar. In his seminal work on art and art worlds—the invisible support system that, when acknowledged, upends the enduring myth of the solitary artist—sociologist Howard Becker notes that "art" is an honorific title intended to separate certain products and practices from "mere craft."[28] In a culture that has been littered with mass- and machine-produced "schlock," "craft" itself has come to signify something "authentic," handmade, and artisanal. As such, distinctions and symbolic boundaries between art and craft are less important today than are those between "mass-produced" and craft.

According to sociologist Colin Campbell, combining the first dichotomy to create the second is more analytically and empirically accurate: "The artist craftsman (or craftswoman) is still set against a division of labor that involves the separation of design and manufacture—a dichotomy that carries with it the implied, if not explicit, contrast between inalienable, humane, authentic and creative work, on the one hand, and purely mechanical, unfulfilling and alienating labor, on the other."[29] Art and craft, then, serve similar purposes in a time and place where machine and machinelike production and labor are the overwhelming norm. In such times and places, "the artist craftsman (or craftswoman)" stands out not merely as a premodern romantic, but instead as a modern *bricoleur* cobbling together old and new practices for the sake of creation and re-creation.

The artist, artisan, or craftsmaker engages in a type of creative and *aesthetic entrepreneurship* that forges the new and the novel out of already existing cultural objects and ideas. Such objects and ideas can pay homage to the past or seek to destroy it. Some even embrace the paradox of honoring the past while ushering in the new. For example, New Belgium Brewing—a popular and successful craft brewery in Fort Collins, Colorado—is best known for its mass-distributed amber ale called Fat Tire, though craft beer aficionados tend to pass over it in favor of their more aggressively experimental Lips of Faith series. Of note, the name of the brewery is intentionally referential and reverential. New Belgium was the first American craft brewery to re-create and specialize in Belgian-style beers, mimicking seventeenth-century Trappist monks with their Abbey Ale. In the early 1990s, the American beer scene was unprepared for the arrival of this and other rich, malty ales, so much so that the Great American Beer Festival had to add another category—simply called Mixed, Specialty—to make room for them.[30]

New Belgium is not only a telling example of the creative reappropriation of place and the things that come along with it, but also one of the largest and most successful craft breweries in the United States. This was not always the case, however. In 2002, when New Belgium first began branching out beyond their safe home territory where their beer had "become wildly popular amongst Colorado's outdoor enthusiasts who flocked to the mountains to mountain bike, hike, Nordic-, downhill-, and backcountry-ski, road bike, mountain climb, kayak, and fly fish,"[31] they quickly discovered their "localness" didn't translate elsewhere, especially in the Pacific Northwest, where local craft beers were already readily available. And those breweries were already brewing sweet amber and brown ales that tasted similar to Fat Tire, New Belgium's flagship and iconic bottled brew, adorned with a single-speed bike resting on a path that wanders through lush green rolling hills interrupted only by a meandering river.

Despite their best efforts to market their wares beyond the Rocky Mountains, they kept hitting road bumps that flattened their proverbially metaphorical tires. New Belgium's owners Kim Jordan, a former social worker, and her then-husband Jeff Lebasch, who fell in love with Belgian beers during a bike tour of the country's famous monastic breweries, consulted marketers to advise them on how to proceed and succeed in these new markets. The brewery's owners were told that instead of "trying to convince drinkers that New Belgium had better beer," they needed to "develop a new ideology for craft beer."[32] After meeting with the owners and staff, they recognized a common strand that would potentially, and eventually did, resonate with middle-class dreamers who, unlike Jordan and Lebasch, haven't quit their day jobs but aspire to do so one day. And if leaving behind their cubicles couldn't be their reality, why not drink a beer that reminded them of those dreams? "Follow Your Folly, Ours is Beer" became a tagline that expanded the idea of craft from product to worldview.

They recognized that New Belgium could offer craft neophytes a gateway into the social world of craft beer, an invitation that promised a new way of being, a new way of tasting, a new way of finding one's own way. Yes. New Belgium's beer was good. But the lifestyle behind the beer was better, especially one that was filled with amateurs learning new skills in pastoral settings divorced from the ubiquitous hustle and bustle of urbanized modern living. According to "brand strategists" Douglas Holt and Douglas Cameron,

> We wanted to say "here's the kind of ideology we aspire to, we celebrate all who pursue the same kind of thing, and this is exactly the ideology that is at the heart of our brewery and the beer that you're drinking." Through lots of creative brainstorming, we came up with a call-to-arms declaration—"Follow Your Folly"—that was our part-serious part tongue-in-cheek response to Nike's "Just Do It" and other hypercompetitive taglines so common at the time. To this we added a hook to say that we are part of this movement as well, not the leaders but fellow travelers who share the same ideology: "Ours is Beer."[33]

A wider audience was more interested in what the beer expressed than in how it was different from similar products. In this way, the ethos of craft itself is the craft, or at least the symbolic anchor for a lifestyle that valorizes both the local and the crafted.

Though New Belgium's new marketing strategy purposely positioned them as "fellow travelers" on their own craft beer journeys, they have certainly been leaders at the forefront of the latest surge of the craft beer movement.[34] They had the fourth highest sales per volume of all US craft breweries in 2014, brewing almost a million barrels of beer, more than the other almost two hundred breweries in Colorado combined. Due to their size, which will continue to grow in their new second facility along the French Broad River in Asheville, North Carolina, their craft label has come under dispute. The introduction of their experimental Lips of Faith series—honed by Lauren Salazaar's learned attention to the brewery's over sixty French oak foeders that house, among other aged elixirs, their influential brown sour ale La Folie—could be interpreted as an indirect response to such criticism. In the competitive industry of beer in general and craft beer specifically, labels and the relative status they imbue matter, especially when courting an increasingly educated and finicky consumer base.

The definition of "craft" and whose products are labeled as such is a point of contention throughout the industry and the scene it rests within. We must acknowledge, though, that squabbles over definitions of beer itself date back at least to the *Reinheitsgebot*, the German Beer Purity Law of 1516 that allowed for nothing but hops, barley, water, and, later, yeast in drinkers' steins.

In 2005, the Brewers Association (which grew out of a merger between the Association of Brewers and the Brewers Association of America and set out to publicize "a passionate voice for craft brewers" and continues to function as a translocal gatekeeper) voted on and solidified the common definition of "craft beer" as a necessary framework for craft industry statistical reporting and trend measurement. New Belgium's Kim Jordan chaired the board—a "Who's Who of the last thirty years of American Beer"[35]—tasked with marking the boundaries of craft. The Brewers Association currently defines a craft brewery as *small*, *independent*, and *traditional*. Breweries that make up to six million barrels a year are considered "small."[36] "Independent" means that "less than 25 percent of the craft brewery is owned or controlled (or equivalent economic interest) by an alcoholic beverage industry member that is not itself a craft brewer." And "traditional" refers to the majority of a brewer's "total beverage alcohol volume in beers whose flavor derives from traditional or innovative brewing ingredients and their fermentation."

As craft beer was on the rise in 2012, the Brewers Association issued a statement to further clarify the aesthetic and proprietary dimensions of craft.[37] Accusing Big Beer of fooling the public, they set out to erect a boundary between "craft" and "crafty." The former fit their imposed definition while the latter pertained to "phantom crafts," beer brewed by Big Beer corporations that *looked* and sometimes even *tasted* like the real deal.

> Witnessing both the tremendous success and growth of craft brewers and the fact that many beer lovers are turning away from mass-produced light lagers, the large brewers have been seeking entry into the craft beer marketplace. Many started producing their own craft-imitating beers, while some purchased (or are attempting to purchase) large or full stakes in small and independent breweries. While this is certainly a nod to the innovation and ingenuity of today's small and independent brewers, it's important to remember that if a large brewer has a controlling share of a smaller producing brewery, the brewer is, by definition, not craft.

Appling the pejorative adjective "crafty" to Big Beer's masquerading products, the Brewers Association didn't hold back, naming names and pleading for an end to purposefully ambiguous and deceptive labeling:

> Many non-standard, non-light "crafty" beers found in the marketplace today are not labeled as products of large breweries. So when someone is drinking a Blue Moon Belgian Wheat Beer, they often believe that it's from a craft brewer, since there is no clear indication that it's made by SABMiller. The same goes for Shock Top, a brand that is 100 percent owned by Anheuser-Busch InBev, and several others that are owned by

> a multinational brewing and beverage company. The large, multinational brewers appear to be deliberately attempting to blur the lines between their crafty, craft-like beers and true craft beers from today's small and independent brewers. We call for transparency in brand ownership and for information to be clearly presented in a way that allows beer drinkers to make an informed choice about who brewed the beer they are drinking.

The distinction between "craft" and "crafty" is even more important today as Big Beer not only continues to produce its craft-like products but also, perhaps more importantly and insidiously, continues to buy formerly legitimate—at least under the Brewers Association's definition—craft breweries. To further distance themselves from Big Beer's crafty counterparts, the Brewers Association introduced an "Independent Beer" seal that approved breweries could put on their cans and bottles.[38] Though the seal helps add some necessary transparency to the beer market, "independence" is also a relative and not altogether straightforward term too.

The Tragedy of Culture and Its Discontents

What often gets lost in grand conversations about craft versus crafty and independent versus corporate, however, is that the local context of craft breweries affects their ability to brew what they want, serve to whom and how they want, and fully participate in the ethos of craft. How independent can breweries across the United States be if they're held at bay by antiquated laws that limit their brewing capacities (in Nevada, breweries with taprooms can produce only fifteen thousand barrels a year) or cap the ABV of their brews (in Utah, draft beer must be 4 percent or less)? After years of fighting the state legislature and Big Beer's lobbyists, Nevada governor Brian Sandoval on June 5, 2017, signed into law Assembly Bill 431, raising the cap to forty thousand barrels per calendar year. Though this was a move in the right direction for Nevada breweries, neighboring states such as Arizona have a huge cap of production at a quarter million barrels, and Washington, Oregon, Utah, and New Mexico impose no cap at all.

Not all places are open to the playful and creative tinkering common in craft beer and, in many ways, necessary for the construction and maintenance of a vibrant local scene. It is not surprising that Colorado, Vermont, and California, states with a critical mass of hippies, hipsters, and hobbyists, emerged as among the first of today's craft brewing meccas. These places are home to a critical mass of residents,[39] those who support the *local* production and consumption of a popular culture that is akin to folk culture rather than one that is mass-marketed, oppressive, or mind-numbing and dumbing.[40]

Popular culture works from the "top down" *and* from the "bottom up." Seminal sociologist Georg Simmel referred to this discrepancy as the "tragedy of culture," which is perhaps nowhere more evident than in and about Las Vegas. The tragedy, according to Simmel, stems from the fissure between creative production and passive consumption.[41] Revered and reviled as "Sin City," Las Vegas is better known for what it imports than for what it produces, including the entertainment it provides for forty million visitors who travel to the city each year.

Las Vegas is really good at top-down popular culture. Celine Dion. Britney Spears. All-you-can-eat buffets. Las Vegas is not so good at locally produced and supported popular culture. Part of this is due to the widespread mediated images of the city and the reputation it stimulates, propels, and reinforces. The neon-infused Strip—a four-mile stretch of concrete littered and glittered with hybrid amusement park–megaresort casinos—dominates public perceptions of the once sleepy, Wild West mining town. Images of the Strip abound in popular narratives from movies (e.g., *Ocean's 11*, *Viva Las Vegas*, *Rain Man*, *Casino*, *21*, *The Hangover*, *The Hangover III*), television shows (e.g., *Vega$*, *Las Vegas*, *CSI*, *The Real World*, *Pawn Stars*), and other pop culture media (e.g., Lil Wayne's "Lollipop," Katy Perry's "Waking Up in Vegas"). These narratives often support the city's dominant image of a place designed for adult entertainments within replicas of other places that span across both national boundaries and historical time periods.[42] An unsettling narrative emerges from the odd juxtaposition of pharaoh's Egypt, the Roman Empire, Caribbean pirates and their displaced sirens, New York City, Paris, Venice, Monte Carlo, the Emerald City, medieval castles, and grand temples to the patriarchs of capitalism (e.g., Donald Trump and Steve Wynn). The sprawling suburbs that stretch outward toward the mountains from the Strip are populated with Mediterranean-style houses on streets and in developments with names that are indicative of other regions and nondesert climates (e.g., Tuscany Village, Spanish Trails, and Providence).

Cobbled together as a menagerie of incongruent styles—styles that match neither each other nor the natural environment—Las Vegas is the cultural analogue to Big Beer. It's a *crafty* city. Or at least that's how it appears at first sight and from afar.

The often paradoxical irreverence for and valorization of the past that is practiced throughout the craft beer scene across the United States and elsewhere is also common in the way that Las Vegas is perceived and understood by visitors and locals alike. As such, opportunities emerge for redefining what the city is, what it was, and what it can become. This malleability of imagery and identity has positioned Las Vegas as a target for critics who see the city as *only* the corporate-driven Strip and, therefore, as a bastion of postmodern hyperreality and inauthenticity.[43] Obsessing about inauthenticity in Las Vegas is more of a common condition of the contemporary cultural critic than of the place in question. Las Vegas is not alone in its importing of styles and traditions from other cultures. Moreover, all cultures are manufactured and fabricated; Las Vegas is just more open about it than are most cities.[44]

Las Vegas provides a perfect setting or medium for "aesthetic entrepreneurs" to take the already existing elements and blend in new ones to foster an emerging local culture. And Las Vegas became even more of a template for reinvention after the Great Recession of 2008.

As the national and local economies plummeted, the Entertainment Capital of the World became the Foreclosure Capital. With too much attention given to the Strip and not enough focus on planning, a lack of oversight led to vast urban/suburban sprawl and overdevelopment during the boom years of the late 1990s and early 2000s.[45] While visitors can playfully visit the simulated ruins of Egypt at the Luxor, they can also see the "newly built ruins" that surround it. Many of the houses are empty even as new ones are being built while I write. Many of the houses are also home to people who can no longer leave Las Vegas as quickly and easily as they were once able to during better economic times when there were more buyers than sellers.

The silver lining of the Great Recession, however, is that locals began thinking about the contours and sustainability of their local urban culture. It is no coincidence, then, that the Las Vegas beer scene arose during a time of social crisis. And not just because drinking highly alcoholic beers can provide numbing relief. There is clearly a difference between craft beers and, say, craft pickles or cheese;[46] although these wares might appeal to people with similar aesthetic interests, the alcohol content of beer separates it as both a symbolic and literal *intoxicating* product. Its distinctiveness is evident in the laws—many of which are holdovers from the days of Prohibition—that govern the sale of alcohol in stricter ways than the aforementioned pickles and cheese. Responding to the growing interest in craft beer elsewhere and then in Las Vegas, legislators worked with brewery owners to write new codes to enable businesses to sell beer without providing food or gambling.

Bars throughout the Las Vegas Valley are dotted with video poker machines. They are reportedly great for increasing revenue, but they have kept local brewpubs from fully embracing a different cultural logic than the Strip, which remains tied to gaming and outdated laws that force independent breweries to sell their goods through licensed distributors rather than by themselves.[47] Such structural constraints are not only contradictory to the supposed libertarian, Wild West mentality of "Sin City" but also thwart locals' abilities to create businesses that can serve the public good both financially and culturally.

By trying to craft a local urban culture in a tourist city, those within the Las Vegas craft beer scene have used their collective imagination to initiate a Las Vegas *for* Las Vegas *by* Las Vegas. Through the products and practices they revere and hold dear, they actively make claims about *their* local culture. Both their products (craft beer) and their practices (brewing and drinking craft beer) are atypical, or at least atypical to common perceptions of Las Vegas. They go against the perceived norm about what "happens in Vegas." And by brewing, drinking, and talking about craft beer together, they make claims about, and lay claim to, a part of their city that is often overshadowed by bright lights and drunken fights.

The burgeoning craft beer scene in Las Vegas is made up of people who believe that the way of craft is the good life, or at least a means to at least taste it. The scene now supports about a dozen independent breweries (see Appendix A).[48] Despite making award-winning beers, no Las Vegas brewery has come close to garnering the recognition and accolades of its distant neighbor's top breweries, brewers, and brews. To understand why, we need to focus on both the context and the content of the scene.

Scenes and Significant Objects

Craft beer enthusiasts love to talk about what they're drinking, what they just drank, or want they want to drink. For them, craft beer is about more than what is in the glass. It's about the conversation about what's in that glass. Where did it come from? Who made it? What type of hops did they use? How did you get it? Are you getting any more? So many of the people I talked to about craft beer in Las Vegas and elsewhere told me how much they loved talking with other people about craft beer. Some even said that was the main reason why they got into and stayed into craft beer, "into" indicating a passion for or attachment to it. Though one person told me "beer speaks for itself. Beer does the talking," most people were more than willing, even giddy at times, to explain their passion. This made my job as a professional listener fairly easy. But being an ethnographer isn't just about listening; it's about feeling what others feel, walking in their shoes, or, in this case, drinking what they drink. As such, the whole body becomes a research instrument through what sociologist Ashley Mears calls "a process of bodily restructuration."[49] The goal is to immerse oneself / one's "self" in the ordinary acts of locals and then produce descriptions that reveal the "normalness" of people's culture without reducing its "particularity."[50]

While simultaneously recognizing both the promise of ethnography and its limits, I set out to describe and interpret the experiences that define and depend on a local scene joined together by a particular cultural object. When I began this project, I didn't know that craft beer was a thing that mattered. Did I drink craft beer beforehand? Yes, for many years. But I hadn't thought of it as something people might rally behind as a means for expressing themselves on both individual and, more importantly, collective levels. As an ethnographer interested in local culture living a city where the very notion of such a thing is a subject of debate, I started to see craft beer emerge as a form of "re-enchantment," as a response to the overrationalization that has diminished the wondrous possibilities of happenstance in favor of predictability and control. Re-enchantment provides purpose and meaning through collective action, effervescence, and even intoxication. We tend to think of intoxication as an individual feeling or reaction that may have consequences for other people, from the toilet puker to the drunk driver.[51] But the intoxication that comes from the shared intimacy of strong aesthetic experiences, and consequently the stories of them to be retold, lies at the foundation of the human condition.[52]

I've set out to tell those stories and have done so in a way that extends the "community found" as opposed to the "community lost" narrative that has dominated tales of American cities since scholars first started studying them.[53] Ironically, I suppose, I do so without using the term "community," and I do so for two reasons. First, it is a historically imprecise term that is a proxy for both small groups and global populations, with very little connective tissue between the two. Second, there are other ways and forms in which people congregate to combat the forces of alienation emanating from a world where people move fast and ideas move even faster. Moreover, it's not what I found. I found a scene, a scene composed of embodied individuals gathering in concert across various stages locally and beyond. As such, I follow and, in turn, provide support for sociologist Gary Alan Fine's call for a "sociology of the local" based on a "puny program" of cultural sociology where the local scene is a "stage" for interaction and "lens" to view such interactions for exploring the empirical connections between aesthetic choices, the performance of taste, and an interactive social order that paradoxically allows for both stability and change.[54]

While moving across and between stages and chatting with folks during festivals or beer release parties and throughout my interviews with brewers, distributors, bartenders, and drinkers, the term "scene" was used by many to demarcate the social phenomenon they were actively playing roles in. When local journalists began recognizing the emergence of craft-beer-related happenings, they used the term too, and they did so repeatedly as the scene started to ferment. The *Las Vegas Weekly*'s first "Beer Issue" came out in late October 2010. No use of "scene" is to be found throughout the various articles including lists of locally brewed favorites and the places to find them and other craft beers, as well as a profile of a local homebrewer identified as "an engineer by day and *a confessed beer geek* by night."[55] The need to include "confessed" indicates how rare beer geekery was in Las Vegas at the time, as if it were some veiled secret, like superpowers or pornography addiction, that can be reveled only under the cover of darkness.

Three years later, things had changed so much that the cover featured Tim Etter, local Tenaya Creek Brewery owner and then head brewer, standing in front of a large copper fermenter holding a pint of what looks to be their Hop Ride IPA, wearing a typical brewer's striped button-down short-sleeve Dickies shirt, knee-high rubber boots, and a "my beer is better than your beer" grin. You can open up the magazine to find an article that acknowledges the "steadily growing craft brewing *scene*," declaring that "2013 could be the year of beer in Southern Nevada."[56] Turn the page to find a "handy guide" to "Las Vegas' craft beer *scene*." Clearly, not only the scene but also the uses of the term to describe whatever it is have grown.

But what is a *scene*? What does the term mean? And why is it important?

Some scholars disagree with using vernacular, everyday terms used by participants and members, like "scene," because of the potential to create analytic confusion.[57] Yet others argue that the actual words that people use, their "situate vocabularies," can "provide us with valuable information about the ways in which members of a particular culture organize their perceptions of the world."[58] The language that people employ when describing what they do or what they are part of is just as important and instructive as what they do. That nobody I spoke with used more academically generated terms like "subculture" or "neo-tribe" tells me something about how *they* think of *their* social world. And that's the ethnographer's mandate: to describe and interpret the creative power, interactions, and meanings of a social collectivity.[59]

Perhaps "subculture" is too bounded, so people stay away from it out of fear of being labeled as only this or that type of person. And there are plenty of scholars who see the term as too rigid and inflexible to account for the in-group diversity of participants.[60] Perhaps "neo-tribe" is too hokey or even culturally insensitive due to the problems of projecting "premodern symbols on to putatively new phenomena."[61] But "scene" works well because it provides a way to identify a collection of diverse people, places, and things devoted to or at least connected to a similar aesthetic disposition without having to fully identify with it. It helps us define a fairly amorphous and shifting entity that is simultaneously inclusive and exclusive, where, for instance, craft beer—the brewing, serving, and drinking of it—sits squarely in the middle surrounded by the myriad of people who brew, serve, and drink it.

While the use of "scene" by participants gives us insight into their labeling processes, the rich yet scattered tradition of scholars who have used the term as their primary unit of analysis offers greater analytic precision to a phenomenon that is itself loose and flexible. Cultural studies scholar Will Straw writes that the concept of scene has been and can be used "to circumscribe highly local clusters of activity *and* to give unity to practices dispersed throughout the world. It functions to designate face-to-face sociability *and* as a lazy synonym for globalized virtual communities of taste."[62] I emphasized *and* twice to highlight that scenes are inclusive enough to allow for studies of meaning-making and communicative actions between people who are within the same proximity *and* those who are far away yet share similar affinities and affiliations. More to the point, following the lead of sociologists Andy Bennett and Richard Peterson, we can categorize scenes as *local*, *translocal*, and *virtual* to show the connections between multiple levels of sociability and geographic propinquity.[63] That is, practically all scenes today, even the most locally emplaced and distinctive small groups, are touched by the ideas and actions of those living, working, and playing elsewhere. Long gone are insulated small groups; even today's "idiocultures"—those small peer groups that have their own inside jokes, memories, and traditions[64]—are affected by the flow of people and ideas moving across diverse geographies by foot, car, or internet connection. As such, instead of treating the local, translocal, and virtual scenes as separate phenomena, I use Bennett and Peterson's distinctions in concert as a heuristic device to explore the various social levels and cultural contours of the Las Vegas craft beer scene.

The flow of people and ideas beyond local contexts does not, however, mean that all scenes are the same. Far from it. Mostly. Instead, scenes—like the Las Vegas craft beer scene—often emerge out of contemporary individuals' paradoxical dual desires for *both* eccentricity *and* solidarity. To be different and alike is the crux of (post)modern identity politics, especially in urban areas where the choices are plenty.

The combinations and assemblages of varied ideas and influences are endless and, in the best of circumstances, can lead to a staggering diversity of options rather than a uniform and stale homogenous similitude.

This, of course, is not always the case. A trip to *any* downtown of almost *any* American city will reveal the frighteningly similar whims and wants of the so-called "creative class" and the developers who promote and exploit them.[65] The coffee-shop-slash-art-gallery, the vintage clothing store next to the juice bar in a repurposed body shop, and craft beer. Yes. Craft beer is there too, for better and for worse.

The mottled particularities, the invisible threads that connect those near and far, and the nuances of localities that allow for imaginative appropriation and experimentation have demanded the attention of scholars of popular culture and urban life. Studies of music scenes have permeated the literature, opening up the social worlds and the experiences of rock 'n' roll, heavy metal, punk, electronic dance music, and hip-hop.[66] Others have ventured into the lifestyle scenes of artists and nerds.[67] Though the agenda for "scene thinking" has been strengthened and expanded in recent years,[68] the focus often tends to rest too narrowly on studies of youth or on studies of consumption as the primary or only means for playing a role in the scene.

Recognizing the important roles that scenes play in urban cultures for those across the spectrum of the life course and across the spectrum of both leisure interests and occupational duties, sociologists Daniel Aaron Silver and Terry Nichols Clark offer an analytical model consisting of fifteen dimensions to be used with a "combinatorial logic" when identifying and depicting specific scenes, especially in comparison with others and across cities.[69] Though they have produced significant findings about the presence of urban amenities dictated by scene participation, they do it from the purposely distanced perspective of the "quantitative flâneur."[70] My goals are more modest and more focused than theirs. That is, instead of "zooming out" for the sake of comparative analysis, I have "zoomed in" to a particular scene to uncover the lived experiences of those who make it happen though a range of practices and interactions.

Yet even among those who recognize the promise of scene's analytical prowess, many give only passing attention to sociologist John Irwin's neoclassic book unambiguously titled *Scenes.*[71] Influenced by but not beholden to sociologist Erving Goffman's dramaturgical viewpoint that sees the world as made of actors playing roles on stages in front of audiences,[72] Irwin's work stands as the first systematic theoretical and empirical attempt to outline the function of scenes as collective "activity systems" set to combat generalized feelings of alienation and disenchantment in urban areas. Writing in the late 1970s when "an unpopular war and the presidential scandals" deepened these feelings, not wholly unlike today's cultural landscape, Irwin applied the folk concept to actions, actors, and their respective stages, such as drinkers in bars, disco dancers, surfers, skiers, spiritualists, hippies, and post-hippie "bourgeois bohemians."[73] We can, of course, find these and many other scenes across today's cities, suburbs, and towns.

Irwin's key defining features of a scene, which I embellish to show their relevance for understanding not only what a scene is but also *how* a scene works, are threefold:[74]

1) *Scenes are expressive.* They are collective communicative devices used both for "direct gratification" and to promote an ethos, an idealized version of the world, a way of life, and so forth. As such, scenes are a social mechanism for making collective claims about "the nature of the good life."[75] Those claims come in the form of words, images, or actions.
2) *Scenes are voluntary.* Individuals can freely choose to participate and how much they participate. As such, scenes help put people in contact with the things they desire and find aesthetically pleasing. And they put those individuals in contact with other people who feel similarly and have similar tastes or are in the process of learning the specified techniques of tasting.[76]
3) *Scenes are publicly available.* Knowledge of the scene and its "obvious patterns and meanings" can be acquired by anyone willing and wanting to participate in the scene. "Most scenes provide well-known locations at which participants commingle, act, and

> share meanings which are part of the process" of "plugging in" to the scene.[77] As such, membership is inclusive and liberally open to participants.

Riding the theatrical metaphor, a scene involves actors who can freely accept or improvise upon the scripts they're given, or help co-author, upon a visible stage. These stages are the places where urban culture is empirically located. One of the grand accomplishments of cities is the sheer variety of places they house that foster varieties of experiences for those seeking varied levels of comradery. This is why studying urban scenes, especially those like the local craft beer scene that provide "an ideology that elevates them beyond mere entertainment and gives them some instrumental aim,"[78] can illuminate the ways contemporary Americans set out and build culture(s) for themselves, though not necessarily by themselves all of the time. Scenes exist at the "meso level" of social life where the city and the individual collide, where the processes of negotiating the meanings of the city and one's identity are both constrained and enabled through action and interaction.[79]

All scenes revolve around a core "thing" that scene members—from those in the center to those on the periphery—endow with meaning and value.[80] Paying attention to the thing itself is an important corrective to the vast majority of studies of scenes in cities, across them, or elsewhere. Sociologists have provided valuable works on the social organization of social worlds and local cultures, as well as the discourse and talk of, in, and about them. But these studies have largely ignored the consecrated object that provides the social adhesive as if all adhesives were created equal. Ever buy knock-off duct tape? Don't.

The ideas at the heart of all social constructionist thought have gained widespread recognition at the expense of deep engagements with and understandings of the material objects that provide the impetus for social interaction.[81] Too concerned with our inability to comprehend social reality unmediated or uninterpreted, those who hold the precepts of social constructionism too tightly bypass and take for granted the very thing that is taken for granted by the people within the social worlds we study. Sociologist Tia DeNora refers to this as "a preoccupation with 'what' people think about particular cultural works," rather than with "what culture 'does' for its consumers within the contexts of their lives."[82]

We can't simply separate the valued object from the *valuing* of it; the two work together in tandem. I am sympathetic toward interpretive studies that focus solely on the interactive practices that help people define the situations and the people they encounter. But, in recognizing the social significance of the things themselves, I follow Fine's lead when he argues that "constructionists dismiss the aesthetic characteristics of works too quickly. People respond to objects viscerally and through culturally linked ideas of beauty. While aesthetic judgments are subjective, they are not random."[83] We can push this argument even further when we move aesthetics, as a term, back toward its original definition. "Aesthetics" comes from the Greek *aesthesis*, which means "sense perception." The modern Western understanding of aesthetics was forged in the mid-eighteenth century. Enlightenment philosophers supported the idea that aesthetic judgment should be passionless and disinterested, and thereby dissociated it from the senses.[84] This helped guarantee the autonomy of the elite enclave now known as "art" at the expense of sensuous and emotion-based knowledge. Instead, as philosopher Maurice Merleau-Ponty notes, all knowledge involves sensuous perception in and through the body and is inseparable from our sensuous experience of being in the world with others and the things we surround ourselves with.[85]

As such, aesthetics is not synonymous with art or beauty. Instead, it refers to the sensory knowledge and felt meaning of people, places, objects, and experiences. Reason and logic have often been contrasted with emotion and feeling, but they are all sources of knowledge that generate meanings we rely and act upon. Aesthetics involves the meanings we construct based on feelings about what we experience through our senses as opposed to the meanings we can deduce in the absence of experience, like statistics based on data drawn from survey research. The latter was the preferred method of sociologist Pierre Bourdieu's purposely and aggressively "anti-aesthetic" work that has had an almost unbridled influence on studies of cultural tastes and how they are unequally distributed across social classes and, in effect, determined by social class position.[86] In such studies, both the lived experience of the person and the object of the individual's attention, affection, dismay, or disgust are absent. This has left wide gaps in what we know about the ways people give meaning to their interactive experiences with others and with their "objects of faith and devotion."[87]

It would be a shame to continue to ignore what happens when someone opens a rare and highly coveted limited-release bottle—a "whale" as it's called in the craft beer scene—and shares it with perfect strangers. Socially significant is the care with which someone might carefully unwind the tiny metal of the small cage that surrounds the cork, slip their thumb beneath it to slowly push it to pop open, pour the sour nectar that spent a year sitting in white wine barrels into a tulip glass or some other form of so-called proper glassware, and then fill their nostrils with the oak and fruit aromas before finally letting the spirited liquid roll beneath their top lip to invigorate their taste buds.

I've seen this. I've done this. I've felt this.

And, in large part because I learned how to "tune-up" my body, as Goffman would say, to the aesthetic encounters during my fieldwork,[88] I can say that the attention paid to "significant objects" matters, especially in a world where there are so many things to choose from and between. "Significant objects" move people in ways that we need to grant them at least a sense of agency to affect moods and motivations.[89] As such, in order to understand the social life of things and the people they animate, as well as the ways those things are animated through their use and engagement with said things, we need to move from a sociology of taste to a sociology of *tasting*.

Paying particular attention to the active acts of tasting provides new avenues for uncovering the values of various aesthetic experiences and engagements with significant objects for individuals and collectives. Here, then, is taste not as cultural preference alone but as the physical sensations of the body in response to stimuli. The tongue, as the bodily mechanism for the tasting activity, is particularly sensitive to intruding objects. Yet it isn't isolated; instead it works in tandem with the nose. The eighteenth-century French gastronome Jean Brillat-Savarin poetically remarked that "smell and taste form a single sense, the mouth is the laboratory and the nose is the chimney."[90] Taste as flavor, in all its this-worldly yet often beguilingly otherworldly variations, is indebted to other senses. This was something I learned, and learned to practice, in the field. We hear the pop of a cork or bottle top, watch the beer poured and examine its color and clarity, or lack thereof in the case of classic German hefeweizens or recently popular hazy New England IPAs. We smell the varied aromas as the beer's head fades. And when we sip a brew, we can note the tactile sensation from its texture to describe variations of "mouthfeel," from thin and crisp pilsners to thick and chewy stouts.

Though the palate is certainly intimate and feels subjectively driven, the ecological effect of tasting is inherently social, beckoning a social relationship between the taster, and the scene he or she in embedded within, and the tasted, the "significant objects" that influence, constrain, and, in effect, coproduce the tangible effects and affects.

The learning process is the collision point between the symbolic and the physiological. The abilities and techniques to appreciate and enjoy certain things that overtly range between the material and ephemeral are acquired rather than ascribed. The dynamic processes that foster such learning are the necessary mechanisms for sociability and the cornerstones of scenes. All scenes are defined by core things/significant objects that coproduce aesthetic preferences and performances whereby, as sociologist Antoine Hennion writes, "taste is formed as it is expressed and is expressed as it is formed."[91] In a similar fashion, we can reword this as:

A scene is formed as it is expressed and is expressed as it formed.

How the Las Vegas craft beer scene was formed, how it is implicitly and explicitly connected to other scenes, and what the scene expresses about the "good life" is the story I offer. And what that means for the ways we should think about the relationships between people, places, and things is uncovered and revealed throughout the pages of *Vegas Brews*.

What's on Tap?

Vegas Brews is a tour of the Las Vegas craft beer scene with various stops along the way at some of its most important places and with some of its most significant players. I bring you to the places where the scene happens, where actors—from the leads to the supporting cast—take the stage to make the scene happen.[92] Through the use of rich "thick description" intended to provide both breadth and depth to help you get a taste, so to speak, of the scene,[93] I've tried to represent the scene with fairness and transparency.[94] You will hear from the actors themselves as *social* actors discussing their roles within a scene in order to avoid reducing the social to the level of the individual.[95] In this "peopled ethnography,"[96] I've uncovered and henceforth present the collective sentiments of a cadre of locals as they attempt to connect to and engage with their city and others in it.

A beer brewed in one place by one person will be different from the same beer brewed somewhere else by someone else. Even the most novice homebrewer can recognize and try to compensate for differences in the quality of ingredients, the effects of water quality, and the temperature when fermentation happens in the glass carboy or plastic bucket. Contextual factors affect the ways that local scenes emerge and thrive, just like brewing beer. Just as the yeast that turns sugar into mind-altering alcohol needs the proper healthy environment, so does a scene to foster culture-altering practices. Even as people are affected by their surroundings, they are able to change them as well. The significance of context still remains. Chapter 1 shows how the specific context of Las Vegas has stunted the growth of the local craft beer scene. The way that context is understood in this case is primarily through the city's reputation and dominant imagery. The way that people outside of Las Vegas think about Las Vegas affects how people live inside of it. The city's *reputational constraints* are exposed through a diagnosis of a condition that affects the way Las Vegas is often (mis)interpreted. I call this the "Las Vegas Syndrome." Yet while this dis-ease is most evident on and emanates from the Strip, the Strip plays dual roles as foe and friend to craft beer drinkers.

Chapter 2 emphasizes the importance of both ongoing gatherings and the places that host and play a part in them. We traverse the "aesthetic ecology" of the local Las Vegas craft beer scene, highlighting the key nodes that provide the stages the scene needs to express itself. These nodes are sprawled across the Las Vegas Valley whereby each place needs to compete to draw people to it outside their respective immediate and nearby neighborhoods. As such, some places, even breweries themselves, have continued to follow the dominant logic of Las Vegas by including video poker atop the bars where they serve their locally and translocally brewed craft beers. This common practice, however, is changing, and some have banded together to help create—through the elevation of taste as an act of resistance—a new cultural logic and aesthetic demeanor for the city.

Aesthetic and affective affiliations that connect local scenes to each other create a grand translocal scene that, as I argue in chapter 3, depends on a widespread belief in *translocalism*—a strong valuation and valorization of other people's local. This chapter addresses the phenomenon of translocalism and shows how it, counterintuitively, strengthens the local scene.

Chapter 4 shows how negative ideological baggage can be passed down from the translocal to the local. This is evident in the varying ways that women are treated within the scene as well as the ways that the intoxication of craft can lead to regressive acts of materialism and conspicuous consumption. Such practices run counter to the egalitarian ethos espoused by craft beer scene participants.

"Pics or it didn't happen," the pop culture mandate declares. Chapter 5 shows how the performance of craft beer fans on Instagram, as well as other social media sites, is but one way to create new meanings out of received culture, thereby engendering some form of agency or control over the lived culture of everyday life, on- and offline. Creating and posting pics is a way to gain ownership over the product, a way of turning the objective object into a subjective experience to be shared with others. Instead of viewing the virtual scene as something independent from everyday life, I found that it necessarily depends on, accentuates, and, in turn, reestablishes the importance of place in the physical material world. As such, the virtual scene becomes a conduit to and for both a specific local scene and the multitude of local scenes that make up the grand translocal scene through the ritual practices of "showing and sharing."

Scenes rely on individuals at various levels of their "experiential career." Because scenes are publicly available and open and voluntarily joined and enacted because people are drawn to and thereby choose to appreciate their core object, they are necessarily home to individuals with varying levels of experience and knowledge. This type of diversity offers a necessary degree of dynamism to a scene. Chapter 6 shows the process by which aesthetic awakenings, aesthetic connoisseurship, and aesthetic entrepreneurship happen. All three are forms of socialization that require the acquisition and use of sensuous knowledge.

The concluding chapter moves from tragedy to triumph. During the time of this writing, the worst mass shooting in US history happened in Las Vegas. It was an event the riveted the nation and shocked the city. It didn't change my analysis; instead, the way the local craft beer scene responded reinforced what I had found during my time empathetically engaged with the people, places, and things that define the scene. I use the last chapter to tie the strings together and make a final argument about the socially significant roles of scenes in cities as expressive, voluntary, and public entities.

Together, the chapters of *Vegas Brews* provide insights into some of the ways contemporary Americans have found meaning, purpose, and comradery with and through the things they care about. Following the significant object as it moves through the hands of skilled brewers and across the palates of grateful tasters, it's hard to ignore, and not derive some "ontological security"[97] from the simple fact that we live in a world with others and we live in a world with things . . . and we might as well do our best to find the best in and of both. And if it can happen in Vegas, it can happen elsewhere.

1

Once upon a Beer Desert

Las Vegas is no friend of sobriety. The city has a reputation for being drenched in alcohol and is home to almost six hundred establishments authorized to sell packaged spirits, beer, and wine. That averages out to about four such liquor licenses per square mile of city land. And that's just for people who want to take their alcoholic beverages home, or at least to stick one in a brown bag for a wobbly drunken stroll. And that bag isn't even required on the Strip, where public drinking and intoxication are the norm rather than the exception.

On a typical Saturday night, drinks are served to both paying and "comped" patrons at rapid speeds in bars across the city. Guys crowd around tables with "bottle service" at the clubs, often giving away freshly, yet crudely, mixed vodka drinks to young women who look like they forgot their pants at home. People slither from casino to casino on the Strip or beneath the Fremont Street canopy—the world's largest television screen—holding yard-long plastic vessels that look like Eiffel towers, women's legs, or cowboy boots filled with cheap liquor and bright sugary mixers. Some come with straps to wear around their necks in case the drinks are too heavy or their buzz is too strong. And it doesn't have to be Saturday. This could be Tuesday.

Through a neon echo chamber of hypermasculinity, an image emerges of the city continually puffing out its chest, trying to get others to take it seriously, while it stumbles, slurs, and mispronounces other cities' names. This image, as well as its "open twenty-four hours" reality and mentality, has stunted the city's growth as a destination for finding both quality locally brewed and locally distributed craft beer. Even though the number of breweries has doubled since 2013 and the number of bars, restaurants, and bottle shops that sell craft beer has increased, craft beer—as well as other artisanal wares scattered throughout the valley—hasn't been seized upon by city officials and developers to bolster tourism or entice gentrifying migrants to reappropriated industrial areas. Supporting and using craft-based business to lure the so-called creative class back into older parts of older cities is a common strategy that, for better or for worse, isn't a part of the Las Vegas craft beer scene's narrative.[1] This is due in part to the relatively young age of both the city and the scene, both of which are bound to the whims of the Strip's "power elite."

Local Las Vegans consistently refer to the scene as develop*ing*. Improving, yes, but still in its infancy. When I asked folks within the scene to describe it, they almost unanimously made references to infancy, childhood, or adolescence. Often with a sense of anguish and frustration, locals labeled the scene, as well as the city itself, as juvenile. This was equally as often followed by a dual plea and justification: "But we're trying."

Like any emerging collective entity or cultural product, it has a life course that can be charted from birth to golden age through to its stagnation or eventual death.[2] No wonder people talked about the scene as if it were a living being going through growth spurts.

On a crisp evening in February, Dave Bowers and I sit at a high-top table on the outdoor patio of Tacos & Beer. Dave was then part owner and director of the restaurant's beer program.[3] Tacos & Beer quickly became a favorite haunt for beer geeks and taco gourmands alike, as well as for local techno junkies during late night electronic beat-a-thons. Patrons sit at tables drinking and eating beneath hanging electric votive candles that match an irreverent yet welcoming sacred taco-adorning Virgin Mary painting near the entrance. A large Cheech and Chong wood carving rests above the bar's twenty tap handles.[4] On any given day, you can find beer geeks using these decorations as backdrops for photos of their sipped snifters, soon to be uploaded on various social media platforms.

Dave's almost Master Cicerone and Beer Judge Certification Program credentials have helped him build clout as a local aesthetic entrepreneur, a scene director of sorts.[5] Settling down for our chat, he brings out a three-year-old bottle of AleSmith's Decadence, a syrupy Belgian-style quadruple ale from San Diego. It seemed fitting to be drinking a beer from elsewhere that wasn't distributed here yet went by the name of one of the city's utmost reputational assets. And while decadence, like opulence or indulgence, is synonymous with the image of Las Vegas, though not with locals' everyday reality. The reputation of the Las Vegas stems far less from those who live there than from the predesigned landscape built for partiers and convention attendees.

As we sip our Decadence while discussing the state, or developmental stage, of the Las Vegas craft beer scene, Dave nonchalantly quips,

> Las Vegas is like a kid that is trying so hard to invent itself to be cool instead of just being what it is. So we copy stuff from LA or see trends somewhere else and reproduce them here. Instead of just doing what we think is cool. We have a fake Eiffel Tower, a fake this, a fake that.

Dave points over his shoulder toward the Strip. I can see the newly built High Roller, a functioning yet money-losing Ferris wheel, peeking over his shoulder. He then offers his own take on the "What happens in Las Vegas . . ." motto:

"Everything that happens here happened somewhere else first."

I smile, thinking it has a nice ring to it, though it likely wouldn't gain traction with many locals.

"Las Vegas doesn't try to serve the local populace but instead they focus on people from elsewhere, from all over," Dave laments. "So you bring chefs who have been successful elsewhere. You bring in other things that have been successful elsewhere. Maybe because we're playing for such high stakes people don't want to fail and try something too wacky and out there."

I ask, "Do you see that logic in the craft beer scene too?"

"Yeah, it's everywhere! It's a mentality. It's a problem with brewing here and beer sales and what products are available. It's mainstream, center of the bell curve stuff. If you take any of this stuff—from barrel-aged sours to super fresh IPAs—to an old-school food-and-beverage guy on the Strip, they don't get it."

"What about locally brewed beer? Local products must have some appeal?"

"Local brewers are in a tough situation. They end up following things that were already done elsewhere, trying to appeal to the largest base possible because they think that's what people want. Thing are changing but slow going. I don't blame them; this is a hard city for innovators."

The steep neon slope that those in the Las Vegas craft beer scene have to climb is telling of the ways that a city's dominant culture can constrain the aesthetic choices and experiences of its inhabitants. Craft beer sits at the crux of a conflict between *local culture* and *locals' culture*. The development of the craft beer scene has been stunted by a culture that favors visitors over residents, a dynamic that is unique to Las Vegas when compared to other craft-beer-friendly and craft-beer-saturated cities. While craft beer accounts for 12 percent of beer sales nationally, it constitutes only about 7 percent in Las Vegas.[6]

Cities and the stages they provide have personas, or at least people act as if they do. As such, as an expressive entity, a scene has some sort of agency. A scene says something and makes some things happen. Though dependent upon the actions of individuals, a scene is still greater than the sum of its parts. Because the stages on which scenes play out are not always the same, it becomes easy to notice how particular contexts constrain expressive actions. The physical parameters of the stage affect how actors enact a scene. The boundaries constrain where they move and what they can do as much as a script constrains what they can say and to whom. The physical constraints of cities are often more obvious than their symbolic constraints.

The built environment affects action and the ways people traverse through cities. The suburban sprawl of Las Vegas and the lack of light rail are constraints, for example. The natural environment affects action and the ways that people can grow food or import it. Poor water quality (beer is over 90 percent water) and the inability to produce useful hops in the desert are constraints that Las Vegas brewers have to negotiate. Most brewers filter city water—most of which has traveled hundreds of miles from the Colorado Rockies to the ever-dissipating Lake Mead—using a combination of carbon filters and reverse osmosis to eliminate unwanted minerals.

The harsh climate affects distributors as well. A local rep of a nonlocal craft brewery told me that "Las Vegas is one of the worst environments for maintaining the quality of beer: really long draft lines through casinos, warm storage places. . . . I've heard stories of pallets [portable wooden bases used for transporting usually sixty to seventy-two cases] being left out in the sun until they're pulled into storage. UV rays for days!" High temperatures and severe sunlight can turn the best of beers into skunky cat pee.

Along with these physical constraints, the most damning constraint has been the city itself, or at least how and what people—including tourists, locals, and commentators—think about it. The constraints that key actors in the Las Vegas craft beer scene must contend with reveal the power of *reputational constraints* whereby perception becomes reality with real-life consequences.[7] Plenty has been written about both the benefits and foibles of urban branding and place-making campaigns used to enhance the most desirable, buzz-worthy, and profit-producing cultural amenities.[8] The branding of Las Vegas, however, is both emblematic and exceptional. On one hand, it reflects many recent trends whereby cities vie for tourists' wallets by paradoxically producing *both* locally distinctive attractions *and* homogeneously themed "sanitized razzmatazz."[9] Postindustrial cities have turned to tourism to recoup lost business and thereby follow in the footsteps of a city founded on serving tourists. "When city after city tries to market itself as an attractive location to offset the relocation of traditional businesses and industries south of the border and overseas, they are simply doing what Las Vegas has done since its founding as a lonely desert outpost."[10] In this way, Las Vegas is emblematic of "the city as entertainment machine," to use sociologists Richard Lloyd and Terry Nichols Clark's apt phrase.[11]

On the other end of the spectrum, Las Vegas is exceptional because its branding as a tourist city has been *so* successful that the image it presents obscures the lived experiences of local residents. In this way, Las Vegas is exceptional as a *city as hype machine*, whereby the city's reputation is so connected to the amenities it offers to tourists that other aspects of the city are unseen, disregarded, or lost in translation.[12] The constant hyping affects locals whose numbers have skyrocketed from about a quarter million in 1980 to one million in the mid-1990s, plateauing at over two million for the last decade.[13] But many of those residents aren't likely to stick around, lay down roots, and seek ways to challenge the corporate control of the city's image and culture. The US Census Bureau's 2013 American Community Survey noted that eighty-nine thousand people moved to the Las Vegas metropolitan area within the prior year, with just over seventy-two thousand leaving the valley during that same time.[14] Though this represents a bit of a net gain, the overall situation is plagued by cultural instability whereby short-term residents simply buy into the mythology of "Las Vegas, the tourist city" despite not living in one of the Strip's hotels, as many outsiders seem to assume. These are the folks who still say they live in "Vegas," rather than Las Vegas, which is what locals—both long-term and soon to be long-term—proudly declare as home.[15]

As we move forward exploring the ways that the city's reputation has constrained the craft beer scene from emerging and flourishing faster than a snail's pace, I offer a diagnosis of the distorted view of the city's culture. Such distortions are symptoms of what I call the Las Vegas Syndrome, a disorder promulgated by misrepresentations and misinterpretations of what happens in Las Vegas.[16] It is so ubiquitous that it often goes unnoticed. Affecting both visitors and locals, the Las Vegas Syndrome is the culmination of the city's reputation and, most importantly, how it affects and constrains the actions and interactions of people within and outside of the world's most impossible city.

The dominant image of the city and its effects on locals can be undone, or at least reconfigured, only through a series of not necessarily uniform yet necessarily collective practices. Collectively, these practices amount to a scene's *articulation*, in sociologist John Irwin's terms. The articulation of a scene coalesces participants' wants and desires into a collective claim about what Las Vegas means to them, often in resistance to the city's dominant imagery. The expressive dimension of a scene is a necessary social mechanism for cultural change. And that change is dependent upon the actions and performances of taste by people who participate in the very activities that the scene embraces, identifies with, and practices.[17]

People are storytellers, weaving tales to either fit their reality or change it.[18] The collective claims-making of early articulators and current participants in scenes often takes form as a melodramatic narrative of villains, victims, and heroes.[19] For those in the Las Vegas craft beer scene, from the hardcore beer geek to the causal craft sipper, the Strip—as the epitome of either the sinfully debauched or the bland—often plays the role of villain. The locals along with a smattering of tourists and would-be tourists are the victims. And as this tale is told by protagonists and ardent narrators, craft is the hero. For those within the scene, craft is an antidote to the Las Vegas Syndrome. While alcohol certainly works with the dominant logic of the infamous Strip, craft beer offers a different vessel for alcohol, one that believers argue fights against that logic. For them, craft beer is of greater value than Big Beer products in terms of taste, creativity, and ethos. Craft beer is part of a symbolic battle against the corporate control of popular culture in a city where popular culture is more synonymous with populism than other American cities. With its most heroic fortitude, craft beer matters for those who believe in its capacity to enable experiences, ideas, and comraderies that the Strip and its branded reputation fail to elicit.

The Las Vegas Syndrome

Almost everyone knows a Vegas "night on the town" story pieced together from vague recollections of debauchery and tomfoolery. For men and women, and across the gender spectrum, the story usually involves some combination of booze, limousine rides, strippers (known as "dancers" in local parlance) and other sex workers, body-pounding bass drums, broken heels or bones, drive-through wedding chapels, late-night eating, ogling, tears, vomit, and one nasty hangover. Such narratives were immortalized in the widely popular movie *The Hangover*, where four white males descend upon Las Vegas's adult playground from California for a "last hurrah" before one of them "ties the knot" the following week. Fueled by alcohol and ecstasy, the "wolfpack" have an uproarious night that leaves the bachelor missing, another missing a tooth and married, and a tiger, stolen from infamous boxer and Las Vegas resident Mike Tyson, in their hotel suite bathroom. Today, those willing to spend about two thousand dollars can get married at Madame Tussaud's in a replica chapel from the movie along with wax versions of its main characters.

Along with the thousands of other fabricated tales that tourists bring home with them, as well as those penned by journalists, novelists, and academics, the movie's narrative easily resonates with audiences near and far. A cultural object's ability to be relevant and discernable, whether it's a movie, a pop song, or an "urban legend," is one of the key ways culture maintains a degree of stability and, in turn, gains power from that stability. In his discussion of the power of symbols, sociologist and media studies scholar Michael Schudson calls this "resonance," arguing that certain objects will resonate with people, in part, because of the ways that they have already learned to interpret them. Over time, a particular symbol will "win out over other symbols as a representation of some valued entity and it comes to have an aura. The aura generates its own power and what might originally have been a very modest advantage (or even lucky coincidence) of a symbol becomes, with the accumulation of the aura of tradition over time, a major feature."[20] When applied to a city, this aura manifests itself *in* and *as* its character, building continuity and stability over time as its tradition.[21]

A city's reputation is a composite, the "cumulative texture" as sociologist Gerald Suttles call it,[22] of character and tradition, of aura and resonance, of the ideas and impressions about it. This reputation isn't derived from a single source; rather it develops from perceptions about "hard features" like its physical makeup and economy and "soft factors" like the way it feels, its "distinctive essence" that "poets, songwriters, and novelists have longed to capture."[23] Though similar to a place's identity, its reputation primarily lies in the heads of those outside of its physical confines. That is, outsiders—and there are always more of them than there are insiders—make evaluations about a place that, in turn, when repeated across time, space, and genre, constitute a place's reputation. In effect, a city's reputation is a shortcut for the many judgments, interpretations, and claims people have made about it.[24]

Las Vegas has two reputations, both of which qualify as "difficult" in the way that sociologist Gary Alan Fine addresses the negative and contested reputations of controversial historical figures.[25] The first is perhaps the more benign one, yet it still has some dubious effects, especially on those unimpressed with premade theme park experiences who rather seek out raw authenticity, however illusionary that quest might be in today's or yesterday's world.[26] This is the idea that Las Vegas is the barometer of American populism, embodying the mainstream, the spirit of the common denominator, homogeneity as social glue. Straight middle-brow culture; spawning and spreading a "theology of the profoundest mediocrity."[27]

The second reputation is the more obvious one because it is summoned and paraded around by Hollywood filmmakers and members of the Las Vegas Convention and Visitors Association alike. This is the reputation that movies like *The Hangover* capitalize on and perpetuate. This is naughty Las Vegas. Sin City. This is the place where people come for a few days to exercise their hedonistic demons. A place where cards with near-naked women are handed out to any passerby, to be thrown on the ground, kept as a souvenir of vice, or used later for sexual arousal or contact. This is the Las Vegas where "what happens here stays here," or at least people hope that is the case (though STDs don't care about geography or marital status).

Together, Las Vegas has a strong reputation, one that is readily definable. Just like the reputations that individuals hold, the reputations of cities can have observable effects on the people who live, work, and play in them. Discrepancies between the rhetoric and reality of a city can cause emotional distress on both individual and collective levels for both tourists and locals. The difference between the rhetoric and reality of Las Vegas is stark and has real effects on how people feel about the city and what happens in it. We can call this the Las Vegas Syndrome. Though place-based mental "disorders" haven't made it into the *Diagnostic and Statistical Manual of Mental Disorders*, they don't need to be "officially" listed to detect and define their existence as real. These syndromes are often short-lived, affecting mainly, though not exclusively, visitors who, soon after their arrival at their intended destination, develop symptoms that range from anxiety and panic attacks to visual and aural hallucinations. Cases have occurred in cities where individuals can easily become psychologically and emotionally overwhelmed by the discrepancy between how a city looks and feels in their imaginations than how it looks and feels in reality.

The three most common places this type of disorientation occurs are Jerusalem, Paris, and Florence. All three of these cities have hosted visitors who have experienced some form of neural intoxication. Sufferers of "Jerusalem Syndrome" are seduced by the historical religious intensity of the Holy City, turning some into wannabe messiahs shouting psalms and sermons at seen and unseen others. The romantic images of accordions, flowers, and cobbled streets that define a particular version of Paris often collide with the realities of the city, leaving some visitors in a state of shock and rabid disappointment. Art lovers making secular pilgrimages to Florence can contract "Stendhal Syndrome," named after the nineteenth-century French author who felt deep pangs of anxiety and all but fainted amid the cultural and aesthetic richness of the city. In all three cities, culture shock might be the "cause," but visitors are not the only ones who are susceptible to place-based syndromes. Local residents can be temporarily or permanently affected as well.

Sociologists are well aware that mental and emotional states cannot be reduced to mere biological or psychological factors because they are shaped by social interactions and cultural conditions.[28] To understand how and why individuals react to specific cities—in both orderly and disorderly ways—it is wise to explore the historical context of the city itself rather than digging into the psyches of specific individuals. Though sociologist Georg Simmel's classic statements about the urban environment's influence on the mental life of individuals were made in the context of massive numbers of people transitioning from traditional rural settings to modern cities, his insights remain cogent today. According to Simmel, the pace of life was slower and interactions were rhythmic and habitual in rural environments. The city, however, with its "swift and continuous shift of external and internal stimuli," requires individuals to adapt to surroundings composed of big buildings and unknown others.[29] Simmel's idealized "metropolitan type" was a rational being who could withstand the stimulation that can induce place-based syndromes. But Simmel, writing in the early twentieth century, couldn't foresee how overstimulating cities would become.

The *hyper*-overstimulation of Las Vegas—accentuated by its flamboyant architecture and activities—bypasses rationality and heads straight for the senses, inducing a potential array of disparate and ambiguous physiological responses that are difficult to interpret yet still require negotiation. Such sensorially exhausting tactics are the *au currant* bread and butter of the "experience economy" that Las Vegas helped propel across the United States where people come to delve into rather than retreat from.[30]

The Strip's neon lights are as alluring as they are disorienting, which might be the goal for some wannabe Hunter S. Thompsons. If you stare too long though, they will blind you, leaving even the most trained observer with a distorted vision of the city and the people who live, work, and play in it.

The damaged eye is one of the key symptoms of the Las Vegas Syndrome. The bright lights, the haphazard pastiche of architectural styles and historical references, and the sheer amount of options for entertainment and lifestyle choices can be off-putting to the uninitiated and unprepared. Though the Strip is four miles long, it feels condensed and "in your face." The Las Vegas Syndrome affects individuals' visual perceptions and aesthetic experiences of the city.[31]

For visitors, symptoms include feelings of entitlement, drunken debauchery, loosened moral boundaries, and overzealous fedora-wearing. They tend to purposely ignore the realities of locals, especially the "invisible" maids who clean their rooms while they soak in the desert rays after a late night.[32]

For locals, the syndrome is evident in the "get rich quick / hit the jackpot" mentality that helped foster the overdeveloped sprawl across the valley in the 2000s that, in turn, led to empty homes, empty wallets, and an empty tax base that can't adequately fund basic social services from health care to education. At that time, 40 percent of the population wanted to move elsewhere.[33] The Las Vegas Syndrome is both a cause and an effect of a continued citywide hesitation to become too attached to and invest in local culture and community. This of course allows others (i.e., the "power elite" made up of those who didn't leave) to dictate what happens, and how the rest of the world thinks about what happens, and presumably stays, in the city.

For cultural commentators, those tasked to make sense of Las Vegas, indicators of the syndrome waver between two extreme poles. On one end, there is an uncritical, ardent, and quasi-populist boosterism of all things Las Vegas. On the other end is a nostalgia-driven, elitist ethnocentrism marked by an implicit conflation of moral judgments and aesthetic tastes. The former can be found primarily in op-eds in the local papers, often written in response to an outsider making the hackneyed claim that there isn't any "culture" in Las Vegas. Studies that suffer from the latter ailments tend to focus on the fantastical elements of the fantasy-driven Strip, omitting the lived experiences of the two million residents whose homes surround it.[34]

It is somewhat understandable, though not necessarily acceptable, that scholars' collective gaze has been stuck on the comings and goings of the Strip since the traditions of gambling and sexual deviance remain consistent despite the various incarnations of the city's neon spectacle. While stories of the Strip might be enticing and entertaining to visitors, they are ultimately incomplete. My Las Vegas–based colleague David Dickens correctly chides such studies:

> There is a long, dishonorable tradition of "drive-by journalism" (and what I would call "drive-by scholarship") where writers spend a few days in Las Vegas (or in the case of academics, send a squad of their graduate students), usually staying in a hotel on the Strip, and then return to their hometowns to write an article or book condemning an entire metropolitan area of two million people as wicked hedonists, degenerate gamblers, prostitutes, and so on.[35]

Las Vegas has played the role of whipping post for many "drive-by scholars" intent on showing the cultural depravity that the city supposedly represents. Such accounts, however, say more about the writers than they do about the city. As Las Vegas historian Hal Rothman once wrote, "Las Vegas is a canvas on which people paint their neuroses."[36]

As long as people believe that Jerusalem is the holiest of holy cities, the Jerusalem Syndrome—either as a "real" disorder or as a cultural phenomenon—will continue to exist. In a similar fashion, as long as people continue to allow the neon lights of the Strip to define and dictate "what happens in Vegas," the Las Vegas Syndrome will persist and will continue to affect the ways of life in the city. The craft beer scene is not immune from the city's reputational constraints. The lasting imagery provides a steep neon slope for brewers, distributors, and consumers to climb for the sake of craft. From the early adopters who tried to push craft beer into restaurants on and off the Strip to the travelers stockpiling bottles from other states to the loose connection of homebrewers scattered around the valley, craft beer is the antidote to the Las Vegas Syndrome with varying degrees of intensity and success.

Big Beer's Craft Beer Desert

Until only a few years ago, Las Vegas was a relative craft beer desert. Already established and pioneering craft brews like Sierra Nevada Pale Ale, Anchor Steam, and Sam Adams Boston Lager could be found on tap or in bottles at local bars and restaurants, as well as on the casino floor of many hotels. Yet at the end of the twenty-first century's first decade, the wares of smaller craft breweries were hard to find. Big Beer dominated the landscape by securing tap handles and shelf space as well as sponsoring big events like boxing matches, the World Series of Poker, and nightclub performances by top forty artists and DJs.

It wasn't until post-Recession Las Vegas that some regional (read: large) craft brewers sent representatives to Las Vegas. More often than not, those representatives were connected to the Southwest, and Las Vegas was a low priority within its distanced crowd of urban neighbors. New Belgium, based in Fort Collins, Colorado, was among the first to devote a representative to the supposed neon beer desert. After a few years with one rep—who helped push the brand and the local scene—they tapped a young yet experienced buck to push their wares. Known around the local craft beer scene for his ginger hair, boyish and bright Midwestern smile, and extensive knowledge of both beer and Las Vegas, Nick Tribulato has been butting up against Big Beer's practices since 2006 when he started serving at the city's first craft-centric bar, the now defunct Freakin' Frog. When I ask him why it has taken longer for craft beer to catch on, he immediately points to Big Beer's influence and control.

> The challenge in Las Vegas will always be that this is where big brands come to brand people so they return home and buy six-packs of Bud, Miller, Coors, Heineken, Corona, whatever. This is where they launch

> a lot of their marketing, campaigns. We are a test market. They make it or they don't, and that might determine if the rest of the country sees it or not. There's just such a large market here, with the Strip and all of the tourists coming through it who, when they want to drink a beer, aren't necessarily looking for new. They want to get what they know already.

When those same tourists go out to splurge on a meal, they usually drink cocktails or wine. "High-end restaurants didn't want to serve beer. And their diners, for the most part, didn't want it either," says Nick. "Wine has always been at the forefront of the culinary experience. The margins you can make are unbelievable; you have to sell a lot of beer to make that kind of money. You can't sticker shock a sommelier." Wine still holds a relatively high symbolic value, even across an industry that includes and celebrates "mass-commercial," "limited-commercial," and "exclusive/elite" wineries.[37]

The popular perception of beer, until recently, was that it was something that you "threw back" at a ball game or while fishing or mowing the lawn. It didn't belong on a white table cloth. This speaks to the relatively low value that beer had and, in certain arenas, still holds. Even as the demand for craft beer rises, Big Beer has the means to make sure that they're the ones filling up that space. Throwing around money rather than muscle, some distributors will do their best Robert De Niro impression and quite literally pay their way into bars, restaurants, and liquor stores.

Nick's fellow "rangers"—the name New Belgium pins on their reps—take off from their home base and sell their wares, and their ethos (i.e., "Follow Your Folly, Ours is Beer"), in multiple cities across many states. According to Nick, the majority of them still believe that Las Vegas is the Wild West. And, from what he's seen, that perception is also a reality. "They think that everything is pay to play, especially on the Strip, and they're not entirely wrong."

The practice of pay to play is one of the biggest open secrets in the beer industry, dancing a thin line between or below what is legal and ethical. With the rise of so many new breweries in the last few years, incidents of pay to play have risen across the United States despite the fact that its practice is technically against the law under federal Alcohol and Tobacco Tax and Trade Bureau regulations. By providing extra compensation (in the form of either money or goods in excess of a certain value) to establishments in order to secure taps lines or shelf space, brewery reps and distributors use pay to play to get a leg up on their competitors. When you walk into a bar and see one distributor has eight tap lines and another has two and then you go back six months later and it's the other way around, it's hard not to think something isn't right. The bartenders or owners won't tell you, but the new sixty-inch flat-screen TV on the wall might give it away. Most people won't notice it, which is why it's so successful and hard to enforce legally.

The ubiquity of the practice in Las Vegas reinforces the city's reputation as a place where bland and big are better. Moreover, the practice adds to the pervasive "anything goes" pseudo-gangster mentality of so-called movers and shakers. Such a mentality runs counter to the collective and collaborative spirit beloved by craft beer producers and consumers. And based on simple economics, it keeps a lot of smaller brands from entering the market.

When I spoke with Michael Shetler, the craft specialist at BreakThru Beverage (formerly called Wirtz Distribution) about the role of pay to play in Las Vegas and its effect on the local craft beer scene, he connected the scene's stunted development to the practice: "We're in our adolescence. We've definitely advanced beyond toddler. The amount of brands that are here now compared to five years ago is pretty remarkable."

"What was the holdup?" I ask.

"A lot of the breweries and distributors were either terrified of this market or it wasn't on their radar," he answers. Reiterating Nick's comments about the city's reputation, Shetler continued: "Perception is that Las Vegas is pay to play and you're going to have to spend enormous amount of marketing dollars to get any traction. And you're going to get lost in a wholesaler's portfolio designed to sell macros, and you're going to get lost in a casino."

Not every brand can afford pay to play. Smaller breweries that operate on small budgets don't have the resources to compete with Big Beer. And Big Beer has an even greater advantage as they buy up small craft breweries that they can use to satisfy the growing legions of craft drinkers while boosting their own bottom line.

Even relatively large craft breweries have trouble competing. They can make a go only on the virtue of their high-quality brews with relatively low price points compared to some of the smaller breweries that have to charge more due to their lack of space and use of expensive experimental ingredients. That hasn't stopped bar owners from trying to get things from them, though. Another representative from a regional craft brewery told me with a smirk that "the shamelessness is hilarious. People ask me for all sorts of stuff. I've been asked for Super Bowl tickets, UFC tickets, whatever. It's egregious. People have wanted me to build them a completely new draft system." And if the rep or the folks he or she works for can't do it, there's a good chance bar owners, acting like fiendish gamblers jumping from one sportsbook to the next to get the best odds, will wait for someone else to come along and give them what they want.

That someone else might be an on-premise salesperson like the one who opened up to me about pay to play. He works for a local distributor that is bound to a Big Beer company yet has a growing craft beer portfolio. As a craft beer drinker, he was clear about his view that the practice is a problem for the local scene and isn't going away anytime soon. And he certainly feels a "role conflict" between being both craft supporter and employee at a Big Beer house.[38] As an employee who can use any financial reward he can sow, like many of his coworkers at his company and others, he often succumbs to the "cash money they put in your hand."

Slightly wincing as if he just sipped milk a few weeks past its sell-by date, he says, "Frankly, I've benefitted from it personally. It's easy cash money." He went on to describe the process:

> Let's say I get an incentive to sell a keg from a craft brewery, I get a bonus to sell it to a bar because it's an expensive keg. Well, let's say that that

> bonus includes a free case of some macro Big Beer. So if I know that a bar has a handle available, I can tell the bar manager I'll throw him a free case of that Miller Lite to bring the cost down. And he's going to turn around and sell those for four or five dollars a bottle which basically comes right off the price they're paying for the keg. Which, mind you, they can sell pints of the craft beer for about seven or eight dollars. It's a win-win for the bar and the distributor.

And if this becomes a steady relationship, he'll throw in coasters and cozies and "cool tight T-shirts for the lady bartenders." His face grimaces again in recognition of the blatant sexism that typical Las Vegas bars willingly support.

Big Beer has the ability to satiate such demands, from discounted kegs to free cases to hard-to-find tickets for sought-after events. They can easily match and outdo the offers of smaller competitors. Ultimately, this hurts the local craft beer scene because it minimizes the variety of aesthetic offerings. It takes control out of the hands of the people trying to grow a beer scene in the middle of a craft beer desert. The practice also helps reinforce and uphold the city's reputation and works in favor of the corporate control of the city's culture. The Big Contracts the Big Casinos have with Big Beer companies give the Strip an influence over the aesthetic experiences of locals. But what if that cultural power could be harnessed for the sake of the scene? Could craft beer's great obstacle become an enabler, a catalyst for aesthetic change? Maybe.

Courting the High End

The Strip often plays the villain in the story of craft beer in Las Vegas. It is also, however, often viewed as the Holy Grail for craft brewers, distributors, and sales reps. If you can change what's offered in Strip casinos, on the floor and in their many restaurants, then the overall impression of the city *might* change for tourists and locals alike. At least that was the collective desire of some of the scene's earliest actors who had enough craft beer knowledge and were in positions to push for a grand "aesthetic liberation" for drinkers in Las Vegas.

People's tastes can change, but they often need help. And if enough of those people are in the same place, the city can change. Because of the Strip's cultural power to ride the strongest and most easily profitable waves of taste, it shouldn't be a surprise that the earliest seeds of the craft beer scene were planted elsewhere. Though the city's first microbrewery (Holy Cow, which also doubled as a casino) opened in 1991 and was located across the street from the famed Sahara Hotel, it did little to change the aesthetic demeanor of Las Vegas. It couldn't get out from under the shadow of the Strip's towering casinos. The suburbs, however, had a bit more freedom to move, act, and promote an aesthetic change. Counter to the prevailing accounts of "creative districts" developed in "revitalized" gentrifying neighborhoods in other cities,[39] Las Vegas's craft beer scene emerged in the less-than-stimulating nondescript strip malls a few miles away from the Strip's impeding lights and influence.

When Michael Shetler moved to Las Vegas from Atlanta in 1999, the valley's population was booming. At the time, there was a steady stream of sixty to eighty thousand new residents expanding "the Las Vegas Valley each year by the volume of a medium-sized city."[40] He opened Rosemary's, a high-end restaurant in Summerlin, a grand master-planned suburb west of the Strip. Shetler's craft beer journey in Las Vegas is indicative of and pivotal for the scene's formation by playing the role of an "early articulator."[41] Due in part to his efforts to enhance others' interests in artisanal beer, he morphed into one of the scene's chief script writers, an evangelist with a story to tell and the means to disseminate it.

"When I got here in '99, the beer scene was nonexistent. This was a Big Beer town, Coors, Miller, Budweiser. It's just starting to trickle in here over the last few years, and it's taken a lot of hard work by a lot people who think Las Vegas can do better," says Shetler.

While speaking a bit more about the difficulties of pushing craft beer in Las Vegas, making implicit connections to the strength of the Las Vegas Syndrome that he and his compatriots have dealt with and tried to overcome, Shetler interrupts himself. “Have you ever had a Seef [pronounced ‘safe’] before?”

“No,” I respond. In fact, I had never even heard of it. Not many others had either.

“Well you should,” Shetler proclaims. “It’s an Antwerp ale, that’s the official classification of the style. I’ll order a couple and tell you the story behind it.”

Rose, the Certified Cicerone and bar manager at the popular Atomic Liquors, brings over two bottles, opens them, and pours the bubbly wheat-colored elixir into our tulip glasses. Before I can taste it, I smell a sweet mix of bread and fruit.

After we clink glasses and nod our heads in unison—a typically ritualized act of performing taste—Shetler launches into the story of this lost yet recently re-created style. It was a popular beer in Antwerp from the mid-eighteenth century until World War I. Local breweries in the Seef district made it for the factory workers who found its light lemon taste and dry finish refreshing after, or even during, a day’s work. At the beginning of the war, Germans seized equipment from the breweries, especially the copper vats, to make tanks and bullets for their war machine. At about the same time, mass-produced light lagers hit the market and kept the already dismantled breweries from recovering. The style was extinct until 2012, when Johan Van Dyck, who was the marketing director at Duvel Moortgat, decided to create his own brewery and resurrect the style. Without a recipe, he searched through old newspapers and even went to retirement homes to talk to old brewers. Eventually he met the great-granddaughter of a brewer who had some old notes in an old shoebox. He took the notes to scientists at the University of Leuven, who after experimenting with a few different blends and yeast strains finally got it as close as they thought they could. Now the style is back and the city of Antwerp can taste a part of its history again.

Is this what Shetler hopes will happen in Las Vegas—that people will one day be able to tell the story of a Las Vegas beer that was so connected to local culture that people will want to keep alive or resurrect it if need be? Yes. And he's not alone.

"See, part of the art of craft beer, outside the creative tinkering with recipes and the actual process of brewing, is the story," Shetler explains. "The story is important. Local stories are important. *Local beer by local people who employ local people and contribute to local taxes.* And distributors and wholesalers need to be able to tell the story of those beers to be able to introduce people to new experiences. That is what we were trying to do at Rosemary's."

When Shetler helped open Rosemary's, he curated a beer list that consisted of mainly Belgian beers in part because the craft beer boom hadn't happened yet nationally, even less so in Las Vegas. "It was easier to get imports than it was to get craft, and the Belgians went really well with our food, southern-style rich sauces and deep flavors." These beers are known for their balance between the bitterness of European hops and the malty sweetness of roasted barley. Connecting these particular beers to the "foodie-oriented" dinners was a way to help elevate the status of beer in general. They weren't going to make any brewery or distributor rich because the volume of beer sales was still low compared to wine and cocktails, but they wanted to give consumers something that they couldn't get anywhere else in Las Vegas.

"I don't think in terms of numbers. I think in terms of culture," Shetler says with a grin as he savors the last drops of his Seef.

For him, changing the culture meant pushing food pairings with beer to so-called "foodies" who tend to be more experimental in their aesthetic choices and consumption practices. Foodies are omnivores, according to sociologists Josée Johnston and Shyon Baumann, who are willing and able to break down the barriers between high and low cultural products, especially for the sake of experiencing something authentic or exotic regardless of price. "They understand their food consumption to be of particular cultural and symbolic importance, rather than a matter of sustenance alone."[42] In some ways, then, foodies can act as the perfect catalyst for cultural change since they have the knowledge and means to actively play with the symbolic side of food and, in our case, beer selections.

By bringing beer into the world of fine dining, Shetler elevates what was previously considered to be a low-brow product. And the foodies at Rosemary's—who were then followed by the "cops and firemen sitting at the bar drinking dark pink framboise," notes Shetler—were open to entering the exotic world of beer, albeit through well-crafted Belgian imports rather than the lowly macro lagers ("lowly" in status and flavor).[43] Rosemary's beer dinners were the first of their kind in Las Vegas and quickly became a successful vehicle for Shetler to help craft a scene.

Due to the success of the beer dinners he offered—which many restaurants have now incorporated into their events schedule—Shetler began offering a greater variety of styles, shifting the focus from imports to American-brewed craft beers. Bridging this supposed divide, he once composed a beer dinner with Wendy Littlefield of Ommegang, a craft brewery in Upstate New York known for their Belgian-style beers. Acquiring such brewing star power was no small feat for a city known as a "beer desert."

Creating "new experiences" through the products and the stories about them, Shetler was writing a new story about and for Las Vegas. Recognizing the potential of the Strip as a resource to tap into to change the drinking culture of Las Vegas, Shetler left Rosemary's in 2009 to work at celebrity chef Shawn McClain's restaurant Sage in the luxurious casino-resort Aria, the crown jewel of the newly built CityCenter on the Strip. Though the move was in part prompted by his desire to accrue advanced sommelier accreditations, Shetler quickly turned back to his "first passion" and launched his own beer program where he initiated "beer pairing options with a chef's tasting menu and chef's signature menu. . . . It was like Rosemary's on steroids!" he exclaims with glee.

It is in this way that, as an arbiter of taste, the Strip—the same Strip that has stunted both the local craft beer scene and local culture in general—morphed from foe to friend. Sage was a success. Success breeds emulation. Other restaurants at other Strip locations began carrying craft beer. Then came the gastropubs with their craft beer and crafted eats, where table cloths gave way to wooden tables and benches.

Las Vegas casinos have always been designed to keep consumers on their respective properties. This has often been achieved through a combination of free or ticketed entertainment activities and the physical layout of the spaces. Winding and circular pathways lead toward gambling areas and away from doors to the forbidden outside realm. Though they want to trap visitors in and watch their every move via "eyes in the sky" or other advanced surveillance technologies, the casino-resorts also want to give consumers what they want. Once customers started asking for craft brands while playing slots or lounging at the pool, many Strip properties heeded their requests. And that "paradigm shift," as Shetler notes, "is due in large part to Sarah Johnson at Mandalay Bay doing whatever she can to thread the needle on that front."

The Taming of the Strip

After a few years working her way up from pastry chef to director of food and beverage at Mandalay Bay, Sarah Johnson found herself spending a lot of time in front of a computer crunching numbers and calculating budgets. Then she got an itch, an itch she wanted to scratch with craft beer. Originally from the Pacific Northwest, a region where craft beer is brewed on more days than it rains, Sarah longed to revisit a love she had tempered while living and working in Las Vegas since 2003. In 2011, when her boss Sean DeCicco, the vice president of Mandalay Bay at the time and former executive chef, asked what would make her happy, Sarah unflinchingly said, "Beer, without a doubt. And I told them that to do it right, this is what I needed." She needed time to learn about the current state of craft beer. She needed time to take that knowledge and turn it into professional certifications.

And she needed them to pay for it.

And they did.

The Mandalay Bay top brass already had a growing interest in craft beer and were well aware of the rapidly growing consumer interest in it. Celebrity chef Hubert Keller's Burger Bar, a casual eatery stacked with wagyu beef burgers and craft beer, was one of the first restaurants in Las Vegas to have a beer list, let alone actually being able to offer the beers on that list.

After a year of traveling to various breweries, restaurants, festivals, and conferences throughout the United States, Sarah took what Keller was doing and brought it to the casino floor. For the first time, one could choose from a selection of tasty craft brews while gambling at the tables or slots. I'm not sure how well an Old Rasputin—a 9 percent ABV Russian imperial stout from North Coast Brewing—pairs with rolling sevens at the craps table, but it was an experiment Sarah was willing and able to execute, despite the difficulties and frustrations.

Climbing the neon slope was slippery at best, perhaps even more so for a woman in the male-dominated environment of the food and beverage industry. Negotiating contracts was difficult on the front end, while staff training proved to be a challenge on the back end. Typical cocktail servers, many who had been at Mandalay Bay for over a decade, were used to their regular routines and regular beer lists that were defined by the usual macro offerings. Sarah was happy that craft beers were now being served through a range of outlets, from the bars on the casino floor to banquets that could range from five to twenty thousand attendees. But she was still frustrated by the slow pace of progress. She knew they couldn't offer the "coolest, hippest, most exclusive stuff," but she wanted craft beer folks—brewers, distributors, and consumers alike—to know that her property was craft-friendly. Much of the responsibility fell on the shoulders of the servers.

She decided to pick one craft beer and give it away (i.e., "comp" it to gamblers). She went with Lagunitas IPA. Though the bitterness of an IPA might have turned off a neophyte whose palate was more accustomed to sweeter macro lagers or even imported brown ales like Newcastle, in her estimation it both was relatively approachable and wielded an iconic label.[44] And hop-forward IPAs, though originally an English-style ale, are largely credited with fostering, if not starting, the current American "craft beer revolution."[45] Sarah thought this would be an easy way to gain some momentum on the floor, but training the staff was unexpectedly difficult.

"Even though I was very familiar with the style, it could be pretty challenging for someone who's never tasted one. There were a lot of bitter beer faces during the tasting, so maybe it wasn't the best choice," she admits.

Sarah took training into her own hands, teaching servers and bartenders throughout the property to engage with the product and engage with customers. The "old-school" training from the local union wasn't up to speed with the breadth and depth of craft beer. "A portion of the crew has been resistant. They were trained by the union twenty years ago. . . . You can't train the *passion*. It's hard to *engage* people without it." Over the course of our three-hour conversation accompanied by a few easy-drinking and relatively low-ABV "session" IPA Easy Jacks from Firestone Walker, Sarah used the words "passion" and "engage" a number of times.

One way she tried to increase the servers' passion for craft beer and their ability to engage consumers was equipping them with little beer carts with a list of available craft beers. This actually helped the servers learn on the go what people were asking for and what they were giving them.

"It sounds so simple," says Sarah. The carts were sponsored by New Belgium, yet they listed all of the craft beers available on the Mandalay Bay floor. "It was a win-win; very craft-centric and community-driven. While everyone is in business, the craft brands are much more collaborative. They're all about it. They'll pay to print someone else's beer on their menu. That's the type of thinking that lifts all beer sales," she says with pride as her eyes expand behind her glasses and a grin that reaches toward her ears.

The "simple" move worked. Though she didn't reveal any specific numbers, Sarah told me that they've been "able to move a ton of beer" by opening themselves up to a new demographic. For her, however, the business of beer is only one part of the equation, though it's the part that drives the profit-oriented and profit-demanding logic of the Strip.

> It's not primarily about selling beer but about building a community and a culture. And I've been able to communicate to the craft beer folks who didn't want to come here, who had the same bias I had when I moved here. The thought was that nobody's going to care about their beer; nobody's going to take care of it. It's not going to be refrigerated properly and the beer is going to go out of date. And there's going to be no one who can speak to it or about it. . . . The assumption is that someone in my role was going to treat beer only as a commodity. And that's how it was ten years ago. We didn't have the knowledgeable food and beverage folks we have now on the Strip.

Sarah's aesthetic labor has been aimed at providing better products, service, and events whereby "better" means a passionate engagement with the craft beer scene, locally and translocally. She's built and hosted a number of events to promote the craft ethos, an ethos that rests on good flavors and good stories. Her Beer and Barrel Festival featured top brews and tasty foods. Her "Team Beer vs. Team Wine" event pitted her against the resort's resident sommelier. And the "Ninkasi Space Oddity Ball," the "launch" party for Oregon brewery Ninkasi's Ground Control Imperial Stout, was a beer (and sci-fi) geek's phantasmagoria. Attendees at the event were treated to live space-themed funk music to celebrate the beer brewed with star anise, hazelnuts, and cocoa nibs and its most "out-of-this-world" ingredient: yeast that was launched into space. The delicious beer and the event itself were both so equally gimmicky and authentically creative that they didn't feel out of place in the Eyecandy Sound Lounge & Bar smack-dab in the middle of the casino floor of one of the Strip's most frequented hotels.

As distributors, buyers, and consumers—including tourists who have begun asking for craft beer while playing the tables or slots—are able to tell the story of craft beer as both a culture and a commodity, as something that has aesthetic and fiscal value, the Strip has begun to morph again.

The villain becomes an ally, a foe a friend.

Local brands, many of which have started canning their brews in part prompted by the passing of a 2014 law banning glass bottles from the bustling streets of the Strip as well as to allow their beer to be served at pools, can be found at bars and restaurants inside the megaresorts. High-quality beers can now be purchased mere steps away from Britney Spears– or Game of Thrones–themed slot machines.

Moreover, celebrity chefs of the top-rated restaurants are embracing not only craft beer but *local* craft beer. While local beers are making the lists at these restaurants, the best example of a "creative collaboration" took place at yet another Mandalay Bay joint. In 2015, celebrity chef Rick Moonen, known for both his cooking skills and his advocacy for sustainable fishing, collaborated with CraftHaus on a specialty beer for both his famed RM Seafood restaurant and his hip steam-punk-themed restaurant Rx Boiler Room. Their collective creative drives led CraftHaus to brew a Belgian wit style of beer to pair with Moonen's seafood dishes. Upping the attachments to local agriculture, they incorporated locally sourced flowers, herbs, and botanicals from Desert Bloom Eco Farms—located an hour and a half outside the city in the Mojave Desert—into the beer.

On a hot night in late June, about sixty people—a self-selected local crowd of food journalists and beer geeks—attended a beer pairing dinner at Rx Boiler Room. The collaboration beer, named Gone with the Wit, was paired with New Bedford jumbo scallops as the third course. The three other courses were paired with CraftHaus's other offerings, their flagship saison and IPA as well as their limited Comrade Imperial Stout for dessert (along with sticky toffee pudding). As each course was introduced, co–head brewer Steve Brockman shared the proverbial stage with Moonen, each explaining what they brought to the table that night.

This was the first time Moonen hosted such an event, and he was ecstatic about it and about the changes to the craft beer scene locally and elsewhere. An avid craft enthusiast with love for beer that stretches back in time to his early days in New York City in the 1970s and 1980s, Moonen relished the opportunity to work with a local brewery. When I asked him about the changes to the Las Vegas craft beer scene, he spoke with joy about the CraftHaus dinner and about potential future collaborations.

> It was great getting my staff involved in the brewing process; they're more apt to be able to tell the story, to explain it. . . . The spirit of where you're sitting now is crafting drinks to go with crafted food. And now we can craft our own beer by going out there and concoct our own recipe and make it happen. How cool is that? It aligns directly with our core values.

The values of craft, creativity, and collaboration that were largely missing for so long in Las Vegas seemed to have found a home. How many more events like this will happen remains to be seen. But the fact that it happened is telling nonetheless, even while the sustainability of collaborations between local craft breweries and Strip restaurants remains in question.

Craft Beer versus the Crafty City

When local craft beer drinkers got word that a craft beer bar was opening on the patio at the Paris Hotel, resting at the foot of the Eiffel Tower and offering views of the Bellagio fountains across the boulevard, they cheered. When they found out it was owned by AB InBev and was going to be called the Budweiser Beer Park, they jeered. Well, at least some of them did. Others were happy to be able to drink "good" beer on the Strip regardless of who owned the breweries that made it. For those who choose to drink their politics, the new Beer Park is a haven for all that is wrong with both Las Vegas and beer culture writ large. It reeks of the corporate control of popular culture and the foul business tactics of AB

InBev that include tax evasion, union busting, and safety violations.[46] Chief among craft beer drinkers' complaints about Big Beer is their crusade to buy smaller craft breweries and bring them under their control. Sure, Beer Park offers many products beyond the usual suspects like Budweiser and Bud Light. Most of the taps are, in fact, dedicated to craft beers, or, again, that's how it seems.

To the uninformed consumer, the selections from American breweries like 10 Barrel, Elysian, and Goose Island all seem like worlds away from the company's typical light lager. And they are, at least in terms of flavor. But these brands are all owned by AB InBev, though you wouldn't know that from their website. Under their list of brands, the craft breweries they've acquired since they first bought Goose Island in 2011, a local Chicago staple, are nowhere to be found. The same is true for Goose Island's website, where there is no sign or mention of AB InBev. Even their "Our Story" tab tells a history devoid of the truth about their ownership. The only giveaway, or "tell" in gambling terms, is that both websites have the same age verification application.

Along with the unethical business tactics mentioned above as well as the acquisition of distributors and the incentive programs AB InBev has designed to ensure themselves an unfair competitive advantage,[47] the deceit leaves many in the scene with bad tastes in their mouths. A distinctive distaste was left in the mouths of the folks at local brewery Tenaya Creek—who have been brewing in Las Vegas since 1999—when they wanted to release their bright hop-forward pale ale in 2013. Tenaya Creek wanted to use the 702 area code to name their beer after their city, like Goose Island's 312 Urban Wheat. What they didn't know, however, was that after AB InBev bought Goose Island, they trademarked fifteen different area codes from fifteen different major cities throughout the United States. The trademark expired after AB InBev didn't use the number, and Tenaya Creek seized it in 2015 and began canning the brew with 702 proudly displayed soon after.

Due to their reliance on false fronts and façades, there is something that makes perfect sense that the first open-air beer bar on the Strip is owned by Budweiser and offers crafty beers with a few scattered craft offerings mixed among them to infuse the Big Beer brands with an aura of legitimacy and authenticity. Both the Strip and Big Beer's crafty beers are riddled with paradoxes. On the Strip, there is the feeling of being free to do what you want while being constantly watched; unlike those in most cities, the streets are owned by corporations rather than the public; and the skyline is made up of towering, lushly decorated, authentically fake buildings that play home to temporary visitors rather than providing homes for long-term residents. Big Beer, especially in the case of AB InBev, is also riddled with paradoxes: the transfer of ownership from a craft brewery to a large corporation violates the Brewers Association's definition of craft in regard to the brewery's independent status; Big Beer has the means to distribute craft beers to more places and, in turn, provide more people with better beer, though; and, despite "selling out," some of their former craft breweries still produce very good tasting beers.[48]

These paradoxes have fueled a seemingly growing fissure within the local and grand craft beer scenes. The fissure muddles the story that the scene articulates. Expressivity is a key feature of any scene regardless of whether or not the narrative it tells is clear. This is a consequence of being voluntary and public. Not every idea or every belief is going to fit neatly together. Such instability makes it harder to combat a strong reputation. And the stronger the reputation, the harder it is to engage it in a way that is effective and resilient. So, when trying to assess whether or not craft beer can be an effective and resilient antidote to the Las Vegas Syndrome, it's hard not to see the Strip—where craft and crafty coexist—as both a faux friend and a faux foe.

2

Not-So-Neon Terroir

Across the long oak table beneath a television that remains off throughout the evening, as it does most days and nights, stand a dozen or so open bottles and cans from some of the most highly regarded craft breweries in the United States. A trendsetting can of Tree House Brewing's Julius, a hazy mango-tasting New England–style IPA, butts up against a golden sour ale with apricots from Berkeley, California's, Rare Barrel. Another sour beer sits next to it, a Berliner Weisse with boysenberries from Tillamook, Oregon's, de Garde Brewing. My lips pucker before I even get to taste them. And I do taste them at the behest of those who brought these hard-to-find, out-of-market treats to share with others. And they'll bring different beers next week.

The bottles and cans move around the table. Little one- to two-ounce pours enter tiny glass snifters for those who arrived early and are then smelt, sipped, and swallowed. As the first batch empties, new bottles and cans are opened and passed around.

"Have you tried this one yet?" Rob calls to me from a few tables away.

"No. Is there any left?"

He shakes the Hill Farmstead bottle gently. "Aw, just dregs. Here, take a sip of mine."

He walks over and gives me his glass. I put my nose in it and breathe in funky red wine aromas. Then I taste it.

"Yum." I smile, knowing this isn't the most sophisticated response, while also knowing that as much as beer geeks like to talk about the intricacies of beer, they also like experiences and expressions of fun. I smile again when I catch the name of the beer: Civil Disobedience.

Rob gives me a nod and goes back to his table to finish his beer. "Look at this crowd," says Corey, the man seated next to me. "This crowd, they're all so different." He squints as if to tell me what he means by "different." Unlike the "white space" that sociologist Elijah Anderson describes at a Philadelphia craft brewery in a gentrifying neighborhood,[1] this crowd, typical of the Las Vegas craft beer scene, is a diverse mix of races, ethnicities, genders, and occupations. An IT specialist exchanges barbs with a contractor. A Latino sous chef pours a drink for a female social worker. A young black hotel executive laughs with a female bartender as they clink glasses holding a dark syrupy imperial stout from a relatively new brewery in San Diego.

Though the beers they're drinking aren't *from* Las Vegas, this is a local crowd, embodied and emplaced *in* Las Vegas. The diversity of the crowd speaks to the desire many have for connecting with others in a city where it's not always easy to do so. Such a desire can lead to connections that span across traditional boundaries of social inclusion that are found in urban "ethnic enclaves" and other neighborhoods born from residential segregation. As a significant object of desire, craft beer's intoxicating effects don't discriminate. And as scene members hope, craft beer re-enchants their everyday lives in a city known for its disenchanting disconnect between people, and between people and their city.

Craft beer allows for these types of interactions necessary for building local culture on the basis of aesthetic choices and practices. Drinking craft beer moves its "community of believers" to experience the world around them as just enough off-center to eclipse the taken for granted. Such off-centeredness can be emotionally, psychologically, and sensuously liberating. The potential for feeling free is great, but can easily be wasted on the wasted.

For the people sharing their beers that night or other nights like it, getting drunk is not the goal (though it can still happen to even the most cautious scenester). They tip their bottles and cans for friends and strangers to sip the vast variety of flavors being offered. Taste isn't merely a disembodied and decontextualized marker of difference or social status, as many scholars often deride.[2] Instead, taste is performed together, and tast*ing* is the binding activity. Craft beer acts as both social lubricant and adhesive.

"These folks probably wouldn't talk to each other if it weren't for the beer. They have their own cliques, and some of them stay in them while they're here, but bottle shares like this bring out something in common." Corey pauses, smiles, and offers his reveal: "the taste of really good beer."

The exclusivity connected to other craft or artisanal wares available across today's "tastescape," like wines and cheeses, is supplanted by a greater degree of inclusion, in part because craft beer is more approachable, more egalitarian, and, in this case, more unifying across supposedly rigid and fixed social attributes and identities.

Bottle shares are commonplace at Khoury's Fine Wine & Spirits on Wednesday and Friday nights. It's an open and voluntary practice of giving and receiving that, while less rigidly adhered to, unintentionally mimics the reciprocal exchange of gifts involved in the ancient and cross-culturally ubiquitous *potlach* ritual. Seminal anthropologist Marcel Mauss famously wrote that such rituals are morally bounded yet contested means of sharing gifts among "nobles."[3] Bottle shares at Khoury's are symbolic rituals that establish loose hierarchies between and among the upper ranks of local Las Vegas beer geeks depending on what they shared that week. These nobles, however, are more than willing to give away their goods for little more than a smile or nod of recognition.

Admittedly, I first thought it was odd that a store that sells craft beer would allow people to bring in outside goods to be consumed on premise. And this is a store that notably has one the best selections in the city in bottles and cans *and* on draft. Between sips of Big Dog's Sled Dog—a locally brewed imperial stout with coffee and cocoa nibs—Issa Khoury, the store's owner and namesake, explained his logic for allowing this practice, summoning a relative degree of affective resistance to the typical and typified Las Vegas bar:

> Unlike most places in Las Vegas, we don't have gaming or fifteen TVs blasting all the time. Without as many distractions, people tend to focus

> on what's in front of them and nine times out of ten they start chatting with the person near them. "What are you drinking?" "That looks good." "Here, try this." And that's kind of how the bottle shares started four or five years ago. . . . I get my shipments in on Wednesdays. A lot of my hard-core craft beer guys knew that and started meeting here to see what I got in. So, one person would buy this bottle, another would buy a different bottle, they'd pop them open and swap them around. And that group of eight or nine has turned into a packed room each week.

"But what about when people bring beers to share that you don't sell?" I pushed.

> The fact that people want to share a cool beer with others they just brought back from Colorado or California or traded for and they want to do it here is cool with me. But at the end of the day, we're a business and I have bills to pay. 99.9 percent of the people get that, and respect it, and are cool about it. As long as you make a purchase in the store, you can open up one bottle. More than that, we'll charge a corkage fee. . . . The first couple of years, we didn't have any rules and then some people started rolling in coolers and not buying anything, so we needed to make some rules explicit to make it fair for everyone. We enjoy the bottle shares; we enjoy the vibe it brings. And the bottle shares get people talking to each other. You've seen it, all kinds of people who've never met before start talking to each other, which is really cool.

By recognizing and purposely cultivating the role his place plays for locals as a gathering spot, Issa reinforces the notion of a scene's ability "to evoke both the cozy intimacy of community and the fluid cosmopolitanism of urban life."[4] Both "a recognition of the inner circles and weighty histories" of his patrons and "a sense of dynamism" allow him to make changes and tweak his own practices and the social norms of his place that, in turn, help the scene change the taste of the city.[5]

Khoury's is an important node in the local Las Vegas craft beer scene. Like other places that it is connected to by affect and aesthetics, it helps foster a scene that creates a source of stability beyond individual selves often separated from one another in this geographically and socially fragmented city. Issa and his patrons are "doing scene," as sociologist Pepper Glass puts it, whereby "members, through their everyday interactions, collectively produce these settings."[6] "Doing scene" is both a creative and practical accomplishment. We should also acknowledge that they are "being scene" by using their bodies to engage is the sensuous activities of performing taste. More specifically, Issa and the folks who buy his wares and drink at the bar or on the patio, sharing beers and laughs with friends and strangers, are *doing and being scene* in ways that elevate local knowledge of taste and tasting.

First, by intentionally choosing not to include gaming, Khoury's presents itself as an unusual watering hole. It expresses alternative aesthetic values to the typical ones that saturate the Las Vegas Valley. Instead of making grand declarations about craft versus macro- or mass-produced cultural goods, Issa and his patrons resist the city's dominant aesthetic offerings through the activities they choose and choose *not* to participate in. The acts of sharing, drinking, and talking about craft beers—"fussing" over them, as Budweiser's 2015 commercial, now infamous among craft beer enthusiasts, put it—are embodied rituals of resistance that invert the top-down pressures of corporate popular culture.[7] Only a few craft beer bars have followed Khoury's lead as a non-gaming space, pushing for more focused attention on the acts of tasting.

Second, by regularly bringing in rare kegs to put on tap as well as working with local brewers and distributors to mine their growing lists of craft selections, Issa is performing taste and implicitly elevating it for those who encounter his shop and those connected to it. When "outsiders" come in looking for Budweiser or Coors they are forced to pass full rows and opened boxes of local and regional craft selections to get to the last door at the end of the beer cooler. Arranging the selections as such allows the craft beers to communicate something about the nuances of taste, and what lurks inside the artfully labeled containers, to both the initiated and the uninitiated. As sociologist Antoine Hennion argues, objects have a "capacity to interrupt, to surprise or to respond. . . . Objects are not already there, inert and available at our service. They deliver themselves, unrobe themselves, impose themselves on us."[8] People like Issa and places like Khoury's use craft beer to help others "unrobe" themselves from preconceived prejudices about drinking that have been reinforced by others within a particular context where the bland and boring have ruled the roost.

"Offering some of the top brands—Alpine, Almanac, Cascade, we're getting Modern Times soon—brings a lot of attention to this city," says Issa. "Then other breweries start taking us more seriously and learn that we're more craft-centric than what Las Vegas is generally known for. We have a culture that's growing here; people from out of town are starting to take notice and people here are starting to take pride in local."

The "craft-centric" culture, and the pride that locals have in it, is the product of creative collaborations between people like Issa and through places like Khoury's. In sociologist Michael P. Farrell's analysis of "collaborative circles"—defined as "groups formed by peers who negotiate an innovative vision in their field"—he notes that individuals with "shared values and aspirations" tend to "gravitate toward magnet places."[9] Farrell focuses his attention on the interpersonal dynamics of small groups and friendship pairs and the ways they work together to create new works of art (like the impressionist painters in Paris) or new forms of knowledge (like the "ultras" who started the women's rights movement). In Las Vegas, a more amorphous yet still collaborative scene supersedes Farrell's smaller circles because the scene is made up of multiple "magnet places" where both producers and consumers, from experts to novices, are drawn for social interaction and craft beer drinking. Both doing and being scene are collaborative efforts that require a relative degree of innovation to combat a lingering hangover caused by the Las Vegas Syndrome.

This chapter traverses and exposes the symbolic contours and aesthetic ecology of the local Las Vegas craft beer scene. While the scene is not a physically bounded place unto itself, it is made of many places that create, foster, and accomplish it. These places are more than simply inert stages on which the scene plays out.[10] They are where thoughts and ideas become action. They are where the scene happens. As sociologist Joseph Kotarba contends, scenes exist "in our minds and become visible during interaction."[11] The most significant interactions for the Las Vegas craft beer scene are those between people, between people and places, and between people and a material yet fleeting object (i.e., craft beer) that develop and nurture the local craft beer scene within, through, and near one of the world's most popular urban tourist spectacles. As such, though the local scene is connected to regional, national, and global scenes, I am focusing here on the publicly observable and available constellation of urban sociability and sensuality that composes the aesthetic ecology within this particular context.

The local scene exists because there are people interacting in and with places that make it happen. All local scenes require places for "participants to commingle, act, and share meanings."[12] As a qualifier, "local" is often applied to the production process of drinkable commodities whereby "local" breweries are valorized for their proximity and often tied to marketing strategies that highlight the freshness of their beers, their supposed "authenticity," or their environmentally sustainable practices.[13] This tends to favor production over consumption, cutting off a large portion of the people who make the scene work (i.e., consumers). As such, I prefer to use "local" as a qualifier that highlights and emphasizes embodiment and emplacement, where sensuous bodies interact in particular locales with each other and with the valorized object (e.g., craft beer) through particular practices (e.g., drinking craft beer). The scene's very nature as an expressive entity that connects people and places to one another provides nuanced ways for participants to engage implicitly or explicitly in the performance of taste and an imaginative restructuring of the city's aesthetic demeanor. Those expressions are embodied and emplaced and, therefore, obviously require bodies and places for the claims about local culture to be made and experiences to be shared.

Certainly plenty of craft beer drinking happens in homes across the Las Vegas Valley during family dinners, parties, and private bottle shares. But scenes require public places that are open and inclusive. Though most of the places are not public in the sense that they are paid for by taxes or owned by municipalities, they are small businesses that function as *shared* places. They are places that owners like Issa use to practice a type of "commercial communalism" that has been an enduring means for sharing experiences and knowledge in American cities since the early nineteenth century.[14] Because each local business relies on a consumer base to keep it afloat, the place itself—as both a stage for interaction and a prop to interact with—is a product of what seminal interactionist Herbert Blumer called "joint action" whereby "participants fit their acts together."[15] The scene is a product of joint actions between multiple actors, including the places and the products that are shared and experienced together. The material and symbolic qualities of such places interact with the cognitive and sensuous capacities of people to produce meaning in meaningful and meaning-*filled* places.

As such, the following focuses on places "where the action is" and the people who work and play with and within them.[16] Without these local places, there is no local scene. These places are the literal and figurative stages where social actors negotiate the ways they act in and on their social world.[17] Actors negotiate their roles and the scripts they follow or improvise upon while interacting with others on stages that both liberate and constrain their performances. Craft beer is a core significant object that brings significant others together within a local scene composed of places located throughout the valley rather than in a particular area, neighborhood, or district of the city. Participants enact a "symbolic ownership" of the scene in similar ways that neighborhood residents often do, as sociologist Andrew Deener found in his study of Venice, California.[18] The morphing and amorphous collection of actors share a contentious objection to the dominant cultural logic of the city that, in turn, fosters an alternative cultural logic developed around the sensuous pleasures and fun of tasting craft beer. There are certainly worse things to rally around than pleasure and fun.[19]

The Aesthetic Ecology of the Local Scene

Local scenes rely on places "that contribute to making the city itself a *place*,"[20] one endowed with meaning and value.[21] As sociologist Thomas Gieryn argues, places are "doubly constructed" by their material physical location *and* as social spaces that must be "interpreted, narrated, perceived, felt, understood, and imagined."[22] Participants' investments of time, money, and emotional labor in places coalesce into a definable and observable scene. This shows their connection to the scene itself as they help build and perform within and through it. As in the case of Las Vegas with its kudzu-like sprawling neighborhoods, traveling to and from such places requires work, and signals a collective desire for particular types of embodied experiences. The type of work that a local scene needs to keep it afloat and thwart the "corruption" that taints so many scenes involves more than purely practical or rational actions.[23] Instead, the local scene—as an alternative to the dominant culture it works against—requires actions (doing) that are motivated by arational aesthetic desires, feelings, and judgments (being).

Viewed as a whole, scene participants bring the scene to life through their joint actions in and through the segmented places that support and sustain it. The local scene is a collective accomplishment that relies on voluntary participants who deem the scene and its "significant objects" as valuable and worthwhile. As such, the local scene is defined by impassioned, embodied, and emplaced individuals interacting in significant places. The continual gathering of those people and places is held together by, and in effect constitutes, an overarching "aesthetic ecology." According to sociologist Tia DeNora, a scene's "aesthetic ecology" is defined as

> a cluster of people and their relations to and with each other, as well as the materials and settings, situated vocabularies, symbols, values, patterned ways of doings and—importantly—happenstance. . . . [It is] also the equally important "inside" of action, its pre-cognitive and non-verbal features such as emotion, impulse, and embodiments.[24]

The somewhat serendipitous nature of a scene's "aesthetic ecology" is, as DeNora notes, a product of "happenstance" rather than that of a rationally constituted plan. This rings true for the "aesthetic ecology" of Las Vegas, affording a means for connecting geographically separated persons and places to the same local scene across the city's sprawling neighborhoods and unincorporated townships.

In Las Vegas, the local scene is not confined to a single neighborhood or area. In other older cities, scenes can be played on and within the stages of particular trendy (or trendsetting) neighborhoods. Chicago's "neo-bohemian" Wicker Park is a perfect example of this. "During the 1990s, Wicker Park gained a national reputation as a site of hip urban culture with a thriving music and art scene," writes sociologist Richard Lloyd. "In defining the local scene, both press accounts and participants evoke bohemian traditions of artistic innovation in the city."[25] The local population of "artists and lifestyle aesthetes" was concentrated within this particular neighborhood, making the scene both spatially specific and limited. Neither of these is necessarily negative or positive, though the close proximity of persons with similar tastes can help reinforce the cultural identity of the scene and its participants more quickly.

Such distinctive neighborhoods are uncommon in the so-called postmodern cities of the Sun Belt that have grown outward rather than upward due in part to the availability of land.[26] As such, the physical ecology of the Las Vegas craft beer scene and the spatial distribution of its key stages take on what sociologist Jonathan Wynn, in his study of urban music festivals, calls a "confetti pattern," unbounded and seemingly random.[27]

When locals—either natives or residents from elsewhere—define Las Vegas, the city extends beyond its legalistic boundaries to encompass the entirety of the valley it sits within. Over two million people live in the Las Vegas Valley, from the northwest Centennial Hills area, where the sprawl gives way to rocky desert, to the eastern stretches of Henderson that lead to the Hoover Dam and its dependent Boulder City. I've seen people from various parts join in local craft beer events across the valley. Though they could stay in their specific geographic circles, many of the core members of the scene traverse the entire valley for unique aesthetic offerings and experiences like out-of-town tap takeovers, local brewery releases, and bottle shares at the scene's sacred sites.

On one particular Saturday, I didn't attend a bottle share I was invited to Downtown because there was another event going on that afternoon. Bad Beat Brewing was celebrating its one-year anniversary. When I entered the brewery's taproom around four o'clock that afternoon, I saw someone I thought had attended the share earlier that day. But perhaps, like me, he chose this event instead. I was wrong.

"Where were you?" he asked me.

"What do you mean?" I responded.

"The bottle share. I thought you were coming."

"You went? And now you're here?"

Looking at me with his typical incredulous smirk, Kris replied, "I'm a professional." I knew what he meant. Attending craft beer events was "serious leisure" for core scene members like Kris.[28] His stocky physique, often adorned in brewery T-shirts, is a fixture in the local craft beer scene. He usually has with him a stash of "whales" he's not afraid to share or "treadmill," which is his and his buddies' collective version of "taking it to the dome"—a subversive and hedonistic act of passing around a bomber of a highly coveted and potent beer and drinking it straight from the bottle.

I told him I couldn't handle the bottle share—especially one promising a blurring array of high ABV brews—and then head to a brewery

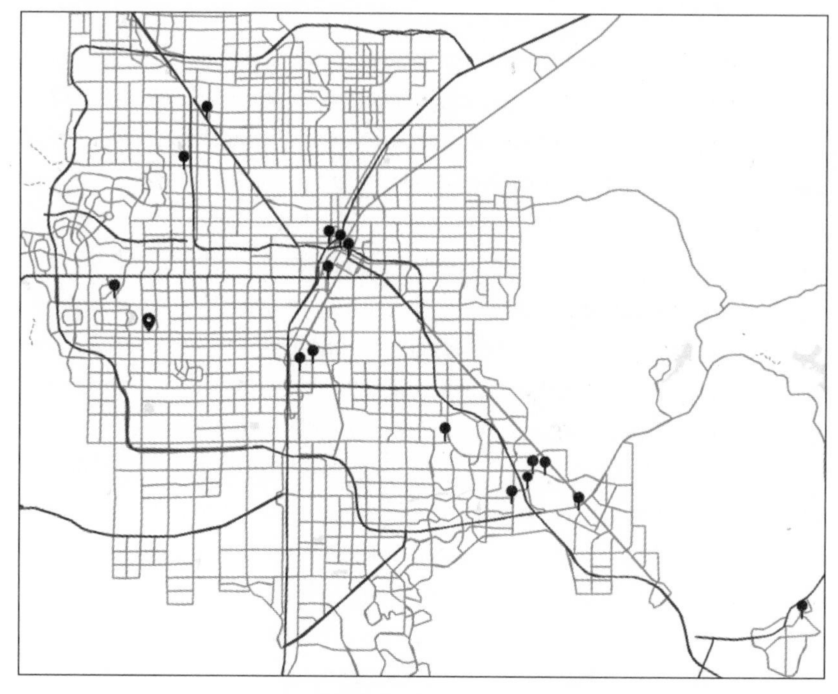

FIGURE 2.1. Map of local craft breweries across the Las Vegas Valley.

anniversary party. And Bad Beat's party was featuring a special beer brewed for the event: the Joker, a 10 percent Belgian blonde ale aged in chardonnay barrels, adorned with a devilish harlequin and hardened drips of yellow wax around the bottle cap. Not only would the alcohol get to me; so would the distance, about a half-hour drive on a Saturday afternoon.

The distance between Bad Beat and Downtown Las Vegas, however, is not the greatest between the scene's magnet places. Add another twenty minutes if you're coming to Bad Beat or CraftHaus in Henderson's "Artisan Booze District" from Big Dog's Draft House. Or for those who live in the deep southwestern township of Enterprise on the other side of the valley, the drive will take about thirty minutes. And I have to emphasize *drive* because Las Vegas is car city built around the asocial, freedom-loving car driver's wants and whims.[29] The city has a fairly inept bus system and, perhaps more importantly, no light rail to speak of. The rising demand for and interest in craft beer in Las Vegas has dramatically increased the number of craft breweries and bars serving craft beer in the past few years (see both Appendix A and Appendix B). This has had the latent effect of increasing the local craft beer scene's footprint. As such, strategizing both physical distance and physical sobriety is required for scene actors because events rarely happen within walking distance of one another.

Despite the spatial distances between breweries, beer bars, and other places offering craft beer, an aesthetic character connects these geographically segmented and isolated places. Invariably, when I asked people to name their favorite local brewery or local craft watering hole, they couldn't, or perhaps wouldn't, name just one. Though some were

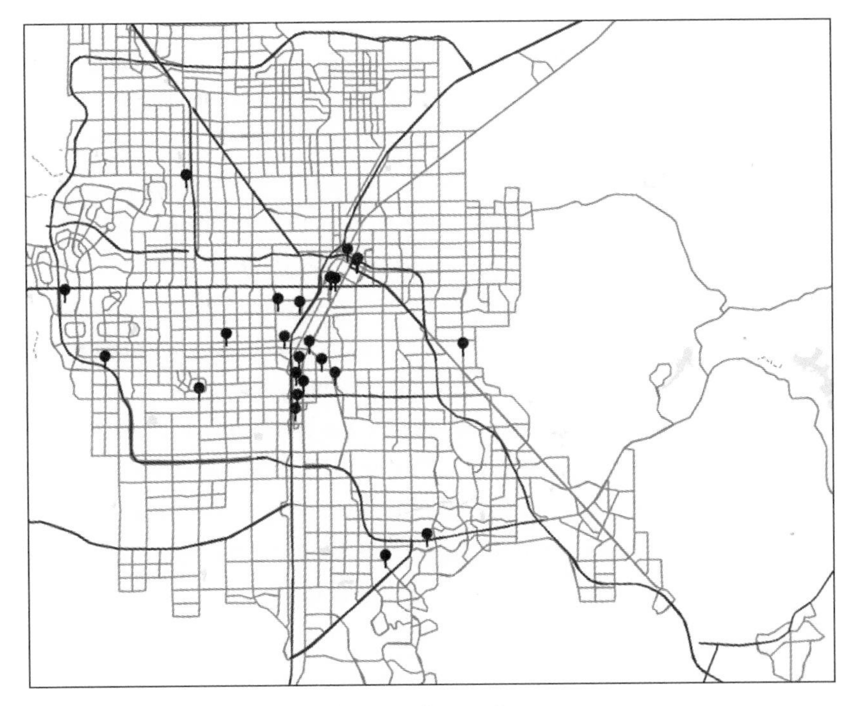

FIGURE 2.2. Map of notable craft-centric bars and restaurants.

partial to particular spots over others, most people seemed to frequent or at least purchase goods from multiple local breweries.

Local breweries, and the places that serve their wares, have helped change the way Las Vegas tastes. I mean that in two separate but related ways. The first implies the way that *people* in Las Vegas taste, whereby taste is a performed activity rather than merely a predefined sensory effect. "Tastes are not given or determined, and their objects are not either," writes sociologist Antoine Hennion. "One has to make them appear together, through repeated experiments, progressively adjusted."[30] Local craft brewers and servers are repeatedly reestablishing a "knowing-through-taste" logic that, as chef and food scholar Roger Haden notes, has been overshadowed and even eliminated by the onslaught of chemical additives that merely simulate flavors in fast food and frozen TV dinners.

"The senses require an 'aesthetic education'—as some European countries offer—rather than the shock tactics of industry," writes Haden. "*Homo sapiens*, the *knowing* human, is simultaneously the *tasting* human. . . . The powers at work in the world of taste today encourage an everyday forgetting of the senses, which is now the behavioral norm."[31]

The acts and arts of craft provide a *re*education to a population surrounded by simulated historical buildings and experiences. As people encounter local craft beer in and from Las Vegas, they begin to perform taste differently and in opposition to the mass-produced and impersonal products that litter the physical and cultural landscape.

With this "aesthetic education," or perhaps *through* it, the taste of the city itself changes. In this way, we can think of places as having particular tastes connected to them that help define the character or identity of a particular place or city. This is what is known in foodie cheese and oenophile circles as *terroir*. The French term is used to identify and label the unique characteristics of a place and the products that, in the cases of grasses and grapes, literally come from its soil. Since the seventeenth century, writers in France, and subsequently elsewhere, have used the term as a means of describing, and later marketing, the "authentic" specificities of locales, the production of high-quality goods in those locales, and their connections to personal and collective identities and memories.[32]

Because terroir means soil, it tends to imply or function as a nostalgic retreat from the urban metropolis to the whistling countryside of an imagined past. In order to update and extend the term to give it a more city-bound vibe, food scholars have recently offered "asphalt terroir" and "concrete terroir" as semantic modifications to redirect the focus from agriculture to urban culture.[33] Though I understand the use of these qualifiers to signify urban-based phenomena, they are both too stereotypical and too static to be of much value. Just as individuals' tastes can change, so can the tastes of cities. "Asphalt" and "concrete" denote only one type of change, a change that solidifies and stabilizes. The rise of the Las Vegas craft beer scene tells a different story, one that is more fluid and amorphous, where the aesthetic ecology of the scene grapples with and pushes against the stereotypical *neon* terroir of Las Vegas with its own not-so-neon terroir. Though that change has been slow to come, in the years following the Great Recession, craft brewers, peddlers, and imbibers have changed the city's aesthetic demeanor for scene participants. Enacting such change is risky, and the biggest risk, perhaps, comes from betting against the house. Gambling, the city's preferred activity for drinkers of all shapes, sizes, and styles, still stands in the way of a full-blown aesthetic payout for the local craft beer scene.

Gambling on Gambling

The first time I walked into Tenaya Creek Brewery in the northwest part of the valley, I was shocked. In fact, I thought I was in the wrong place. Hearing Gavin Rossdale belt out Bush's 1990s alternative rock hit "Glycerine," surrounded by the glowing screens of video poker machines and the harsh smoke from a black plastic ashtray was enough to make me step back through the doors I just entered. This can't possibly be a brewery, I thought. It wasn't like Stone Brewing's World Bistro and Gardens in northern San Diego County, where you can sit next to a lazy stream and sip one-off variants of their typical offerings, like their IPA with kaffir lime leaves and pomegranate. Nor was it a quaint and simple brick-lined room on the outskirts of Downtown Denver where you could sit next to Crooked Stave Artisan Beer Project's twenty copper barrels while sipping on a funky sour Nightmare on Brett.

Was the towering silo outside Tenaya Creek just for show? I later found out that it did, in fact, house grains for brewing in a space that is closed off from the bar area. But the first thing indicating that I was, indeed, in the right place was the glass case in the entry way that held T-shirts with the labels of Tenaya Creek's beers as well as trophies and awards, including a Gold Medal from the 2002 Great American Beer Festival for their pilsner.

So I walked back in, saddled up to the bar, and ordered a Hop Ride IPA, a beer I've tried before, but only from a bottle. The bottle has an attractive label with a hissing rattlesnake surrounded by bicycle gears with prose that warns that riders in the desert will have to hop over the potentially dangerous creatures as they "enjoy the areas beyond the reach of the neon." This one, however, was brewed a week earlier about hundred feet from where I sat. The grapefruit-like hops penetrate my nose. The almost white frothy head sticks to the hair above my upper lip, a small drip trickles down my beard. I use my forearm to wipe it away while I savor the pleasant bite of the bitter aftertaste.

The beer is good but the place doesn't seem right. Sure, it plays host to a diverse crowd of locals, some of whom are devoted craft beer drinkers and some of whom could not care less about the beer brewed and served there. No Big Beer brews are available, but there is liquor. And video poker machines ensconced in the bar top. The bartender tells me I'll have to give up my seat to someone looking to gamble, but until then, I'm free to enjoy my beer there. "Sure thing," I say, squinting from the flashing bright red and blue lights that ricochet off my glass, daring me to slip in a twenty and test my luck.

Video poker at breweries is a common sight in Las Vegas and elsewhere in Nevada. Great Basin's Brewery in Sparks—the oldest in the state—and Big Dog's Brewery—the oldest in Las Vegas (originally called Holy Cow! Casino and Brewery)—have them, as do some of the best craft beer bars in the city (e.g., both Aces & Ales locations, Money Plays, Office Bar, PKWY Tavern, Rebel Republic). They're hard to resist for owners since they bring in extra cash for bars and breweries alike. I've been told that profits can range from ten to sixty thousand dollars per machine per year. And bartenders like them because winners give them tips that can double their hourly salary, and then some.

The intoxication of money, and gambling for more of it, can often trump the intoxication of craft, which has had a residual negative effect on the local craft beer scene because the focus shifts to gamers and, in the end, reinforces the dominant logic and narrative of the city and the prominence and effects of the Las Vegas Syndrome. In Las Vegas, gambling is a "convention," a standardized way of thinking and acting, "embodied in practices and equipment that are totally taken for granted."[34] The ubiquity of places with video poker machines affords gambling an ability to infiltrate and hold power over the local scene despite its translocal and virtual links to a larger grand scene. But, as sociologist Howard Becker maintains, "The limitations of conventional practice are not total. You can always do things differently if you are prepared to pay the price in increased effort or decreased circulation of your work."[35] Going against the grain is a daunting task for even the biggest dog in the fight.

Big Dog's Draft House, now solely located in the northwest region after closing a few outposts throughout the valley, tries to do it all. It has three distinct areas inside its confines, not including the dog-friendly patio and parking lot where it hosts its seasonal festivals. It is a family-friendly restaurant, a sort of transition space that has a classic pub feel, and a bar area for the twenty-one-and-over crowd, which is often also the video-poker-playing, mixed-drink-or-light-beer-drinking crowd. Whether at one of the big Strip casinos or at a local gaming pub, gamblers expect to receive *comped* drinks. Why would a brewery want to give away a prized and crafted barrel-aged stout or an IPA with expensive and hard-to-find Citra or Nelson Sauvin hops? They usually don't.

FIGURE 2.3. Video poker machines line the bar at Big Dog's Draft House, the oldest craft brewery in Las Vegas. (Photo by Maddie Jo Evans)

So they'll brew something else, something likely to resemble a typical macro light beer. Big Dog's former assistant brewer Tom Harwood told me that, like other breweries in the city that have gaming, they made a beer specifically to be given away for free to gamblers.[36]

> Outside this building [Big Dog's Brew House] our Dirty Dog IPA is the most popular, followed closely by War Dog, a double IPA. When we do special beer releases or have one of our outdoor festivals, it's a totally different crowd. People are coming for the beer itself. But on a typical day in this building, Leglifter is by far the most popular. It's a super light beer, only 4.2 percent, if that. It's the beer we serve while people are playing the poker or slot machines. It's our comp beer. When they're not drinking Bud out of a bottle, they're drinking Leglifter.

Just like their former self, Holy Cow!, was devoted to all things bovine, most of Big Dog's beers have canine-themed names. I can't help but wonder how many people who drink Leglifter think about why dogs lift their legs while they drink a pale yellow beverage. This subtle jab at both Big Beer and its consumers' tastes signifies the frustration that brewers have about being constrained by the need to cater to non-craft patrons.

Yet with the guidance of successful marketing, Leglifter slowly morphed into Las Vegas Lager, "crafted for neon lovers" and canned with the famous "Welcome to Fabulous Las Vegas" sign printed on one side of the container.[37] And packaging it in an aluminum can instead of a glass bottle means that it is legally permitted to be carried and crushed on the Strip. With their words, imagery, and actions, Big Dog tries to appeal to both fans of craft and mainstream macro-light lager drinkers simultaneously. This move is a clear attempt to deal with the creative constraints driving them to garner appeal from both their local fan base and a broader population.

Like the restaurant cooks that sociologist Gary Alan Fine studied, brewers, most often at the behest of the brewery's owners, are always negotiating between aesthetic desires and economic concerns. Fine notes that "the proximal source of constraints is a restaurant management that depends on the loyalty of its customers. . . . Management supports and encourages aesthetic presentations as long as good work remains profitable."[38] Of course, all breweries have to serve beer that people want. But at a casino/brewery or brewery/casino (which term comes first is itself a matter of aesthetic judgment), "the loyalty of its customers" takes on greater importance when loyal customers are also placing bets while drinking brews.

Gambling on Beer

The mere reality of breweries that allow gambling—often coupled with smoking because of profits that depend on and feed both rushes and addictions—shocks craft beer fans and aficionados outside of Nevada. Neither the reality nor the shock went unnoticed by Colorado-based writer Lee Breslouer in his 2013 selection of the best craft brewery from each state. After speaking fondly about multiple breweries in western states, he didn't hold back any punches when he got to Nevada. Breslouer decried the "Battle Born" breweries by declaring that "many of the breweries in Nevada have a serious lack of ambition, as they seem happy to own a taproom/casino (seriously, they exist) and not bother to bottle and get their beer out into the world in any way."[39] A case of the Las Vegas Syndrome for sure.

This is a fairly accurate description of the prevailing business model of a few local breweries and beer bars, especially those where gambling takes precedence over their customers' desires for craft beer. Yet, to be fair to other local breweries—some of which allow gambling and neither bottle nor can their wares—many have still won prestigious awards for their beers. Ambition certainly wasn't lacking in 2015 at Chicago Brewing Company (in the running for worst local brewery name anywhere outside of the Windy City). Under the helm of Dave Pascual, Chicago took home Gold and Bronze medals from the Great American Beer Festival, both for Belgian-style beers (a quad and a tripel, respectively), adding to an impressive and growing collection of their own accolades as well as the Las Vegas scene's collective awards case.[40]

Still, the perception remained that the Silver State hadn't fully entered the Golden Age of craft beer. But things have changed in recent years; inherited social conventions and difficult reputations have been challenged. Breslouer named Tenaya Creek the state's best brewery in 2013 when it was still a functioning and wildly popular brewery/casino. The 2015 version of that list—still on thrillist.com but compiled by two other writers—also gave Tenaya Creek top honors. This time, however, they quipped that Tenaya Creek is "perhaps the only business in Vegas that isn't also a casino."[41] The writers also noted that "Tenaya takes its brewing very, very seriously—so much so that it straight-up abandoned everything it was doing, including food service, to concentrate on the beer." They actually "abandoned" food service in 2010. More to the point, they also did away with gambling, but that wasn't until they changed locations in late 2015.

Former Joseph James head brewer turned "beer mercenary" for Tenaya Creek Alex Graham was offended by Breslouer's knock on the local scene, especially the claim about Nevada brewers' "serious lack of ambition," but he conceded that it has traditionally been difficult to get people in Las Vegas interested in craft beer.

Sharing his views on the difficulties as well as Tenaya Creek's effort to change the local culture through the craft beer scene, Alex shifts in his seat across the table from me and his usually cool demeanor fades behind his tightened fist.

> This city is different than any other city. Denver, San Diego, Portland, Seattle, even Phoenix. They all support local craft beer. They don't have bars like us. We've got gaming in almost every single bar and they're comping drinks. They're looking at the bottom line only, looking at prices of kegs because they're giving away drinks. We'll get put on tap and the product's doing great, but I'll come back in and find my handle replaced with another more national, larger scale brand. And they'll say, "Hey, your product was doing fine but we're giving it away, it's nothing personal." Also, we have a bar and have gaming here, so other bars look at us as competition. They don't want to put our handles on because it will promote us and they think it will take away their gaming customers. *It's a really frustrating part about building a local scene here.*

"That must be frustrating," I say reassuringly. Making craft beer only to compete with bars eager to serve the usual Big Beer fare was not why he got into this as a career. The native Las Vegan knows he could move elsewhere, as many would-be brewers have, but he wanted to stay and do something good in and for his hometown.

"We weren't the first in town, but we're a truly local company. We have nine employees and four of us were actually born and raised here in the city. People view us as a really local brand, which is great," Alex announces with pride.

Pushing harder, I ask what he and Tenaya Creek are going to do to help the local scene become less frustrating and foster more local support. His answer surprised me. They actually had a strategy that was already in motion.

> It's all going to be changing when we move into our new facility because we're not going to have gaming anymore. . . . It was time to change course again. We went from a restaurant to a bar/production facility and, well, we don't have room to grow here because we're running out of height. So we're moving to a new location Downtown. The owners have been looking at the way other cities do it. It's very much industrial. I'm looking forward to more production, more distribution. And we'll have a taproom with our beer and guest taps.

Tenaya Creek's game changed because the game was starting to change around them. They wanted to contribute to and help reinforce the changes. So they adopted a new business plan and new philosophy about what it meant to be a local craft brewery in Las Vegas. And they changed locations to make it happen.

Tenaya Creek's geographical shift was a tactical move to boost their identity and, in turn, the reputation of the city's craft beer scene. Relocating helped them redefine who they were, how they saw themselves, and how others saw them. The move was a behavioral, symbolic, and aesthetic act of resistance, a means for redefining themselves and the local craft beer scene. Part of that meant continuing to expand their distribution into and beyond neighboring states—though they somewhat oddly already have a strong presence in Alberta and British Columbia, which Alex credits to the Canadian snowbirds seeking respite in the desert. It also meant finding a better way to connect to local craft beer drinkers. Both approaches are intended to help both the brewery and the scene it contributes to and relies on.

"We're a Las Vegas brewery, a Las Vegas company. I was born here," said Tim Etter, Tenaya Creek's most vocal owner. "Our roots are established. We want this to be our home and our emphasis. We want people to realize that with all there is to see here, *Las Vegas is more than just what you see on the Strip*."[42]

Moving Downtown, though outside of the llama-shaped zone owned by Zappos CEO Tony Hsieh and his Downtown Project, was a way to capture a recently evolving spirit of local aesthetic entrepreneurship that aims to present a side of Las Vegas not seen on the Strip.[43] Riding the wave of redevelopment in the general area, Etter and company found a former plumbing supply warehouse. The fourteen-thousand-square-foot building was built in 1952 and sits across Bonanza Road from the former site of the Moulin Rouge—known for being the first racially integrated hotel-casino in the city, where greats like Sammy Davis Jr., Ella Fitzgerald, Frank Sinatra, and Judy Garland performed during its short life span in the mid-1950s.[44]

"Adaptive re-use" is a common strategy employed by small craft breweries.[45] Old industrial buildings across the United States have been taken over by hop-sniffing, barley-carrying brewers. Critics have been quick to see this as a form of or in concert with broader gentrification processes or, perhaps even worse, as "symbolic violence" against the place's history, new neighbors, or both.[46] But leaving a building without occupants, attracting vandals and vagrants while property values plunge, doesn't seem like a good strategy for promoting and uplifting a local culture. Granted, it's a complicated issue, but the craft beer scene players are far less harmful than the moguls who have historically bought massive swaths of land to build casino after casino. At the very least, Tenaya Creek's move signals a shift *away* from gaming, providing a publicly accessible, open setting in a formerly vacant warehouse.

The building has a spacious area in the back that now houses Tenaya Creek's new brewery equipment, including new fermentation tanks set

FIGURE 2.4. Tenaya Creek's new brewery sits just below the highway at the edge of the Historic Westside. (Photo by Maddie Jo Evans)

to produce six thousand barrels of beer a year, three times the amount they were doing at the old location. The front of the place has some "mid mod" quirks that the brewery uses in a productive fashion to create quasi-intimate spaces that are both connected to and somewhat shut-off from the rest of the taproom.

"This is what we wanted for our locals and for visitors," Tenaya Creek's longtime brewer Anthony Gibson told me when I stopped in to see the new place a few weeks after it opened. He points to wooden tables made by local arts, then to the chalkboard listing about ten of their own beers and another ten or so guest brews, and then toward the plexiglass wall that separates the consumers of their beers and those who make them. "When people come to a craft brewery, this is the type of atmosphere they expect, and *deserve*."

Anthony's goal of creating a new "atmosphere" is apt for the situation he was moving from and now helping create in the brewery's new digs. In her study of the relocation of a coffee house in Northern California, sociologist Melinda Milligan notes that the visual appearance and *atmosphere* of the site influences its "interactional potential," a key characteristic of "place attachment."[47] "The specific physical details of a site," writes Milligan, do not determine yet still influence "the types of interactions that are likely or able to happen within it, meaning its interactional potential, or the 'expectations' an individual has for interactions there."[48] Employees of the coffee shop she studied tended to have negative responses to the new location's atmosphere. This was due in part to their perception of the ownership's newly adopted values represented by the replacement of wooden tables with fake granite tops. Anthony moved in the opposite direction for both employees and customers of the old and new Tenaya Creek, especially those who situate themselves deeply within the aesthetic ecology of the local craft beer scene. While some bemoaned the move, citing frustrations about proximity and propinquity, or *positioning* as Milligan calls it, others embraced the change.

"I have so many great memories of the old place. Those won't go away," declares a regular patron of Tenaya Creek's old location. "But this place is great. It's a brewery with a taproom attached."

"Instead of a casino?" I ask provocatively.

"Exactly," he replies, pointing to the see-through wall. "They're back there working on making great beer, bottling it, canning it, getting it out there. Around town. In other states. They're thinking about distribution, but they're letting us come here and drink their beer while they work. I think that's great. It works for me."

The move has been a success, but was a surprise to most when first announced. Perhaps we all should have seen the move coming, especially *this* move. Tenaya Creek even provided a clue about where they might relocate, though maybe it was just pure coincidence or the product of happenstance. I haven't been able to get a clear answer about it. In 2014, they changed the name of their Great American Beer Festival (GABF) medal-winning English-style brown ale from Calico Brown to Bonanza Brown. The label still opines about their "love of the surrounding area of Red Rock Canyon" where Calico Basin is, urging craft beer drinkers to "get back to nature," even though Bonanza Road runs through the predominantly low-income neighborhood known as the Historic Westside and crosses near the recently demolished F Street wall that, in effect, kept residents out of the so-called revitalizing Downtown.[49] Perhaps they'll pay homage to the history and culture of their *new* surroundings in future batches of the brew.

Regardless of the exact reasons for the name change, it was allegedly prompted by the threat of an impending lawsuit from a much larger and well-known brewery in a neighboring state that produced a beer with a similar name.[50] So maybe calling it Bonanza was just a simple twist of fate. Maybe not. What is certain, though, is that their move *to* Bonanza wouldn't have happened if another brewery hadn't already been fighting their own legal battles. Not with another brewer, but with the city of Las Vegas instead.

Banging on the Doors of City Hall

Sometimes it takes a mixture of a little naïveté and a little chutzpah to get the wheels of justice turning. Tenaya Creek wouldn't have been able to make their move if the new kids on the block—totally coincidental that they're five young men—hadn't paved the path that made it legally possible. Enter Banger Brewing.

Even before they had secured a firm brick-and-mortar location, the "Banger Gang" had made their local presence known.[51] They showed up to festivals, pouring relatively left-field beers like a jalapeño hefeweizen and a watermelon wheat ale underneath a maroon tent announcing their name, their logo, and the words "fresh," local," and "Las Vegas." Together. With pride.

Like the folks at Tenaya Creek, Banger Brewing drew their "local cred" from their individual upbringings in and around Las Vegas. And each of them grew up professionally working on the Strip. Though some of them knew each other beforehand, happenstance brought them all together while working at different high-end restaurants at the Bellagio.

There's a bit of poetic irony in the coming together of a racially mixed working-class quintet in the middle of one of the first properties to usher in the era of garish opulence in Las Vegas.[52] And they came together to brew beer, which eventually brought them Downtown.

The brewery's namesake, Michael "Banger" Beaman, got his nickname from unintentionally knocking into pans hanging in the kitchen of Olives, an award-winning restaurant by celebrity chef Michael Mina that anchors the Bellagio's dining collection. Beaman had been homebrewing since 2005 and eventually turned his buddies onto it. Putting together about fifteen recipes they could replicate with consistency, they decided to leave the garage where they initially brewed five gallon batches and take a shot at the professional craft beer game. After looking at other locations, mostly on the east side of Las Vegas Boulevard (it's not called "the Strip" in Downtown Las Vegas) in the area now designated as the Fremont East Entertainment District, the guys settled on an unpredictable yet seemingly prosperous spot.

The three-thousand-square-foot space lies in the shadow of Slotzilla, a twelve-story monster slot machine where people pay twenty-five dollars to zip-line through the Fremont Street Experience. Their neighbor is the hospital-themed and glutton-grabbing Heart Attack Grill, a restaurant with a scale underneath one sign promising a free meal to anyone over three hundred fifty pounds and another sign promoting their three-thousand-calorie butterfat milkshake. The location is even more surprising for anyone who's been to Downtown Las Vegas before former mayor Oscar Goodman's prized spectacle became an umbrella of flashing lights and classic rock. Tipsy tourists grasping sugar-saturated frozen drinks in plastic footballs and street performers who pose for pictures with them have replaced prostitutes, drug dealers, and the homeless. Of course, these "deviants" didn't just go away. They were pushed further north and east.

Nick Fischella noted the unusual setting while sitting with two of his partners, Eddie Quiogue and Roberto Mendoza, in their window-lined taproom that looks out onto Fremont Street.

FIGURE 2.5. Banger Brewery is located on the tourist side of Fremont Street, squeezed in between unlikely neighbors Slotzilla and the Heart Attack Grill. (Photo by author)

"If you told folks who've been here a while that this was where we were opening a brewery, they'd think we were crazy. We even thought that! We looked elsewhere first, where Inspire Theater is, but it was tied up in a foreclosure at the time. We looked where Le Thai is before they began construction, and the hookah lounge that became Park on Fremont." Despite its imperfections, the space they settled on was one they could afford with the help of the recently "revitalizing" Downtown Project and a few hundred thousand dollars in personal savings as well as loans from loyal friends.[53]

The space where they would build their place, it turned out, was the least of their worries. Licensing, or more pointedly the *lack* of the *existence* of the right license, was their biggest obstacle. They wanted to brew beer and pour it, but the city didn't have that license. The influence of gambling is so pervasive that a license for brewing beer and serving it on premise without food and without gambling didn't exist within the confines of the city of Las Vegas. So the Banger Gang set out to create one.

To do so, they collaborated with the city's attorneys and Mayor Carolyn Goodman to write a new type of business license.

Within the city proper, most businesses that sold alcohol, of all types, held a "tavern license" that required a seventy-five-thousand-dollar origination charge along with annual fees. Because of the recent boom across the street on Fremont East, the city had recently introduced a "tavern limited" license for twenty thousand that could be waived if the venue hosted entertainment three nights a week. There was, however, a "beer and wine room" license for seventy-five hundred that provided an important step to the license Banger actually needed: a brewpub license.

"This almost didn't happen," says Eddie. "We stopped construction [when] we were like two-thirds done with it, and we were supposed to open in two months! Our last-ditch effort was to go directly to Mayor Goodman and she put us in touch with the city's attorneys. And we worked with them for the next couple of weeks and got the ball rolling in the right direction."

"So what was the pitch, what did you say to her"?

"We need this!" they shout in unison, laughing.

"The tanks were in here, the walls were rebuilt. . . . Basically, [we said] the city can't have this *not* happen. The city has to let this business open," Nick says, reliving those struggles in his head.

Roberto chimes in, saying they used the idea and appeal of *local*—as both a commodity and a cultural artifact—to help sway the mayor.

> We told her that you're not allowing tourists to take home something that is locally made in Las Vegas. That's where the growlers came in. We wanted to do premise and off-premise sales, for tourists and locals. . . . We have a local product made locally that you're saying "No" to because of the license, so clearly we need to amend this license in order for us to sell a locally made product for people to take home with them. They still said "No." But they called us back two weeks later and said, alright, let's get this going.

Together, Banger and the city created what is called an "ancillary brewpub" license that has no fee outside of the "beer and wine room" license, but allows them to sell beer that customers can take off premise. Locally brewed craft beer from a "true tap tasting room with a brewery connected to it," as Roberto calls their place, was henceforth able to survive and thrive in the heart of Downtown Las Vegas.

"Our license says Banger Brewing and Ancillary Brewpub #1," Roberto says, smiling alongside his partners. "And that's pretty cool."

With less of a headache, yet with the same amount of fortitude, Dave and Wyndee Forrest were fighting similar battles across the valley in Henderson. Instead of laying their eyes on a central location, they wanted to open up a brewery in a recently built industrial park where both the craft spirts producer Las Vegas Distillery and the winemaking school Grape Expectations recently opened. Those two businesses also had to haggle with the state, county, and city over out-of-date licensing.

Like with Banger, the problem for the Forrests and their would-be CraftHaus Brewery was that the city didn't differentiate between brewpubs with and without gaming. "It's almost assumed [in Las Vegas] that if there's alcohol there has to be gaming," Wyndee told me. "That was never a part of our plan. You can get that all over the valley." She and Dave worked almost two years with the city's licensing board, with input from Paul Gatza, director of the Brewers Association, to come up with a new license alternative that would reduce the fee from sixty thousand to ten thousand dollars.

The reduction in cost for the "non-gaming brewpub" license would allow them to bring their dream to life. And at that point, it wasn't only their dream. Through a campaign on Kickstarter—a crowd-funding website for creative projects—the Forrests exceeded their original goal of $20,000 in twenty-eight days and finished with $25,859. Those who donated to the CraftHaus cause were dubbed "Propagation Members" and can now find their names on the wall of the brewery's taproom surrounded by cuckoo clocks that Dave and Wyndee fell in love with while traveling and tasting their way throughout Germany. The Propagation

Members were treated to a party in their honor soon after the brewery opened in September 2014.[54]

"They get to feel some ownership, which they totally deserve. We wouldn't be here without them," says co–head brewer Steph Cope as we sit with her brewing partner Steve Brockman under the watchful eyes of cuckoos while sipping their Evocation Saison. Steve adds that they try to do things for those members like giving them early access to tap releases or a first chance to swing the hammer at a firkin on Fridays.[55] The relationship between the brewery and it's Kickstarter donors turned CraftHaus elites is reminiscent of and, more to the point, a continuation of one of the most vital ways that businesses have helped shape local culture in cities, and vice versa, throughout American history. Kickstarter is a digitized version of "subscription campaigns." In his social history of urban community building, sociologist Daniel Monti shows that "the essential feature of subscription campaigns was that persons . . . gave money to a project that was deemed good but probably would not have been initiated otherwise. The cash or assistance stood as a 'donation' when there was no expectation that the contributor would profit from it."[56] If the business prospered, so would the people who supported it in the beginning and those who patronized it thereafter. This olden tale is the story of CraftHaus. They asked for help. They got it. And they've given back to Las Vegas locals by providing them with tasty craft beer and a place to enjoy it.

Though Dave had been an established and respected homebrewer, pouring at local festivals (one way they attracted people to donating to their Kickstarter fund), he and Wyndee decided to stick to operating the business. To do the brewing, they hired two Australians who had been traveling in the United States and stopping to work at different breweries over the course of eighteen months. Though Steve and Steph had experienced "some of this country's best 'brewing cities' [such as San Diego, Portland, Denver, and Boulder]," Steve tells me that doing something in "a virtual craft beer desert" piqued the brewing couple's interest.

"We had some other job offers but nothing really felt right," says Steve. "[We wanted] the opportunity and ability to build not just a brewery but a community, an awareness. Not a lot of people are aware of craft beer here. And we liked the challenge."

From the outset, they knew they were starting not only a brewery but, instead, a brewery that would help a young local scene mature. "We want to be that brewery that makes the beer that's in people's fridge," says Steph. "We want to be their go-to beer, the one they keep at home *and* the one they look for when they're out on the town." So they were one of the first to put their beer in cans in Las Vegas—and their distributor sent them to stores across the valley. Their kegs went to bars and restaurants, where their tap handles can be found in an increasing number of places. And they eventually went on to produce the first-ever Southwest IPA in 2017 to rival the sometimes overwhelming popularity of New England–style IPAs. Brewed with southwestern named hops Amarillo and El Dorado as well as indigenous, organic agave syrup to dry out the beer, it is aptly named Mojave as an ode the desert that Las Vegas calls home. Though the idea superseded the execution, CraftHaus's Mojave is the most pure example of "not-so-neon terroir."

Golden Tap Handles

A growing collection of bars and restaurants have embraced the ethos of craft by replacing handles of Big Beer products with local and top-rated craft wares. Handles are props that both brewers and bartenders use to show off their identity and local influence. And craft beer drinkers take notice. Eyes quickly dart to the taps behind the bar even before a beer list on a chalkboard, electronic screen, or sheet of paper is consulted.

Grinning with his mouth and eyes, Kyle Wenniger, the head brewer of local Joseph James, declares, "Tap handles are gold!" Kyle and crew have struck gold all over the city where their malt-bomb-decorated handles rub elbows with other local handles as well as taps for beers from elsewhere. Because of their production-only license, they can't have a taproom. And because of the three-tier system in Nevada, breweries cannot sell their products off premise and have to go through a middleman. If they had a taproom somewhere else they would have to send their bottles, cans, and kegs through their distributor, even if the taproom was across the street from the brewery. As such, Joseph James relies on their local distribution to bars, restaurants, and stores. They're able to contribute to the aesthetic ecology of the Las Vegas craft beer scene through events they hold at other people's places for new beer releases and through tap handles that bartenders pull to serve their wares.

The New Jersey–born, but Las Vegas–raised, "skate punk" started homebrewing when he was nineteen, motivated by what he frankly calls "delinquency." A few years later, Kyle became a devout member of the local homebrewers club SNAFU (Southern Nevada Ale Fermentation Union) until he took on a position at Joseph James in 2012. He became their head brewer in 2014 at age twenty-nine. After a brief rant about the laws holding back their taproom, Kyle tells me about the brewery's relationship with the places that serve their beers.

> Places like Khoury's and Shakespeare's and the Atomic; we love working with them. They're all our friends. And they're all centered around craft. Khoury's and Shakespeare's are right down the road from us. Khoury's is able to get all the craft beer heads to come around, and Shakespeare's, we did beer for them, the Milkshake. Yeah, they came up with that one.

A chocolate milk stout, the Milkshake, was served almost exclusively at Shakespeare's Grille & Pub, a British-themed spot known for attracting fans of soccer, fish and chips, and craft beer. They've hosted a few Joseph James "tap takeovers," including one that featured eight variants of the Milkshake.

> I asked those guys what they wanted to do and they said a milk stout, so I said, yeah, I'm game. I'm good at doing sweet stouts, people seem to like

> them, I did one for Alex Graham [local brewer and beer rep] called Baby J's German Chocolate Cake that was for his daughter's first birthday. But I really lean toward IPAs and pale ales.

As if on cue, we both look over at the beer being poured and handed to a young woman. It was one of his beers, his pride and joy and a fan favorite: Citra Rye Pale Ale. As one local scenester told me, "If that was the only beer Kyle ever brewed, and he didn't bother with the sweet dessert stouts he brews, which would be our loss, he would still be among the top three brewers here."[57] Citra Rye was named Best New Beer in Las Vegas by *Vegas Seven* when it debuted in 2013 and earned Best Local Beer from *Las Vegas Weekly* two years later, among other local accolades. It has also earned honors outside its origins: a Bronze Medal at the 2013 Great American Beer Festival for the category American Pale Ale, a 96 out of 100 score from Ratebeer.com, and *Men's Journal*'s Best Beers in America list in 2015. As the Citra Rye name implies, Kyle uses rye malt that makes it a bit thicker than most pale ales and helps enhance the passion-fruit-like aromas and flavors of the Citra hops.

One of the first places I saw Citra Rye on tap was at Money Plays, a bar that has one of the weirder relationships to and with the local craft beer scene. Planted in a strip mall a mile west of the Strip under the shadow of the Palms Hotel and Casino, this beloved dive bar was once a strictly macro beer and cheap wine swinging and slinging joint. Though an old-school juke box was replaced by a digital touch-screen system, the air remains filled with the "beats, rhymes, and life" of late 1990s hip-hop without a hint of irony. That's what Stan Henderson's been listening to since he was a barback there. Now he owns the bar and the shuffleboard, foosball, darts, and Golden Tee that tempt those not glued to the craft beer pouring from almost all of the bar's twenty-four taps. Bud Light's always available for the gamblers.

Money Plays is physically located at the gateway, or barrier, between the Strip and local residents' homes on the western side of the city. And it shares a similar symbolic location. It is physically close yet culturally distant from the Strip. The neon green sign above the bar's windows often goes unnoticed by those driving past on Flamingo Avenue. It blends into a landscape filled with similar signs and bars where locals stop for a quick drink and a run at taking away some cash from the video poker machines that sit atop two-thirds of the rectangular bar. But for those who look closer, there's something peculiar about this place wedged between a taco shop and massage parlor. Like Las Vegas, the bar constantly battles itself over who it is, who it wants to be, and who its clientele want it to be. Money Plays hosts an active open mic night where neophyte hip-hop groups, acoustic guitar strumming waifs, and awkward comedians vie for the audience's attention late into the night. On an average day, Ethiopian and Tamil taxi drivers down light lagers or the sweet dark tan liquid of a Jamaican Red Stripe next to random beer geeks who "heard" on social media that Stan finally tapped an aged keg of "something special."

Even when Stan isn't there, he is always present. A poster of his large and intimidating physique hangs above the register. Wearing one of his signature knit caps over his well-kept dreads, Stan dramatically points his finger like Uncle Sam. In large print above his head, he sternly warns "I'M STILL WATCHING YOU!!!" This paternal demonstration seems to be pointed at his bartenders, who seem to turn over just as often as his kegs.

One former employee never received the scorn of Stan, in part because he still relies on his advice about new craft beer releases and the state of the local craft beer scene. Stan gleefully refers to Nick as his "son" regardless of their obvious physical differences; Stan is a tall, muscular black man while Nick's red hair shines atop his pale face. They both have infectious smiles, though, and a deep love for craft beer. In between his stints as a bartender at Freakin' Frog and, as we saw earlier, his position as a New Belgium Ranger, Nick worked at Money Plays and helped Stan redefine the bar that would go on to earn a spot in the Las Vegas Bar Hall of Fame's Class of 2013 for its combination of dive bar atmosphere and vast selection of craft beers.

When Nick started bartending during the graveyard shift at Money Plays in January 2011, a few craft beers were available, but not many people even knew that. "They had Speakeasy Double Daddy and Rogue Hazelnut Brown," Nick reveals, "so they were dipping their toe into craft but didn't know how or if they wanted to take that leap and jump in fully." At the time and since its opening in 1989, Money Plays had a limited liquor license that didn't allow them to serve anything over fifty-five proof, confining them to remain a beer and wine-only joint. Nick talked to Stan, and they both agreed they weren't going to become a wine bar; there were already plenty of them on and off the Strip, and boosting wine was unlikely to appeal to either their regulars or the slowly growing demographic of craft beer drinkers. Together, they set out to distinguish Money Plays as a craft beer bar, a process that, as Nick notes, has to be done slowly and with precision.

> You can't just jolt in there and go ahead and turn a bar into craft because you'll freak out the regulars, and there definitely was some freaking out. And it's expensive also, which gets passed onto the customer when you buy beers of this caliber. And if you don't have an educated staff that's going to protect the product and serve it and talk about it properly, the whole venture can go south really quickly.

He took it upon himself to train the staff—about the beers and how to serve them properly—as well as the customers, old-timers and newbies alike. For the first time in the bar's tenure, they printed a beer list. Like tap handles, beer lists are key props for craft beer bars. A typical list presents the name of the brewery, the name of the beer, the style of the beer, and its alcohol percentage. Noting beer's ABV is an ethical responsibility and absolute necessity when a bar serves beers that range from the relatively low 5 percent pale ale to barrel-aged behemoths in the low to mid-teens. Money Plays seems to always have high ABV beers on tap from local and out-of-town breweries and rightly gives patrons what they need to make informed choices about their respective levels of intoxication.

Once Money Plays gained some recognition for their craft selection, more locals started popping in. Visiting beer geeks—many of whom would ask around or on online forums for places to find craft beer in Las Vegas—started showing up as well. Due to its proximity to the Strip, tourists had often visited the bar to get away from the Strip's sensory overload and enjoy a low-key locals' dive experience. Now they come for the beer too.

"Stan and I wanted to enhance Money Plays beyond *just* a dive bar. If you look at some of the most famous craft beers across the country, a lot of them are dive bars." Nick mentions Toronado in San Francisco and O'Brien's in San Diego.

"They both have great beer lists," I respond in agreement.

"And they're not all shiny and put together. They're bars with really good beer. Craft beer and the dive bar can coexist in Las Vegas as much as it can elsewhere." He pauses for a moment and returns to a topic that seems ever present in the minds and discourse of those responsible for *staging* the scene.

"The biggest animal has always been gaming and trying to figure out how to make gaming work with craft beer. It's something that no other market has to deal with," Nick says, echoing the sentiments of others across the valley.

"It's a problem for everyone who wants to attract gamers who expect comped beers and also offer interesting beers."

Whether at Money Plays or somewhere else in Las Vegas that has both gaming and craft beer, the decision to give away craft beers is usually a judgment call made by the bartender. This puts added pressure on bar managers and owners to keep their staff trained as to the difference between, say, Sierra Nevada Pale Ale, which is much less expensive and has a much lower ABV, and Narwal, an imperial stout made by the same brewery. Two craft beers, same brewery, different price, flavor, and effect.

Some bars—like some of the breweries mentioned earlier—have tried to make the two work together with mixed results. As the name connotes, Aces & Ales mixes gaming and craft beer at both of its locations

FIGURE 2.6. A Dogfish Head 120 Minute IPA sits atop a video poker machine, making for an odd pairing for most craft beer enthusiasts. (Photo by author)

and has been successful at attracting a local craft beer following across the valley. Former Alice Cooper and Winger guitarist Keri Kelli took over a former Big Dog's outpost in 2010 on the east side of the valley. Nestled in between Sam's Town and Boulder Station, hotel-casino resorts catering to the not-so-rich or famous, a serious beer bar emerged. Kelli opened a second location near the old Tenaya Creek brewery in 2014. Both locations host out-of-town tap takeovers, scrumptious beer dinners, and seasonal/style-specific festivals. Yet, for all the tasty brews they serve, they still follow the dominant local conventions of gaming and smoking. I can't seem to ever get used to sipping a rare release next to a guy alternating between pulls off his cigarette and swigs of Bud Light. Even during their Stone Domination events—where all the taps are dedicated to Stone's vast array of brews and key members of the brewery make the trip from San Diego to Las Vegas to drink and chat with local beer geeks[58]—I watched two "regulars" poke away at the video poker machines in front of them, one clutching his Coors Light bottle and the other nursing her glass of red wine with floating ice cubes. Though Aces, as the locals call it, still deserves credit for bringing to town kegs of beer that otherwise wouldn't have been available to local craft beer fans, another bar, with a deeper local history, was rising as the preeminent node of the local craft beer scene.

When brothers Lance and Kent Johns took over the Atomic and hired Rose Signor to curate the tap list, it exploded on the scene.[59] And they did so without gaming. Las Vegas's oldest free-standing bar is a testament to and of time.[60] With plush velvet lining the bar, and the original neon accent that runs along the stucco above it, it summons a time long since passed. Martin Scorsese's epic ode to the city of Las Vegas, *Casino*, embalmed an early portrait of the Atomic into the halls of popular culture.[61] Now, as a place that attracts foodie evangelists like the late Anthony Bourdain, who filmed the finale of *Parts Unknown* at the bar, it has also proven to be a key "magnet place" for local craft beer enthusiasts. The Atomic provides a stage that offers about twenty rotating taps and a fifty-plus bottle and can list, as well as the events like their annual Sour Saturday Festival and various beer release parties throughout the year.

Atomic Liquors opened in the early 1950s shortly after the US Army built a nuclear testing site a mere fifty miles north of the city. Patrons would gather to sit on the bar's roof to watch mushroom clouds careen across the horizon. Even after the nuclear fireworks stopped, the Atomic became a popular stop for folks who worked westward down Fremont Street at the casinos. Along with the cocktail waitresses, dealers, and pit bosses, celebrity performers—like the Rat Pack and Barbra Streisand—would make their way there for a drink.

> Atomic Liquors was the essence of Vegas in the golden days of the 1950s and '60s. From the Atomic testing just up the road, the celebrity patrons of the day, casino workers, mobsters and law enforcement officers, it represented Vegas as it was: a melting pot of talent, dreams, criminals and the workers that made the fantasy of Las Vegas possible. But then in the 1980s and '90s the bar fell victim to the downturn of Fremont Street, the downturn in the economy, and general urban decay, and vagrants replaced the stars and casino workers and Atomic Liquors went from the "go-to" bar to the bar to avoid.[62]

Having survived Downtown Las Vegas's worst times, the Atomic emerged from the ashes to greet an eager crowd salivating for craft beer (and craft cocktails).

Through her *staging* of the Atomic for the local craft beer scene, Rose Signor quickly became a local torchbearer for the virtues of craft. And craft, from her point of view, is about both *education* and *expression*. Before taking on her role as general manager, she left Las Vegas for a few years and learned about the variety of styles of craft beer while residing in Seattle. Sour beer particularly piqued her interest. During her explorations across the Pacific Northwest and while she studied for her Cicerone exam, she became keenly aware that "brewing is an expression. Someone is expressing themselves through the beer they make."

I point to the tap handles and the chalkboard list hanging between them and ask if this was how she expresses herself. She replies,

> Yes. Absolutely. . . . Nobody else orders or picks the beer but me. I just want to put something out there that I like and that I stand behind. . . . I try to create a balanced tap list. You'll see it's all American. We have a guest international tap. . . . I just want to create awareness because, when I first started doing this, we were the underdog, but I feel like now we're pushing boundaries and pushing the limits and putting out some really interesting beers.

Her use of "underdog" is, on one hand, odd because the bar has such a long-standing devotion to it and a continued presence in popular culture. Atomic Liquors is part of a shared history between locals, newcomers, and visitors alike. But, on the other hand, underdog is a common label that actors who produce, stage, and consume craft beer in Las Vegas often apply to themselves and their scene. (Recall Bad Beat founder Nathan Hall's comment in the introductory chapter.) The underdog mentality inscribes and enacts a narrative of marginality and resistance, regardless of however real or imagined, where tenacity and creativity are required to keep up the good fight for the "good life" and the ability to taste it.

One way to summon people to the stage is to give locals locally crafted wares. "It gets people excited. They can be proud of it. *My hometown made this beer*," says Rose, showing off the same pride she hopes to instill in the people across the bar from her.

Rose continues,

> Highlighting local. That was the concept from day one. Trying to stay as local as possible. Las Vegas has some solid breweries these days putting out some really good stuff. I always try to have at least three local taps on at all times. People who are into craft seem to appreciate it, and our numbers show that. Sometimes tourists come in here because of the history and are confused by our beer menu. The pickiest beer drinkers are your Bud Light drinkers, your Coors Light drinkers. But there's really a huge range of people into craft beer nowadays. People you wouldn't expect. I have hoity-toity little old ladies asking me what IPAs I have on tap. It's kind of awesome.

Whether serving those old ladies or one of Atomic's regulars who orders only Busch Light—always on tap and listed as a "Crappy Lager"—Rose embraces the ethos of craft by introducing people to beers they haven't had or wouldn't find elsewhere. This takes both tenacity and creativity.

For the Sour Saturday festival that she's been running since 2013, Rose works extra hard to get some of the best sours from breweries that don't distribute locally. "There's a lot of emails going out, a lot kissing ass, trying to get people interested in having their beer here," she says.[63]

Whatever she's doing, it's working. I'm pretty sure that most locals had their first taste of a Jester King beer in 2014 because of her.[64] And these weren't just any of their beers. Delicate pours of Snorkel, an earthy umami-flavored farmhouse brewed with oyster mushrooms and sea salt, and Aurelian Lure, a sour beer aged in oak barrels with apricots and wild yeasts, engaged the palates of the city's most hardcore beer geeks and adventurous craft neophytes.

With the success of events like Sour Saturday, which has sold out each year, Rose has been able to experiment more with her regular offerings.

Distributors of rare and odd beers often go to her before they approach other buyers. Making those beers available consequently draws more craft beer fans to the bar, further helping her, and the scene itself, make a case for both the aesthetic and fiscal value of craft beer in Las Vegas. This process of "call and response" makes up a great deal of any functioning arena of social life.[65] And as more bars and restaurants put on "golden" tap handles of both local and highly coveted craft beers, they communicate to others that Las Vegas is emerging as a craft-friendly destination.

Changing Tastes, Tasting Change

Across an increasing number of American cities, a clustering of craft breweries has led to the emergence of recognizable brewery districts. You can easily hop between breweries in the Pearl District in Portland, Oregon, the Ballard District in Seattle, Washington, and the River North Art and Lower Downtown districts in Denver, Colorado.[66] This type of clustering doesn't exist in Las Vegas, with the exception of Bad Beat, CraftHaus, and the newly opened Astronomy Aleworks in a relatively young office park. There are also smatterings of craft-centric bars in the Downtown area whose distances between them are walkable, but that is far from the norm. Yet despite the fact that the aesthetic ecology of the Las Vegas craft beer scene is geographically dispersed, the collective claims made by those who traverse through it are growing stronger.

With their brewpubs and taprooms, ritualized bottle shares and homebrew supply stores, beer pairing dinners and tap handle takeovers, the taste of the city has changed. That is, craft beer enthusiasts have changed *what* can be tasted in the city and *how* people taste in the city. The success of the local scene's participants, from those in the center to those on the periphery, is evident in the shift in not only what people drink but how and why they drink. Their collective labor rejuvenates a city that too many think only deadens the senses. Instead, the brewers, bartenders, and consumers enliven the senses and the city with each beer that is brewed, sipped, and shared.

3

Think Globally, Drink Locally

During the summer, board shorts and bikinis float in and out of the water to the beat and bass of electronic house music pumped across the beach. The wave pool, the size of a football field, and the imported sands and "exotic" rock formations that encase it are surrounded by massive masts of gold, otherwise known as the Mandalay Bay Hotel and Casino. When summer ends, though, the pool calms to a still, until the shaggy-haired and big-bearded brewers from Arizona Wilderness Brewing decide to jump in. With their clothes on.

An unlikely spot most days for a craft beer festival, but come September, the soft sands of Mandalay Bay Beach serve up a sensuously bombastic buffet of scrumptious eats and fermented treats. Tables stretch around the circumference of the beach loaded with jockey boxes and coolers with unopened bottles yearning to be popped. Attendees kick off their shoes to drift through the sand, wetting their cups with craft beer to be sniffed and swallowed. Though the golden towers of the megaresort loom over the festive crowd, they never impinge on the aesthetic experiences, the shared history in the making, the scene performed in all its presumptive glory.

Drawing in interested industry insiders and core local beer geeks, Sarah Johnson, the hotel's food and beverage director as well as the first female Certified Cicerone in Nevada, knew how to host a standout beer festival. During the four hours of the festival, as well as the ancillary events connected to it, the craft beer scene seemed to have gained some stability in the heart of the city. The typical homogenized spectacle of the Strip gave way to an aesthetic experience that brought the scene's most devout craft aesthetes together with neophytes looking for a sensuous arousal that didn't depend on gambling or sexual exploits. The

FIGURE 3.1. Craft beer brewers and drinkers and celebrity chefs comingle on the imported beaches of the Strip. (Photo courtesy of Mandalay Bay)

Las Vegas Syndrome, or at least some of its symptoms, was cured with fermented elixirs for a few hours. The intoxication of craft, reflexive and eminently social, peaked on the beach. And, regardless of how stumbling and mumbling they left, participants in the local craft beer scene surely *felt* a sense *communitas.*[1]

The aesthetic best of Las Vegas comingled with the aesthetic best of elsewhere. The city's celebrated celebrity "foodscape" offered tasty treats to tantalize beer-soaked taste buds. For example, local celebrity chef Hubert Keller, with his starkly glistening white beard and ponytail, was seen handing out savory pork tacos as well as sampling the evening's liquid offerings. The second year, another local celebrity chef, Shawn McClain, cooked and served delicately designed small bites to attendees at the "Culinary Brewing" seminar led by brewmaster Jared Rouben. The food was paired with Rouben's Chicago-based Moody Tongue beers, one of which was a pilsner brewed with black truffles (the crisp rush of earth never tasted so good). Both McClain and Rouben were seen later that night making their way through the offerings from top regional craft breweries like New Belgium, Stone, and Brooklyn, as well as SoCal stars like the Bruery and Pizza Port, which shared the beach with local brewers ready to show off some of their best wares.

Rouben wasn't the only brewer who had traveled to Las Vegas for the festival. Matt Brynildson from Firestone Walker in Paso Robles, California, Grady Hull from New Belgium in Fort Collins, Colorado, and Alex Ganum from Upright in Portland, Oregon, among other brewers and brewery personnel, as well as Brewers Association director Paul Gatza, all dipped their toes in the beach's imported sand. They were as excited to be there as the attendees were that they had come to be with them.

"This is a far cry from my little house in the woods," Brynildson tells me while gazing upon the faux volcanic rock across the water from where we stand. "This is a fun place to be serving our beer."

Bringing folks from various breweries and having them pour the beers they made was a unique feature Sarah was able to orchestrate. At most beer festivals (which have grown in number and popularity locally, nationally, and globally), a local brewery rep or an anonymous employee or volunteer usually does the pouring. For many, drinking a beer served by the person who brewed it can be as intoxicating as the beverage itself. Similar to going to a concert and watching and hearing a band play songs you've heard only through stereo speakers or earbuds plugged into a phone, the disembodied and displaced product becomes *re*humanized.[2]

I saw Las Vegas local Mike Gaddy on the beach, sipping one of Brynildson's brews a few feet away from the brewer. Later that night, Gaddy walked away with one of the local brewery's surfboards. The boards were wedged into the sand to show where each brewery was pouring. Craft beer fan and local scene staple, Gaddy was giddy like someone who caught the drummer's sticks.

Chatting a few months later, Gaddy explicitly compared his music and craft beer fandoms. When he was younger, he would happily travel four hours for a band. He isn't likely to do that anymore. But he'll do it for a beer and a brewery, though.

> I can enjoy a good pop hook, but there's something about a band that has something to them. There's sincerity to what they're doing, with the lyrics, the hook, the non-hook. . . . The singer believes what he's saying and singing about. He's had his heart broken. This translates to beer for me. I love knowing what brewers went through to produce their beers, all of the stuff they go through to make sincere beer. *Craft beer is sincere beer.* Beer made with sincerity, rather than just a hook.

Appreciating how a beer is made and the labor expended to brew it can bring out its *sincerity* through its humanity. That is, no longer can the product—whether music, literature, food, beer, or anything else touched by human creativity and physical determination—exist magically as something that emerged from an anonymous person or place. Instead, the product is intimately connected to action, taking on the *aura* of an activity rather than a static object. When the producer is present, the product reflects and enacts a degree of agency as an extension of the producer's creative work and can influence the experience of the product itself. The discerning drinker raises the beer to sip it under the watchful eye of the brewer, and the beer, in turn, responds to the attention directed toward it. Tasting becomes an act of coproduction as the beer is consumed and then talked about, fostering an intensity of attention, reflection, and experience.[3]

The performance of taste doesn't have to involve serious furrowed-brow analysis, though craft beer drinkers are somewhat notorious for initiating both wanted and unwanted talk of beer minutia. The joy of consuming pleasurable delights in the company of others is a driving emotive and affective force behind beer festivals. Fun and frivolity are the norm, not the exception. They are part of the "interaction membrane" that, as sociologist Erving Goffman notes, allows participants to become euphorically engrossed in the event.[4] This became clear to me while standing behind a few guys who joked with Preston Weesner, a blender from Portland, Oregon's, Cascade Brewing.[5] Weesner was pouring an apricot sour ale and a blueberry sour ale.

"Did you try the third beer you brought?" asks one of the guys standing a few feet to my right, leaning slightly on the table that holds up the box taps. Weesner gives him a quizzical look. Weesner is then handed a cup to sip from.

"It's a blend of both!"

Weesner tastes it. Pauses. "Not bad."

The four of them share a laugh and clink glasses, and then the three locals go on their way still sipping on Cascade's "third beer." And by the end of the night, the spontaneous blend was being poured for others by Weesner himself. Craft beer might be a catalyst for cultural change, but it doesn't always have to be so serious. The fun of trying new beers, or even coming up with your own blends and pairings, is what draws so many people into craft beer fandom in the first place. But fun is more than just a personal feeling of pleasure; it involves a collaborative commitment to the collective.[6]

As I watched the impromptu amateur blenders joke with the pro, it was clear that they were having fun. And their fun was a way of "doing scene" where producers' and consumers' interests where entwined and enacted through their interactions.[7] Encounters between festival attendees and the belles of the ball—the blenders and the brewers who traveled to Las Vegas to pour their respective beers—at times played out like a weak version of what sociologist Chris Rojek calls the "St. Thomas Effect."[8] Like the New Testament tale of Doubting Thomas, fans want to photograph, be near, or even touch the person of their admiration, the person granted with ultimate status. Though the "St. Thomas Effect" is an exaggeration for the vast majority of craft beer fans that night, the idea leads us to two interrelated points of interest. First, the craft beer star—and all scenes and local cultures have their stars[9]—relies on the perceived quality of the product rather than their personality. Yes, charisma and cool can help propel the brewer's status. But in the social world of craft beer, personality can't gloss over off-flavors and poor execution. Craft beer's grand celebrities are adored for the fruits of their labor rather than "being known for [their] well-knowness."[10]

Second, for fans of particular beers or breweries, meeting the people responsible for those respective beers and breweries brings them closer to the act of creation. As I've heard many times from both brewers and consumers, brewing is both an *art* and a *science*. Though art and science are often erroneously believed to operate in different social spheres, there are great similarities between them.[11] A successful craft brewer must be able to see those connections and exploit them to the benefit of the product and future consumers of it, as well as the beer's relationship to the historical guidelines of its particular style. Of course, that relationship to history isn't always about unilateral adherence, especially for those who have followed Sam Calagione's Dogfish Head Brewing into the once unusual world of "extreme brewing."[12] Regardless of how traditional or nontraditional a beer or brewer might be—homing in on an old, beloved, and common style like a pilsner can be just as artful and methodical as crafting a spontaneously fermented wild ale that sits in a barrel with citrus fruit and then is dry-hopped before it is bottled—the poetics of a recipe depend on chemical actions, reactions, and interactions.

The blending of artistic passion and scientific aptitude is at the heart of the craft ethos shared by both producers and consumers. In his discussion of the important role that "craftwork" plays in contemporary culture as a counter to the dominant modes of both production and consumption, sociologist Colin Campbell shows how "craft production" and "craft consumption" are co-dependent "as part of the widespread aestheticization of everyday life."[13] The craft producer, writes Campbell,

> chooses the design for the product, selects the materials needed and generally personally makes (or at least directly supervises the making of)

> the object in question. Thus, one may say that the craft producer is one who invests his or her personality or self into the object produced. . . . And it is, of course, on these grounds that this form of work activity has traditionally been regarded as expressive of the more humane, creative, and authentic aspects of human nature.[14]

The craft consumer is drawn to those aspects of humanity. Campbell notes that craft consumption is equally "important because of the opportunity it presents for the manifestation of similar valued human qualities."[15] The values of self-expression and creativity connect drinkers with those responsible for the beers they are drinking as coproducers.

The connection extends beyond individuals as well. Individuals are conduits that link local scenes to translocal scenes of craft production and consumption. This is especially the case when local drinkers comingle with nonlocal brewers. A connection between consumers and producers can range from obsessive fandom to mutual respect. At Mandalay Beach most of the connections were of the latter, despite the fact that brewers from elsewhere received the most praise in part because being from *elsewhere* increases their supposed value.

From living in a city composed of imported styles and persons, Las Vegas locals know the value of elsewhere better than anyone.

Because it is a relatively young city with a notorious transient population that plays host to over forty million tourists a year, Las Vegas is a primed context for incorporating other people's cultures into its own. This sets Las Vegas apart from other cities that have more deeply held shared local histories. Those more historically anchored cities, not coincidently, also tend to be well-known craft-beer-centric cities. Writing in the late 1990s, geographer Wes Flack noted how San Francisco, Portland, and Seattle, among others, marked by "the strong environmental sentiment of the region," became leading microbrewing centers in part because "the idea of a fresh local brew seems to fit very nicely into

Ecotopia."[16] He argued that the success of microbreweries—the popular parlance before the "craft" label for small breweries caught on as qualifier and identity marker—in these cities and those with similar aesthetic demeanors, as well as the rising interest in farmer's markets and "even the defensive battles that towns are waging to keep Wal-Marts from opening," should be understood as part of a cultural countercurrent he calls "neolocalism."[17]

What makes neolocalism different from traditional local ties is that today's local ties are cultivated by choice rather than necessity. There is clear evidence that neolocal or "locavore" interests have been growing over the last two decades along with a wave of other "lifestyle movements."[18] There is also clear evidence that "locavores" are a loosely connected heterogeneous population whereby some use local goods to build an identity as savvy or artisanal or environmentally friendly, while others are supporters of *all* local communities, theirs and other persons'.[19] Either way, "local" is often held up with honor and righteous fortitude, giving credence to a *festishized* object as if it held some magical powers that guarantee greater quality and a better sensuous experience.[20]

Counterintuitively, what is considered "local," however, doesn't necessarily have to consist of material goods or ideas from a single proximate location. That is, local culture—any local culture in the modern world—is never a stable and hermetically sealed and bounded entity. "Cultural diffusion" in its many forms of practices and products moving across and between varying scales of populations (e.g., between nations, between cities, between cultures within the same city) is a constant feature of a globalized and globalizing world.[21]

The scenes that play out on local stages are not built from scratch. They are neither fully self-referential nor self-contained. Rather, their symbolic boundaries are porous and flexible enough not only to allow for outside influences but to even depend on them. Props and scripts are borrowed and reworked. Scenes from elsewhere provide "models of" and "models for" shared and common expectations and practices that are adopted and adapted by locals within particular contexts.[22] A model *of* something shows us what something *is* like, while a model *for* something shows us how something *ought* to be.

The interest in other persons' local goods and products indicates an aesthetic shift from homogenized mass cultural products. It's not an all-encompassing shift; Wal-Marts still dominate towns across the United States and Budweiser is still the king of beers. But it is a shift that is under way, a shift that appreciates local products inside and outside of their "home territories."[23] At the center of the shift is a vibrant *trans*-localism that seeps through the dispersed grand craft beer scene and throughout the scene in Las Vegas. Incorporating "trans" as a prefix moves the focus from issues pertaining to one specific locality and place to issues of connectivity across localit*ies* and places. And like any other "ism," it can be understood as a belief system or worldview whereby translocalism reinforces the desire to pursue and acquire other people's local wares to be consumed on premise or, more to point, to be transported back to one's *public* home territories. As such, a beer from *your* city might be symbolically worth more than a beer from *my* city, at least for scene participants who want to expand their aesthetic knowledge of the scene's core significant object.

Cities and their respective locales have reputations that influence aesthetic judgments of the things, like beer or food, made within them. There is a relative congruence between a place's character and the cultural objects produced by persons in those places.[24] It shouldn't be a shock to learn that northern Vermont is home to both the most outstanding maple syrup inspired and utilized beer—Lawson's Finest Maple Barrel-Aged Fayston Maple Imperial Stout—that my palate has ever experienced. And some of the best not-from-concentrate and no-sugar-added craft hard ciders come from Citizen Cider in Burlington, which uses apples from local and regional orchards.[25]

Many craft beer enthusiasts will either travel to other cities to pick up bottles and cans that aren't distributed locally or have beer mailed to them from elsewhere. These transported beers—the outcome of either physical travel or "porch bombs" delivered by FedEx—become the targets and progenitors of "oohs" and "ahhs" at bottle shares often for their rare status and quality. The "local" of local beer that is transported across state borders takes on a different meaning than "local" as simply something produced in a nearby locale. A loose connection, but a connection nonetheless, is forged between the locally produced product and the translocally consuming consumer.

Translocalism clearly has a tinge of Orientalism with the credence it lends to the vigor of the exotic Other.[26] Yet translocalism allows for a sense of comradery because the exotic goods are appreciated for both their not-from-here localness and their acceptance as part of a larger collectivity. Because it tends to celebrate local particularities rather than smooth them over or adhere to "a view from nowhere" attitude, translocalism differs from cosmopolitanism as well. In effect, it stands between what sociologist Robert Merton defined as the differing "basic orientations" of locals and cosmopolitans.[27] It serves as a bridge between the two, connecting the local to the wider social world and vice versa. Moreover, local particularities are appreciated rather than merely tolerated.[28]

Whether an object is consumed in its original locale by a visitor or in one's own locale after it's been shipped, carried, or smuggled, the same process of valuation is at work. In both scenarios a symbolic and affective bond is created between people and places that supports both the original location and its newfound home. As such, the act of pursuing someone else's local products creates social bonds as part of an "imagined community" or grand scene—weak and abstract, but nonetheless social and significant—across geographical areas, transcending the symbolic yet legalistically functional boundaries of cities, states, and nations.[29]

The collective imagination of aesthetic entrepreneurs—in the roles of both producers and consumers—not only connects the translocal to the local, but incorporates it into the local, becoming the essence of the local itself. The "culture from elsewhere" becomes a "culture from here" in new and novel ways. Ironically, this is something that Las Vegas has always excelled at, but primarily for the sake of wanderers (i.e., tourists), those who come and leave tomorrow. But at least in the way it has played out in the local craft beer scene, translocalism for Las Vegas's natives and its overwhelming hordes of relocated strangers, those who come and stay tomorrow,[30] is a means for establishing affective affiliations to and between the local scene and local scenes elsewhere.

How the Translocal Becomes the Local

Some observers of and participants in the recent rise in craft beer production and consumption in the United States call it a revolution, a movement, and a community or culture. All of these terms are used to evoke connections that stretch beyond physical borders and morph local symbolic boundaries into a translocal grand *scene*. The translocal scene connects local scenes by "producing affective communities that transcend the need for face-to-face interaction as a necessary requirement for scene membership."[31] Though the local and translocal are necessarily connected, their relationship differs across and between particular contexts, much of which depends on a city's reputation and its "place" in a status hierarchy of other cities.[32] Not all scenes are created equal, nor are their respective abilities to affect the translocal scene. Regardless of such differences in cultural or symbolic power, we can safely say that the local affects the translocal, and the translocal, in turn, affects the local. This point became clear to me during a conversation with Rose Signor as we sat across from each other at one of the high tops on the patio of Atomic Liquors.

A light breeze skips down Fremont Street while Rose and I both sip on one of the Bruery's pucker-inducing tart bombs, Sour in the Rye. I ask her what Las Vegas needs to take it to the proverbial next level as a respected craft beer scene.

"To be considered a great beer city," she begins, "it often boils down to the local breweries. When we have a really solid group of local breweries here, I think that we'll be taken more seriously in the craft beer scene across the country."

"We have some good breweries now, no?" I probe.

"For sure, but we need more, and we need more breweries taking more risks."

"So to elevate the scene, the brewers have to do it. Not the distributors?"

"It has to start with the local breweries. And then when that happens, then other cities and other breweries around the country will want to send their beer here. *We have a real problem with not being able to get some of the great beers from some of the great breweries across the country; at least that's how it's been up until the past year or two.* We're starting to get some cool stuff from some cool breweries now."

She points to the lightly rust-colored beverage in our glasses. "The Bruery is finally starting to send us really good stuff. And they're not far away, in Orange County. They're just starting to turn their heads and look at Las Vegas as a city that's serious about craft beer."

The point that Rose makes is important for our understanding of the connections between the local and the translocal and the way it is articulated on the local stage. A local scene cannot depend upon its local breweries alone for its vitality. For a local scene to be vibrant, the thirst that craft beer drinkers have—to be able to go to a bar, restaurant, or liquor store and be able to purchase and consume a wide variety of nonlocal offerings—needs to be quenched. And those nonlocal offerings should be from some of the highest rated and coveted breweries like the Bruery, which, as Rose notes, is less than a four-hour drive away from Las Vegas.

The Bruery, a playful adaptation of founder Patrick Rue's family name, is known for both its intense experimentation and equally intense price point of many of its 750-milliliter bottles. The Bruery's beers run the gamut from light and tart saisons to heavy beasts like Black Tuesday, their bourbon-barrel-aged imperial stout. Many of their releases are offered only to members of their exclusive and stratified societies (Preservation, Reserve, and invite-only Hoarders). A good number of core scenesters in Las Vegas hold memberships and drive to the Anaheim area to bring back their coveted elixirs.[33] The Bruery's rare special releases often show up at bottle shares around the valley, always receiving attention from vets and newbies alike. The market in Las Vegas has seen an uptick in the amount and variety of beers from them.

Having a slew of publicly available out-of-town translocal beers is a good sign of a strong local craft beer scene. But they don't just show up on shelves and tap lists magically. Not only does someone need to order and buy them, but breweries must be willing to sell their goods within a particular market. Beyond simple economics, craft brewers want to know that their beers won't just sit untouched but will be enjoyed within a reasonable time period. This is why you often see the dates when beers were canned or bottled. Despite the mythical tales of British sailors using hops to preserve their ales as they traveled to India, giving India pale ale its name, beer does not travel well. Most beers, especially styles that rely on hops for flavoring, like today's India pale ales that have been at the center of the spike in craft beer interest in the United States, are not meant for aging. The command to "drink fresh" is as common as the command to "drink local." The general rule for hop-forward beers is to drink them within a month to three months before the flavors from the hops recede. The appropriate shelf life of a beer is relatively (or even ridiculously) short compared to, say, a record or a CD or the virtually immortal MP3. As such, for brewers who want to send their wares beyond the walls of their respective breweries and states, a knowledgeable local consumer base is necessary at the other end.

To help extend and escalate a local scene's reputation, local brewing is an important indicator for outside brewers considering selling their product in that specific market. A collection of local brewers is a sign that a city and its craft beer production and consumption are actively engaged. When Rose claims that "it has to start with the local breweries," she is telling us that small craft breweries from elsewhere look to see if and how beer is produced, sold, and consumed by locals.

Without turning this into a fermented version of the chicken and the egg, we can say that a local scene needs to be strong locally in order to

FIGURE 3.2. The relationship between the local scene and translocal breweries.

attract the attention of respected translocal craft breweries, whose presence in the local scene will, in turn, strengthen both the reality and the perception of the local scene itself. The process looks something like the diagram depicted in Figure 3.2. Here, the local scene changes by way of its relationship to the translocal.

Though local breweries are certainly important signals of a vibrant local scene, the burden of supplying locals with nonlocal craft beers, as well as local products for that matter, falls on distributors. The way the industry is structured, however, often links distributors to Big Beer simply due to mainstream consumer demand. Small companies that aren't connected to a Big Beer brand have had more freedom, though fewer resources, to bring craft beer to Las Vegas.[34] Yet even the biggest distributors in Las Vegas are making room in their portfolios for nonlocal and regional craft breweries. For example, Chicago-based Breakthru Beverage has offices in Las Vegas and Reno and is considered a "Coors house." Despite their connection to one of the largest macro brands, Breakthru has a diverse portfolio largely curated by "craft specialist" Michael Shetler, one of the city's early craft beer adopters. The increasing demand for a variety of craft beers in Las Vegas, he told me, is coming from both consumers and brewers. Though the transient population of the city is often noted as having a negative impact on community attachment or quality-of-life issues, from his vantage point, Shetler sees its positive side.[35]

"Everyone knows that there are lot of people who live here from elsewhere. I know a lot people who moved from the Midwest where there's a well-established beer culture with breweries like Founders and Bell's."

"And that's just Michigan," I add.

"Right. You have Three Floyds and Two Brothers in Indiana and all the great breweries in Chicagoland, new breweries are cropping up every day. In places like that they don't ask if you're local, they ask which neighborhood!"

"Then they move here, what happens?"

"People come here from other places and they want to experience variety. They want to experience great beer from all of the country, especially from their hometowns or states. That's had a big influence on both suppliers and distributors and what's available in the market."

Though he didn't use the term, Shetler is telling us how the local scene is affected by *nostalgia* for not merely a romanticized or idealized past, but for the tastes connected to a past place. Thinking of nostalgia in this way does three things. First, it connects the term back to its original seventeenth-century meaning as a type of homesickness, whereby place is as important as time.[36] Second, it can be understood as a mechanism for connecting the places where someone once dwelled with his or her current residence to thwart the effects of identity loss.[37] And, third, for the displaced person, whether by choice or not, it is an embodied feeling that can be aroused by a sensuous interaction with materials from back home.[38]

Thinking of nostalgia in this way moves it from its more pejorative meanings about longing for a romanticized lost past to a "social emotion" that affects individual and cultural change in the present and for the future. Nostalgic sentiments, as literary scholar Svetlana Boym writes, not only are "retrospective," but can also be "prospective." She notes that "the fantasies of the past, determined by the needs of the present, have a direct impact on the realities of the future."[39] Nostalgia, then, has the capacity to foster symbolic connections between the "then and there" and the "here and now," providing continuity and coherence to individuals acting on the stages of local and translocal scenes simultaneously.

Craft beer can offer a taste of home for new residents. In this sense, and in a somewhat paradoxical way, being able to enjoy and share beers from one's hometown with newfound friends and acquaintances in the local scene becomes a way to both establish new relationships and kindle old pleasures. When Founders Brewing came to Las Vegas via Nevada Beverage, traditionally a "Budweiser house," local Midwesterners rejoiced. One Las Vegas local, who has lived in the city for about eight years but spent most of his life in Michigan, not too far from Grand Rapids, where Founders brews its "highly acclaimed" KBS, told me that being able to buy a Founders beer at a local bottle shop or bar would make him a little less home sick on those days the neon desert frustrated him. His cure was soon to come.

Founders seemed to know that local ex-Midwesterners wanted their old local favorites in their new destinations. They also wanted to introduce the uninitiated to their wares. In a press release on the Founders website, co-founder and CEO Mike Stevens wrote, "We're thrilled to continue to expand our distribution in the West where there is such appreciation for craft beer." He followed this statement with an unprecedented one about Nevada. "Northern California and Nevada are *hubs for beer enthusiasts* and we're excited to add Founders to their list of choices."[40] Perhaps more important than the increase in local consumer demands are the changing perceptions that breweries have of the Las Vegas craft beer scene and market.

Shetler tells me that this is the first time that "suppliers—reps from breweries—have started contacting local wholesalers in Las Vegas. Five years ago, this was not happening nor did anyone really expect it to at the current rate." This is due to the local scene's changing reputation coupled with the simple geographical fact that Nevada is surrounded by well-respected local craft beer scenes and their respective markets, namely California and Arizona. "If you're shipping to California, north or south, and going through Nevada," says Shetler, "it makes sense to maximize loads and drop some beer off in Las Vegas."

It's a bit odd, Shetler notes, that you could find beers from Colorado powerhouse breweries like Avery and Great Divide and smaller operations like Funkwerks and Paradox in San Diego or Los Angeles.[41] Unless they're equipped with wings or an ill-functioning navigation system, trucks carrying those beers have to cross through Las Vegas. Interstate 15 demands it.

The same can be said about coveted Southern California beers that skipped over the neon desert in route to destinations farther east. Of note, San Diego's Modern Times—a brewery that devotes an entire wall to a mosaic image of Michael Jackson and his monkey Bubbles made of Post-It notes and includes quotes from urban historian Lewis Mumford on its cans—tested the Las Vegas market in late 2015 and solidified and celebrated its presence in early 2016 with a week of tap takeovers featuring special releases throughout the city at some of the local scenes' most important craft beer nodes. Modern Times is now a staple for Las Vegas craft beer drinkers who enjoy their year-round beers like Blazing World, a hoppy "dank" amber ale, or their rare releases like Monsters' Park, an imperial stout offered in multiple variants. AleSmith didn't wait too long to follow their younger counterparts to Las Vegas. The inclusion of beers from these two breweries, as well as others increasingly making their goods available to the Las Vegas scene has, however, enticed even more local beer geeks as well as SoCal transplants to travel to the brewery to get the releases that don't come to town.

It's a fine line to dance. I was at Khoury's the night that AleSmith bottles became available. Plenty of people rejoiced that they could buy a Speedway Stout or an Ol' Numbskull Barleywine without leaving Las Vegas. But the hardcore beer geeks were already a few steps ahead. A bottle share was happening that night, as it usually does on Wednesdays, and one of the beers opened and shared was a Speedway Stout. But it was one available only from the brewery in San Diego, a Hammerhead variant brewed with espresso rather than coffee. Was this a sign that the scene was moving too fast? Were locals interested only in what couldn't be found locally? Maybe for some. For the majority, however, the proliferation of translocal brews into the local Las Vegas market, available for locals and tourists alike, has helped the city's newly reinvented reputation as a destination for craft beer. Increasing the variety of beers has changed and will likely continue to change the way the city is experienced. It will also likely continue to drive the local scene forward into new terrain, baiting local brewers to push their abilities and local consumers to push their palates further. The creative wares from afar can push the creative yearnings and workings locally. Influenced by translocal trends, many Las Vegas breweries have started barrel-aging programs as well as experimenting with purposely infected sour beers and unfiltered hazy IPAs.

All signs point to continued growth, especially when the acts of drinking and the performance of taste are accomplished collectively. And opportunities to do so have increased dramatically in recent years. Festivals, in particular, as well as other ritualized social gatherings, provide important routes for connecting brewers, distributors, and drinkers to each other and to the significant object they've made, moved, or yearned to try.

Festivals as Translocal Rituals with Local Roots

One of the best ways to facilitate the connections between local and translocal scenes is through festivals that highlight both local and established or newly emerging nonlocal breweries. Because festivals occur less often than the regular events that provide the lifeblood of the local scene—like bottle shares and special release tappings at local shops, taprooms, and bars—"the *intensity* of a festival compensates for its infrequency."[42] In their comparative analysis of music festivals as translocal scenes, sociologist Timothy J. Dowd and colleagues show how the intensity of such happenings affects the ways that both organizers and attendees experience the festival itself. Festivals demand commitment from participants who invest both time and money to be able to attend and taste what usually amounts to only a sample of the litany of a festival's offerings. Such investments are made with hopes to gain connections to others, human and nonhuman alike. The sites where those gatherings are made possible are conduits for connecting spatially bounded local scenes to translocal scenes as well as grounding the translocal in a geographically empirical and meaningful place.

Religious studies scholar Jennifer E. Porter argues that a fan's pilgrimage to a shared site—in her case "Trekkies" and *Star Trek* conventions—is a liminal journey of transformation to find *communitas*, a "communal fellowship," with other like-minded fans.[43] The site of fan tourism becomes a locally emplaced form of the translocal scene and provides "a time and space for fans to be free to explore their love of something deep and meaningful in their lives."[44] Pilgrimage sites, then, should always be considered *emerging*. The place's meaning changes, modifies, and transitions throughout the event as individuals' experiences change through their sensuous participation. Everyday places morph into "festival spaces" for attendees.[45] Encounters with other individuals—so very important in the emergence of *communitas*—is not significant simply because it challenges or solidifies the social order of everyday life outside the event, festival, or ritual. Rather, the significance to the scene emerges as an embodied creative act that symbolically shapes the meaning of the site itself, fostering connections between individuals and localities.[46]

The intensity and liminality—the sense of being "betwixt and between" the norms of everyday life[47]—of festivals help define the local setting and, thereby, the scene itself. That is, the festival and all of its translocal influences can bolster the bonds of local scenes via its pilgrimaging participants and its revered offerings. A festival's intensity—in the ways it produces heightened multisensory stimuli—can also affect the ways people experience the significant object itself. Is there music playing? If so, does it jive with the crowd? Is the festival outside or inside? Does it feel hot or cold? Are there plumes of cigarette smoke or perfume in the air? The extra stimuli can enhance or damage the intended aesthetic affect and effect of the sought-after brew.

Spending about four hours (either one day or repeated over the course of a few days) waiting in lines while holding small cups or snifters made of plastic, metal, or glass—the last of which is usually avoided for fear of drops from not-so-sober hands—to receive one- or two- or four-ounce pours certainly influences the experience of the beer and, in turn, of the festival, the local scene, and the translocal scene. As an affective prop, the small vessels help transform the pilgrims into rule-following tasters rather than obnoxious overdrinkers. This is also true for the pourer at the booths who must abide by the festival's rules to thwart against either planned or accidental overindulgence by overzealous participants. Adhering to the rules of the small pour allows actors to play their roles according to a loosely defined script that promotes socially reflexive intoxication over hedonistically regressive intoxication.

Addressing the various yet rule-bound roles of the key actors on the stage of wine festivals—namely the servers, tasters, and wine itself—sociologist Phillip Vannini and his colleagues note that taste is performed both as a personal evaluative act and as a collective endeavor. The relatively loose yet still explicit rules help frame individual embodied experiences as a collective emplaced experience where participants can give maximum attention to their significant object together.

> By listing and evaluating the material qualities of wines and by outlining both the pouring procedure and the range of techniques available for wine appreciation, pourers set tasting apart from everyday drinking, allowing a group of tasters-qua-spectators to become aware of the special quality of the performance writ large and the performance of the objects laying before them. In so doing, they also become aware of the unique qualities of themselves as a group. Certainly, *while these ritual rules are organized around a pleasure principle, they are no less effective or forceful than rules laid out in more traditionally sacred rites.*[48]

Regardless of the scene's core object, from *Star Trek* to wine or beer to opera, the liminality of performing taste is restrained by both explicit and implicit rules. Some rules, particularly those that have emerged *from* participants rather than organizers, become part of the lived mythos of the event.[49]

The first time I heard the convention hall roar I jumped a little and almost dropped my plastic taster, which would have elicited another roar. This ongoing ritual, a sort of inebriated call-and-response, is an interactive part of Denver's Great American Beer Festival (GABF), the preeminent beer festival in the heart of one of the most vibrant craft beer cities. The sound of a small plastic chalice bouncing on the concrete floor brings laughter to and hollers from onlookers, and momentary embarrassment for the now empty-handed drinker. Unlike the applause after a server accidently breaks a plate in a restaurant, this ritual is less about shaming and more about sharing. It's a collective experience that breaks up the aural monotony of a thousand voices slurring at once.

Another shared ritual that aides the translocal scene's sense of aesthetic comradery is the growing presence of costumed attendees at the festival. Along with common beer festival adornments like dangling pretzel necklaces and brewery shirts, a good number of GABF attendees wear "carnivalesque" costumes for the sake of frivolity and innocuous role play.[50] Making my way through the crowd, tightly holding my plastic sipper with my wet fingers and thumb, my elbows inadvertently rub with many folks dressed in the same "costume" I had on: a beard and a plaid shirt.

My elbows also meet human-sized hops, Belgian monks, popes, a cadre of seven or eight bespeckled red-and-white-stripe-shirted Waldos, and the Dude and Walter from the cult classic film *The Big Lebowski*. Las Vegas's own Kat Sassafras, a Certified Cicerone and craft beer program director, could be seen traipsing around the festival in her "brewnicorn" hat and matching gear. The festival allows individuals to act as both performers and spectators, adding visually stimulating and aesthetic complexity to the otherwise mundane confines of the convention center. The costumed "characters" are often stopped by other attendees for pictures of and with them, some of which are posted to Instagram or other social media sites.

Even as the event has expanded in size from year to year, tickets sell out within a few hours, and increasingly so. Some years it has taken

FIGURE 3.3. A large map stands at the entrance to the convention hall, greeting pilgrims to the Great American Beer Festival in Downtown Denver, Colorado (with an unexpected photobomb by Brooklyn Brewery's veteran brewmaster Garrett Oliver). (Photo by author)

only about half an hour for all publicly available tickets to be snatched up. For the 2015 event, the Brewers Association—the main organization behind GABF—added ninety thousand square feet of space in the convention center to accommodate eleven thousand more attendees than the previous year's event. What started as an industry-oriented event where brewers could talk shop or meet with distributors has become a four-day party that hosts sixty thousand people, about half of whom come from outside Colorado to sample as many of the four thousand beers from about eight hundred breweries as they can.[51] Visit Denver, the city's convention and visitor bureau, estimates that GABF generates an annual economic impact of about $28.6 million for the Denver area. Both the economic and cultural effects of the translocal festivals spill into and across the local scene and its host city.

Though many who have attended the festival often call it a "shit show"—due to its immense and intense physical size and the immense and intense amount of drunken wobblers soaking up as many beers as possible, especially during the last hour of a four-hour session—GABF is accompanied by a wide variety of events in Downtown Denver and its surrounding areas that happen before, during, and after the festival. As the festival itself has grown, so has its reach by supporting local events that often provide more intimate and intense tasting experiences for pilgrims.

The festivities get started quickly for travelers who fly into Denver International Airport, where a temporary beer garden, called "Beer Flights," operates from eleven in the morning to seven in the evening each day for about a week. Many attendees who make the annual trek to GABF reinforce Denver's status as a craft beer mecca, and do so even more by attending other ticketed or nonticketed corollary events. Some skip the festival entirely and opt instead for special release tappings at bars and pubs, beer-centric themed parties (like "Offensively Delicious: A Craft Beer Comedy Show" or the "Kenny Lagers" celebration of easy drinking and easy listening), and dinners where crafted beers are expertly paired with crafted foods to stimulate even the most dulled palate.

On the Wednesday evening before GABF in 2014, each of the sixty or so attendees of the beer pairing dinner at the Kitchen in LoDo (Lower Downtown Denver)[52] was greeted with a white wine glass half filled with Crooked Stave's Veille, a refreshing and slightly funk saison with a crisp light citrus nose. This was the second year the popular "community bistro"—a chalkboard lists the local farms that provide the restaurant with their meats and vegetables—put on their "Young Guns Beer Dinner." It's named as such to celebrate some of the grand scene's quickly burgeoning newcomers. The night's beers, and honored brewers, came from five of the newest yet extremely well-respected breweries from across the United States: local Denver's Crooked Stave Artisan Beer Project, the Bay Area's Almanac Beer Company, Tampa's Cigar City Brewing, Austin's Jester King Brewery, and Tulsa's Prairie Artisan Ales.

The crowd is an even mix of men and women ranging from their late twenties to their late sixties and ranging in dress from suit and tie to flowery sun dress and shawl. All attendees sipped their "aperitif" beverage in anticipation of the big wooden doors sliding open, inviting them to take their seats. Picking seats feels important because a meal like this will last at least two hours. Choose wisely. But how? Turns out there wasn't much to worry about, though. Not like prom or your husband's cousin's wedding.

Though each actor was embodied and emplaced on the same local stage that evening, everyone was taking part in a translocal scene defined by a common valuing of the same core object. Temporary or fleeting as that particular collective may have been, the prefabricated bonds between those with aesthetic affinities made the seating question moot. Everyone there willfully ponied up $130 for what was bound to be a sensuously intoxicating evening of food, drink, and conversation.

Though only one brewery was local to the area, the event *felt* local. Maybe it was because the food was made primarily from local ingredients. You could almost hear the porchetta oink through the cherry demi-glace. Maybe it's because Kyla Ostler, the Kitchen's beer director, invited breweries that cared about *their* local scenes and said as much when they introduced and explained the beers they brought with them. Maybe it's because of Prairie Artisan Ales' Coolship Truck, a wild ale spontaneously fermented in the back of their pickup truck. This was the same truck the brewers drove from Tulsa to Denver, arriving about an hour before they told us this story. Drinking that beer was the first time I thought "old tennis shoe" was an appropriate descriptor, and a positive one no less.

The dishes were served family style with big plates for folks to pick from. This type of setup could potentially be awkward when eating with strangers. But it wasn't. Perhaps it was the alcohol. More likely, it was a consequence of the diners' common aesthetic interest in and desire for the beer and food pairings. The evening started well when the smoked mussels and corned beef tongue were paired with a sour guava beer and a rum-barrel-aged coffee stout, both brewed by Cigar City. Though the people at each table fed themselves and drank out of their own glasses, they did it together with a communal sense of purpose. The "civil inattention" between strangers that is common on city streets and across public places was replaced by an *attentive civility* reinforced by a shared desire for a similar aesthetic experience.[53] And it is the embodied and emplaced experiences of these crafted wares that elicit and enact taste together.

The performance of taste is as important as the tasted objects themselves, perhaps even more so. The performance is a public and shared action, an activity, a practice that provides a bit of social stability in contrast to the sensations felt by a lone body. This follows sociologist Antoine Hennion's contention that

> in the act of tasting, in the gestures that allow it, in the know-how that accompanies it, in the supports sought (in other people, or in guides and reviews), in the tiny ongoing adjustments that lay it out and favor its felicity and reproducibility—it is on the basis of all these responses that objects return to those who take an interest in them.[54]

The gestures signify the know-how, supported by confirming affective gestures from those sitting around the same table, sharing food and beer that were produced—cooked or brewed—to elicit sensuous reactions and aesthetic judgments that are felt by individuals and fashioned by both translocal and local scenes. The translocal and the local blend into each other during big festivals. The "Young Guns Beer Dinner" wouldn't happen, at least at its magnitude and with its breadth of offerings, if GABF weren't going on the following three days at the convention center, a short walk down the street.

Translocal festivals take place somewhere. They rely on specific places to house and host them. As such, translocal festivals are always local events; they're always rooted in a particular local economy and culture, even when they attract attendees and participants from elsewhere. For that matter, they depend on out-of-towners to increase their intensity and reinforce the significance and reputation of the host city or town. For example, for most people, the thought of going to Munster, Indiana, isn't much of one. But for craft beer enthusiasts, Three Floyds Brewing's Dark Lord Day turns Munster—a real place with real people—into a modern fairyland, a place where people yearn to experience and sip on variations of the soy-sauce-like imperial stout that is sold only on that designated day at the end of April each year. It's safe to say that over 90 percent of the pilgrims who come to northern Indiana to bow at the feet of the Dark Lord aren't from Munster. The local needs the translocal as much as the translocal needs the local. Entertaining out-of-towners might be a rare event in Three Floyds' hometown, but it's right in the wheelhouse of Las Vegas. We go back there next.

Festivals as Local Rituals with Translocal Roots

As a global tourist destination, Las Vegas has an excellent track record of making strangers less strange by providing them with places to stay and things to experience. They transform from strangers into tourists, willingly taking on the role scripted for them by staying within the neon bubbles of the Strip or Downtown. Big name restaurants (e.g., Le Cirque, Momofuku) and big shows (e.g., Blue Man Group, Cirque du Soleil) that cost less than they would in other cities, if you can even get a reservation or ticket for them in those other cities, provide attractions for those on vacation, or taking a break from their professional convention, to briefly escape the banalities of everyday life. Las Vegas's ability to consistently re-create spectacles to satisfy the changing collective aesthetic whims of tourists is noteworthy, marking it as perhaps the preeminent example of a city built on the precepts of the "experience economy."[55]

Featuring a variety of "shopertainment" and "eatertainment," cities vie for tourists by providing opportunities to experience something stimulating and distinct. The goal for city officials and stakeholders, according to urban planner Anne Lorentzen, is to produce an "attractive atmosphere, which comes from place-bound activities, events and services, attractive places and diverse social spaces, which make *visitors and residents feel inspired, involved, and connected to the place*."[56] Because the staging of experiences and the events that foster them in Las Vegas are primarily aimed at attracting visitors, locals have often been left out of the equation to "feel inspired, involved, and connected." Instead, they end up feeling pushed to the side, seeing the events as unwelcoming or partaking in them either as workers or as tourists in their own city.

Ranging from those that celebrate and showcase music to those that celebrate and showcase particular ethnic identities, festivals have emerged as key sites for displaying a city's image in a quick and affordable way as opposed to building more costly permanent structures for cultural amenities like museums or stadiums.[57] Festivals have been primarily used this way in Las Vegas, as an *outward-facing* happening to attract visitors from outside of Southern Nevada. Since the Great Recession, however, some of the festivals, in particular beer festivals and related events, have become more *inward-facing*, set to entice locals who populate the city and the local scene as it plays out on local stages. As such, if we approach the "experience economy" as more than simply a supply-side business strategy and instead as a way that individuals and groups learn to be in the city, feel it, and act upon it, we can begin to appreciate the demand side of urban festivals and the experiences they offer.

Local festivals help "communicat[e] something meaningful about identity, community, locality, and belonging."[58] Unlike translocal festivals, local festivals are intended to bring locals together in a common place with a common purpose. Yet like translocal festivals, they tend to follow a script that's been written elsewhere. This does not mean that by borrowing from festivals that have happened elsewhere local scenes are contributing to the devious sides of cultural homogenization or standardization. Rather, it highlights a translocally shared history that influences the staging of local events and, in turn, the expectations that participants have about them. Those expectations, either implicit or explicit, are learned through embodied participation in the grand translocal scene and then become anchored locally. When the festival acts, as most rituals do, as a means for transmitting and acquiring the "interactional grammar" of the scene, beer geeks are invited to share their passion with thirsty neophytes. Newcomers, then, can learn not only what to taste and appreciate but *how* to taste and evaluate.[59]

The need to educate locals about the intricacies of craft beer was a claim made by the majority of people I met throughout my field research. At first glance, a beer festival might seem like a place where the brain and body are comfortably numbed rather than enlightened or awakened. This is especially the case during the last hour of a festival when broken palates try to suck down their money's worth of the beers still flowing.[60] But one of the main ways that festivals serve the scene, and the culture that supports it, is by providing a springboard for *aesthetic socialization*. For local scenes, local festivals—especially in a city like Las Vegas where interest in craft beer was initially slow compared to other cities—help foster and transmit knowledge about three separate but related subjects: the city and its changing image, craft beer in general, and craft beer brewed locally. The Great Vegas Festival of Beer (GVFB) hits all three.

Motley Brews—a beer-centric events company—moved their annual craft beer festival from Sunset Park, a three-hundred-plus-acre public park a stone's throw southeast of the airport, to Downtown Las Vegas in 2014. By changing the geography of the festival, they explicitly and implicitly rode, and in turn helped push, the currents of local culture and the local craft beer scene. Craft beer, according to Motley Brews founder Brian Chapin, "can be a portal into a portion of the city, the culture, the flavor." That "flavor" is experienced locally, but relies on translocal influences, from the festival's organization to the beers served, to propel it as a cultural force. The move to the Fremont East Entertainment District was a clear "strategy of action" that Chapin pulled from both his local and translocal cultural "tool-kits." As sociologist Ann Swidler argues, "Strategies of action incorporate, and thus depend on, habits, moods, sensibilities, and views of the world. . . . People do not build lines of action from scratch, choosing actions one at a time as efficient means to given ends. Instead, they construct chains of action beginning with at

FIGURE 3.4. Old Vegas and craft Vegas come together Downtown during the Great Vegas Festival of Beer. (Photo by author)

least some pre-fabricated links."[61] At the time, Chapin was seizing upon a mood in Las Vegas, and built his line of action out of "pre-fabricated links" that connect craft beer with a population looking for new and novel enlivening experiences. Chapin told reporter Alan Snel of the *Las Vegas Review Journal* that "Downtown captures the spirit about us."[62]

Like "Life is Beautiful"—a music festival accompanied by crafted food, drink, art, and learning—which Rehan Choudhry founded and, through his connections with Tony Hsieh's Downtown Project, placed within Downtown's refurbished footprint, GVFB took over a few streets and parking lots to create an inclusive space. In 2014, 2015, and 2016, a fence circumscribed the area, a clear sign that the city approved of it (and the potential revenue it brought to the Downtown area despite the closing of its regular shops and restaurants).[63] Perhaps more importantly, at least for the symbolic "rhetorical force"[64] and aesthetic experience it fostered, festival attendees walk across the normally car-infested grid without care or fear of being run over. This is surely reassuring after a few hours and a few sheets to the wind. Moreover, the closed-off streets provide a temporary yet revised sense of place for both locals and visitors alike. The reimagining of quotidian space into a "festival space" aids participants' pursuit of a good time as well as their implicit socialization into the spectacle of both the festival and the city.

Chapin brings his knowledge from elsewhere to help Las Vegas, his home since 2009, showcase its brews to a local and translocal audience, even though the majority of beers served at the festival are from elsewhere. The 2014 festival featured notable out-of-market breweries like Lost Abbey. Alpine, another popular San Diego brewery, made its debut in Las Vegas at the 2015 festival. In fact, the heavily IPA-producing brewery helped sponsor it that year. It seemed odd, then, that the line at their tent was relatively short or even nonexistent. I ran into local Las Vegan Dave Moore drinking one of Alpine's offerings a few feet away from the mini-trailer that held Alpine's kegs and the tent that helped keep them cool. I recognized him from the distinctive shaved head, gauged ear plugs, and sleeve tattoos that I had seen on Instagram under the handle @beerelevance. He was sipping a hop bomb and clearly already anticipating a refill.

"Can you believe that nobody's here?" Dave asks me. "This is a freakin' Duet, probably the best IPA at the entire festival, and nobody's here?!"

"More for us, I suppose," I joke.

"You bet!" he retorts with a smile and a "Cheers." We clink glasses, small four-ounce snifters actually made of glass, a rarity at most festivals. After digging into the intense piney nose and citrus aftertaste from the Simcoe and Amarillo hops, Dave and I walk toward the blinking "WE HOT" neon sign that's supposed to read "WESTERN HOTEL." The old hotel had been refurbished as an event space by Hsieh's Downtown Project. Today, it's home to BrewLogic, a series of seminars about a variety of beer-infused topics. In a press release before the festival, Chapin noted that the response was so positive the first year they did the seminars, he had to bring them back again: "We want to continue to explore the diversity of craft beer through innovative ideas to keep the festival fresh and exciting for beer lovers and novices alike."[65]

The seminars appeal to both demographics. Each session packed in over a hundred people, with twice as many turned away at the door. Popular local chef Justin Kingsley Hall showed people how to make beer vinegar, Michael Shetler offered an introduction to wild and sour ales, and Stone Brewing ambassador Bill Sysak officiated a beer and doughnut pairing session. No stranger to Las Vegas, "Dr. Bill" as he's known from here to Escondido, has hosted a number of Stone events, including a cigar and beer pairing at the Atomic, which not coincidentally served as the VIP "Brewers Lounge" during the festival. Cigars were lined up with beers from Stone as well as local beers like CraftHaus's boozy Russian imperial stout, the Comrade.

"Even though he's not from here," the Atomic's Rose says of Dr. Bill, "he's all about improving the local beer scene here in Vegas. He's an educator; he's somebody that wants people to get excited about beer."

Not only did the seminars return, but for the second year in a row, Chapin's Motley Brews crew designated a space for local breweries strategically placed near the entryway, itself a spectacle. Beneath a large banner declaring "Great Beer Lies Ahead," former mayor and mob lawyer Oscar Goodman, accompanied by feather-headed classic showgirls, greeted attendees. The juxtaposition of old Vegas and the newly *crafted* local Las Vegas was a bit jolting. But it provided a fun and noteworthy instance for those more focused on the drinks being poured rather than Goodman's somewhat notorious reputation, almost as dirty as the gin martini in his hand.

When the festival moved a bit eastward down Fremont Street, the Western Hotel and the entrance on Sixth Street provided a grand open setting to display local breweries ready to pour their beers. The term "local" was stretched to include Northern Nevada breweries like Great Basin and Brasserie St. James from Reno. An elongated booth for the Nevada Craft Brewers Association, an active yet relatively small guild that lacks the organization and funding that other state guilds receive from the national Brewers Association and local supporters, served a collaboration beer by Las Vegas brewers. They called it Banana Split, a German-style hefeweizen brewed with vanilla beans and cacao nibs.

I couldn't hear what they were saying, but I wanted to. So I turned around. A couple standing behind me waiting in line at Tenaya Creek's tent were having a good old time. "You must have found something you liked," I say to them through a goofier smile than I had hoped.

They both smile back, fortunately, and the woman, in her late thirties or early forties sporting sun-kissed cheeks and an empty glass, tells me they're from Minnesota. They usually visit Las Vegas every other year or so but had never been Downtown. And they had never had a beer brewed in Las Vegas either. With a tinge of embarrassment she leans forward and half-whispers, "We didn't even know there were any breweries here!"

"We're craft beer drinkers," her husband interjects. His Twins cap keeps the sun away from his cheeks, yet the gray hair in his goatee still reflects white. "We love our Surly [a popular brewery in Minneapolis]. We love trying all sort of beer. But we didn't know they were doing this much good stuff here. . . . I'm happy we just happened to be here this weekend."

The three of us get pours of the same beer, the Old Jackalope Barleywine. Our conversation would have likely lasted longer, but I'm distracted by a dancing duck in the middle of the lot. I'm not the only one staring. There seems to be an unspoken acknowledgment and sympathy for the person underneath that full-bodied feathered costume skipping around above the reflected asphalt heat. Maybe that's why people took pictures with him or kissed his beak, or, as one young lady did, cupped his genitals. The Atomic Duck belongs to Able Baker Brewing, which, despite the coveted beers available from popular out-of-towners, consistently drew the longest lines of the day, as it did the year before.

The new local brewery provided some strong beers—in both quality and alcohol content—to eager crowds. James Manos and Randy Rohde used their dancing Atomic Duck—also the name of their IPA—and their brewery's name to connect to local Las Vegas history, specifically the so-called Atomic era. "Able" and "Baker" were the names of the first two atomic bombs dropped at the Nevada Test Site and a duck, reportedly, was the one animal that managed to survive those tests. Women dressed in either bomber jackets or rockabilly-style poodle dresses served their treats to intrigued locals and visitors.

With the attention that the new brewery was able to grab along with its local compadres, despite being surrounded by more established translocal breweries, Able Baker helped turn the festival into a celebration of local culture. That celebration continued the next month during the first Locals Only Beer Fest, hosted by Banger Brewing. Tucked away from tourists entertained by fat cupids and Jack Sparrows beneath the Fremont Street digital canopy that, when night falls, shines a mishmash of visuals and videos choreographed to the sounds of classic rock hits every half hour, the Neonopolis rotunda provided a safe haven for locals that day. And instead of the plastic yards of iced sugar vodka slushes their counterparts imbibed that early afternoon, they held plastic snifters of locally brewed beer.

This was a first of its kind event in Las Vegas. The city had reached a point where enough breweries were making enough good beer that the folks at Banger thought it would be a "great way to show off what local breweries are doings," Banger co-owner Eddie Quiogue tells me with a big grin across his face. "We want to bring awareness to what's going on here and help put Las Vegas on the map for craft beer." Along with their beers, many local brewers took their turn in the "dunk a brewer" tank as local homebrewers competed for "best in show" judged by the one thousand attendees of the sold-out event.

"It was one of the best festivals we poured at," reports Steph Cope, co–head brewer at CraftHaus. "We weren't sure how it would pan out, but it was a total success. There were a lot of old faces but there were a lot of new faces, people we've never met or seen before, and that was great. Local pride was well and good that day."

Whether its attendees were trying to find the "best" IPA, as a small group I talked to set out to do that day, or trying some of the new beers that were being poured only during the festival, or even taking a break to sip a brew and sit on the imported faux grass, the festival emitted a communal sense with a communal message of local pride waving in the

FIGURE 3.5. Closed off from the Fremont Street Experience by the Neonopolis, the Locals Only Beer Fest provided local brewers a stage to show off their translocal skills to the local scene. (Photo by author)

wind without guilt. And that communal message seemed as if it was meant to be heard by both the local and translocal scenes: "We exist!"

Translocalism and the Local Scene

The relationship between what happens in one place and what happens in another is difficult to measure, but can be felt or sensed in other ways. The variety of local scenes and the grand translocal scene are beholden to one another, in part because of the contemporary valorization of all things "local." Though that might seem at odds with the trans- or nonlocal, a valuing of the local doesn't have to be confined to one's sole geographic location. Translocalism is, as discussed earlier, a belief in or desire for local from elsewhere, for other people's and other places' local.

Local beer scenes necessarily rely on identification of both neolocalism and translocalism. Local breweries are important, but so are the products brought into the city by distributors and traveling or trading beer geeks alike. Beyond the products, the practices of scene participants span across geographical boundaries. Even at GVFB or the Locals Only Beer Fest, many of the ways the events were set up as well as the ways attendees performed taste—from beer exchanged from servers to tasters with small vessels to hold their small pours to pretzel necklaces wrapped around and hanging from sweaty necks—were imported ideas from elsewhere. Yet without local scenes where people enact the key taste performances that define the grand translocal scene, the grand translocal scene would drift into an aimless abyss. Yet again, without the grand translocal scene, local scenes could grow stale and stagnant where no "celebration of us" could be heard beyond the immediate confines of familiarized locales.

4

Fussing over Status

The door opens with a squeal that grows louder the slower you push it. A sticky linoleum floor and an endcap stuffed with Wonder Bread welcomes you and a quick peek at the back cooler reveals cases of silver bullets and skinny Clydesdales. Is this the right place? This was a question I've asked myself all too often in Las Vegas. All over the city, signs advertising "craft" share wall space with pictures of Big Beer eighteen-packs. I walk past the packaged pastries and bags of flavored potato chips. Then suddenly the place changes. Taking a slight step up—a step that was more symbolically blunt than it was physical—onto the wood flooring, I'm exposed to a variety of artisanal cheeses and a grand selection of craft beers staying cool behind glass doors.

The deli counter stocked with Boar's Head meats and French baguettes once saw prescription drugs handed across it to local residents including one of Downtown Las Vegas's most (in)famous pill poppers, Elvis Presley. The White Cross Drugs sign that I saw before walking in is a remnant of and "artifactual witness" to bygone times.[1] The pharmacy, which had been dispensing medicine since 1955, closed in March 2012 and then reopened in July 2013 as White Cross Market. Located at the center of "Naked City," a neighborhood nestled between the towering Stratosphere that symbolically signals the northern point of the Strip and the 18b Arts District a few blocks north, the market served a diverse population as one of the few, if not only, places to buy groceries.[2]

I pick up a few beers to bring home. Going back out the way I came in, I keep thinking about how different the two sides of the store are from each other. My thoughts are interrupted by a voice outside my head.

"You got craft beer in there?"

I ignore him. He says it again, this time a little bit louder. "You got craft beer in there?!"

"Yeah," I answer reluctantly.

"Well, that shit sucks. Too fucking expensive and tastes like shit," he gnarls through bits of spit that fell onto his stained blue T-shirt. "All you hipsters are ruining this town."

I stare at him blankly holding my box of bottles in one hand and fumbling for the car keys in my pocket with the other. As I settle into the driver's seat, I hear him again.

"Got any change to go with that beer?"

The key's in the ignition before I could fully grasp let alone answer his question. But his voice and what he said with it lingered in my mind for much longer than my drive home. Though I couldn't verify it, he looked like he was drunk, at one thirty in the afternoon. Stumbling and spitting as he yelled at strangers like me, he embodied—at least in that moment—the very dark side of alcohol that puts even the best intentions of craft drinkers into question.

Alcohol is a toxic poison linked to increases in vandalism, sexual assault, and other social problems. How could such a liquid—even when made with the best artisanal ingredients and crafted techniques—function as a mediator for contemporary urban re-enchantment when so many of the city's "underclass" remain beholden to its addictive and numbing properties? Maybe he was homeless; there's a significant homeless population that "resides" in that neighborhood.[3] Or, even more likely, maybe he was one of the many people who come to Las Vegas with little to their name who try to make money gambling and then find themselves trying to survive other ways.

This random encounter spoke to a key issue about craft beer: the relationship between taste and status. Our exchange occurred outside of a place located smack-dab in the middle of a neighborhood boasting both wealth and poverty. And inside its walls, it showed both faces. Moreover, the man gave a label to the people perpetuating what *he* saw as a problem: hipsters. And he certainly wasn't alone in his assessment.

Both casual craft beer drinkers and serious beer geeks have been lumped in with the tragically hip and the unbearably pretentious. "Hipster" is as notoriously ill regarded as the label is ill defined. Despite both lay and scholarly attempts to explain and apply it to a particular type of social character, the term remains too amorphous and too far-reaching to have much analytical value.[4] Though I support the use of vernacular terms for urban cultural analysis, as I've argued and done throughout with the term "scene," this one is just too weighed down with negative connotations to be of much use to describe the lived realities of actual social actors. Regardless, that hasn't stopped social actors themselves from pinning the hipster label, and all of its supposedly irony-infused and ironically tattooed baggage, to their adversaries.

A few weeks after I was charged with hipsterdom, a commercial aired during the 2015 Super Bowl that gave visual life to the clichéd hipster craft beer drinker. It was a Budweiser ad replete with hypermasculine overtones and homophobic undertones aimed less at Bud guzzlers and more at presumably less-than-masculine craft sippers. With a heavy-handed sneer and pulsing soundtrack, the commercial showed well-groomed bearded and mustachioed men with and without Warby Parker glasses holding snifters of dark ales—rather than pints of translucent yellow lager—talking and "fussing" about the drinks in their hands.

The "king of beers" threw down the gauntlet between Big Beer and craft, poking fun at and besmirching their smaller yet encroaching foes. This sixty-second, nine-million-dollar "us versus them" declaration was a display of power and force from the top down, from the corporate elite, from the industry's top grossing company. Accompanied by visuals of men chopping wood, tossing beers to buddies, and being served Buds by women, the following verbiage ran throughout the commercial:

> Budweiser. Proudly a Macro Beer. It's not brewed to be fussed over. It's brewed for a crisp smooth finish. This is the only beer Beechwood aged since 1876. There's only one Budweiser. It's brewed for drinking not dissecting. The people who drink our beer are people who like to drink beer

> brewed the hard way. Let them sip their pumpkin peach ale. We'll be brewing us some golden suds. This is the famous Budweiser beer. This Bud's for you.

Ironically ("hypocritically" is probably the more accurate word), the commercial aired shortly after one of AB InBev's craft brewery buying sprees. Between 2011 and the airing of the Super Bowl commercial in early 2015, AB InBev purchased four US craft breweries: Goose Island Brewing in Chicago; Blue Point Brewing in Patchogue, New York; 10 Barrel Brewing in Bend, Oregon; and Elysian Brewing in Seattle. Notably, Elysian's Loser Pale Ale was inspired by the Seattle grunge legends Nirvana and carries the slogan, "Corporate beer still sucks." Moreover, the deep-throated captions closed the commercial by reassuring Bud drinkers that their beer is "brewed for drinking and not dissecting," so let the silly and effete craft beer snobs "sip their pumpkin peach ale." Well, Elysian also makes a beer called Gourdgia on My Mind. It's a pumpkin peach ale.

The commercial was the proverbial shot heard around the beer world. And it was loud. Equally so was the response. Agitated craft beer brewers and drinkers quickly flocked to their computers and smartphones to fire back across the internet on websites, forums, and blogs. Elysian cofounder Dick Cantwell, who opened the brewery in 1996 and lobbied the lone dissenting vote to sell it, responded in an email to the *Chicago Tribune*:

> I find it kind of incredible that ABI would be so tone-deaf as to pretty directly (even if unwittingly) call out one of the breweries they have recently acquired, even as that brewery is dealing with the anger of the beer community in reaction to the sale. It doesn't make our job any easier, and it certainly doesn't make me feel any better about a deal I didn't even want to happen. It's made a difficult situation even more painful.[5]

The shock of the commercial clearly jolted Cantwell to further question his brewery's recent allegiance to Big Beer. Despite his long career in craft beer that predates its current rise by two decades as well as his position as the president of Washington's brewers guild, his status was clearly in question, and he was doing the most ardent interrogating of himself by himself. We can say he was in the process of both spoiling and repairing his identity.[6] He wasn't the only one. The pangs of the aesthetic conflict were felt across the grand scene.

The folks gathered at Bad Beat's taproom to watch the "Big Game" laughed with a mixture of nervous glee and defensiveness as the Budweiser commercial aired, especially when the throaty voiceover declared that their beer wasn't "brewed to be fussed over." "Who wants to fuss over that piss?" was a common sentiment and knee-jerk brush off.

"I like fussing over my beer," Mike Gaddy told me. A local craft beer enthusiast who turned his "hobby" into a career as an on-premise distributor and brewery representative, Gaddy is an unabashedly devout believer in the virtues of craft.

"I like sitting and talking about beer. It's a fun social hobby. I can spend eight hours at a bar with people and not get drunk. Because that's not the point," he exclaims between deep inhales followed by tiny sips of the dark syrupy beverage in his tulip glass. "It's fun and positive and I learn something about beer and science and the people I'm with and what they appreciate and sometimes we agree and sometimes we argue."

To Gaddy, like so many others in the craft beer scene inside and outside of Las Vegas, the "fussing" about a beer *is* the point. Swirling, sniffing, and then sipping a beer, whether it's the first or fiftieth time someone has had it, examining it with the tools of both a surgeon and a mechanic, is how taste is performed with others. It's the key practice, along with the significant object, that connects craft beer drinkers as and into, according to Gaddy, "a neat social circle that we created that didn't exist too long ago. . . . The people behind that commercial don't understand our mind-set, they don't understand how we choose to participate in the way we drink, think, and talk about beer. Which makes no sense since, they're buying craft breweries and they just told the people they want to buy that beer to fuck off!"

"Fussing" about beers is a key practice that, in effect, defines craft beer drinkers as craft beer drinkers. The interactions with the beer and with others in a social setting are primary ways of enacting the scene and acting within it. It is through these types of shared engagements and practices that scenes are "interactional accomplishments."[7] By showing the products craft beer drinkers consume and *how* they consume them with disdain, Budweiser disparaged and consequently alienated the exact market segment they were supposedly trying to woo. The overtly negative and pejorative tone seemed at odds with the rising market for craft beer and Big Beer's own practices of buying breweries to satisfy and benefit from that segment.

"When the commercial started, I thought they were celebrating macro, which would have been fine," says Mike Dominiak of Bad Beat Brewing. "But then I realized they were making fun of us. They were attacking craft beer!" Mike nudged Weston Barkley, Bad Beat's head brewer, and told him to watch. And he did. And he looked at Mike. And they were mad. "Brewed the hard way," Budweiser pronounced. That's even the title of the commercial.

"That really ticked us off. For the most part, Weston is back there brewing by himself, lugging fifty-pound bags of grain on his shoulder, pouring into the grain mill by himself. *That's* brewing the hard way, not pushing buttons." Mike notes that most macro beers are brewed by machines; the hard labor is done on the backs of robots rather than human beings.

"Whatever they were trying to do, it got the craft beer world talking. If it was meant to make us mad, to make craft beer people mad, it certainly struck a chord. Maybe it was meant to defend themselves. I don't know. But we must be doing something right."

The Budweiser commercial and the reactions to it provide competing narratives that illustrate a cultural fissure about taste and status. They didn't create the divide between Big Beer and the craft beer scene, but they certainly helped reinforce it. This type of contentious, line-in-the-sand action is called "boundary work," defined by sociologist Christena

Nippert-Eng as "the strategies, principles, and practices we use to create, maintain, and modify cultural categories." Though it is primarily mental labor, "it must be enacted and enhanced through a largely visible collection of essential, practical activities . . . that help us tangibly reinforce and even challenge cognitive and situational distinctions."[8] Boundary work is often a practice used to foster an "us" that is opposed to a "them." And clearly it can come from both sides of the dividing lines.

The tangible practices within the translocal craft beer scene—from "fussing over" the various stimuli from their brews in hand to lugging large bags of malted barley—are at odds with Big Beer's message and intent. Budweiser's commercial shows that they not only accept the disagreement but also hope to distance themselves from the effete feminized fussers by reinforcing their own brute masculinity.

Boundary work and the status distinctions it creates, however, can move in two directions: externally *and* internally. That is, while cultural classification systems are used to demarcate insiders and outsiders, protagonists and antagonists, us and them, they also develop as a means for ranking, organizing, and evaluating *within* particular scenes. For example, while much of the early writing on punks focused on their countercultural normative ethos and their relationship to "conventional" society, sociologist Kathryn Joan Fox's seminal study showed how punks created internal divisions of membership based on a range of criteria including commitment to their core beliefs and presentation of self through style.[9]

In his discussion of in-group dynamics within social movements, sociologist Joshua Gamson notes,

> The maintenance of group boundaries involves movements in bitter disputes not only with those everyone agrees is not a member (that is, with antagonists) but also in often uglier conflicts with those who might reasonably be considered members or protagonists. The *us* is solidified not just against an external *them* but also against *thems* inside, as particular subgroups battle to gain or retain legitimate *us* standing.[10]

At the same time the craft beer protagonists are engaged in an aesthetic battle with Big Beer antagonists, distinctions *within* the scene have emerged. And those distinctions have as much to do with commitment as with the contradictions and paradoxes of competing and often ambiguous ideologies.

In their review of contemporary cultural consumption practices, sociologists Omar Lizardo and Sara Skiles write that "within [scenes], consumption norms are organized not according to a logic of compliance with or resistance to external ideology, but rather by identification with internally created and maintained codes and boundaries."[11] Though they add an important dimension to our understanding of symbolic boundaries, they nevertheless incorrectly present internal demarcations as more powerful or important than those that divide varying taste factions. Instead of one or the other, symbolic boundaries are often constructed in relation to *both* outsiders *and* insiders. The case of the contemporary craft beer scene shows that attempts to create stable identities through consumption tussle against *both* external *and* internal ideologies. This conflict transcends social spheres whereby the translocal scene passes on some of its constituted ideological shortcomings to the local scene.

Though they don't connect the translocal to the local, and thereby overlook the lived effects of place, sociologists Josée Johnston and Shyon Baumann nevertheless found a similar tension among and between gourmet food writers and self-defined "foodies." They aptly reveal and explicate two competing ideologies of *democracy* and *distinction*. The former, they write, is based on

> normative liberal principles of human equality and meritocracy. . . . Democratic ideology is connected to normative conceptions and populist ideals of the United States as a classless, multicultural society, where immigrants of multiple races and ethnicities have equal opportunities for socioeconomic and cultural advancement, at least in theory.[12]

At a more "covert" level, however, an ideology of distinction exists that emphasizes the autonomy of individuals and an assumed belief that value is derived from hard work. Johnston and Baumann find that

> an ideology of status and distinction operates implicitly to suggest that only certain individuals can appreciate and understand "quality" culture. This ideology recalls the hierarchy of old-fashioned snobbism, but is reformulated in individualistic, meritocratic language for a democratic era. . . . Because the focus is on the autonomy of individual tastes and lifestyles, the collective underpinnings of high-status cultural forms are not readily transparent or discussed . . . particularly in the U.S. context where democratic populism has such strong currency. The overt ideals of liberal democracy work in dialectical tension with a covert ideology of status and cultural distinction, informing a belief in equality of opportunity that emphasizes cultural openness, but say little about the power relations, class inequality, or ethnic hierarchies of cultural outcomes.[13]

Though not all status distinctions are inherently detrimental or damaging to scenes and their actors, their tendency to reproduce inequalities of status power can be palpable. Craft beer brewers and drinkers are part of a scene that prides itself on inclusion and an egalitarian fervor for merit-based judgments and evaluations. Yet, in part due to its public openness where anyone is purportedly free to take part in the scene, inclusivity can, paradoxically, breed both latent and manifest forms of exclusivity within, across, and through local scenes.

The practices and symbolic codes of either inclusivity or exclusivity, or both, in local scenes are not created anew. They come from and are connected to somewhere else, or, more accurately, to a collection of somewhere elses. Translocal connectivity can negatively impact local scenes when locals reproduce status hierarchies that have been internalized and taken for granted. This often happens when classification systems become more than tools for constructing social reality and become the very basis of social reality itself. From the outset, craft beer—even when it was called "micro" rather than the more elevated and honorific title—has been and continues to be defined in opposition to macro Big Beer. Because the logic of creating distinctions was part of its origin, it is bound to continue to create them. First externally, then internally, playing out across the translocal scene and onto local stages.

Internal boundary work reveals itself in two salient and readily identifiable ways, though there are certainly others worthy of discussion, that act against the scene's opposition to external adversaries. The first is the varied roles that women play, from the stereotypical exploitations of sexuality through names and labels to the slowly growing number of female brewers, beertenders, and beer drinkers. Sometimes it seems like male craft brewers and drinkers feel the need to assert their masculinity by demeaning women, as if they want to win favor from the Big Beer crowd rather than oppose them. The second is the perilous intoxication that mimics the worst of American "conspicuous consumption" and materialism.[14] The scene's "core object" can become so revered and sacralized that, instead of being consumed, it becomes a status symbol encased in designated beer fridges and cellars like trophies, simple notches on a belt or, in contemporary craft beer parlance, ticks on an app.

The status hierarchies that have emerged around gender and materialism rest at the crux between the ideologies of democracy and distinction.[15] And they show the paradox of taste as *both* a sensuous property open to all *and* a means for making choices and judgments that affect social relationships and the symbolic boundaries that constrain and contain them.

Taste judgments are not only made about popular culture. They are a necessary part of it because of popular culture's ubiquity and the overwhelming choices contemporary individuals living within cultures of abundance have to make about what they choose to consume day to day. "Good taste" is a mark of distinction, in the double sense of setting apart from, and conferring honor to, those who claim to possess it. Yet taste and the focused acts of tasting require action beyond mere passive consumption. That is, in the same way that sociologists Alan Warde and Lydia Martens found that "dining out" is "a perpetual experiment,"[16] craft beer consumption and scene participation require negotiations of taste, social status, and allegiance to a broader ethos. Taste is turned both inward and outward to define membership, even if that membership is not fully defined or articulated and more temporary than or even more subservient to other attributes. Craft beer consumption and scene participation, then, become a means to perpetually experiment with taste, identity, and popular culture as consumers confront feelings of alienation and anxiety through their choice of drink. As with any experiment, the results are not always good. But, like a well-kept cellared and aged stout or sour ale, they can change too.[17]

Brewing Gender

A simple Google image search of "craft beer labels" presents a vast array of colors, fonts, and innumerable versions of hop flowers as well as depictions of mythical, religious, and working-class characters. Adding "women" to the search terms yields a menagerie of cartooned bikinis and lingerie draped on and off female bodies.[18] Big-bosomed and big-eyed women ride bottles, rockets, and hops. They're French maids, *mer*maids, pinups, erotic masseuses, and "wenches." And they're ready to undress (e.g., Pig Minds Brewing's Panty Dropper Blueberry California Ale), show off their seductive tattoos (e.g., Clown Shoes Brewing's Tramp Stamp Belgian IPA), or offer not-so-subtle sex acts (e.g., SweetWater Brewing's Happy Ending imperial stout). The label for Happy Ending—a reference to a post-massage male orgasm—includes a box of tissues, an open-mouthed man at the pinnacle of pleasure, and the silhouette of an Asian geisha. It drew not only the attention but the ire of a craft beer store manager who refused to put it on his shelf. "This label is about a female Asian sex worker manually masturbating a man to orgasm and cleaning up the ejaculate with tissues," he noted. "Why is that appropriate on a beer label?"[19] Craft beer was supposed to be above that, or at least he thought so.

Though beer is a living organism, it doesn't have a gender, nor does beer drinking. These labels, and others like them, suggest otherwise and have the potential to alienate women who make up roughly one-third of the American craft beer market.[20] Moreover, by presenting women as mere objects in the service of men, these breweries alienate themselves from the long and storied history of women's role in brewing. That history reaches back to ancient Sumerian and Egyptian societies where Ninkasi, the Goddess of Beer, was worshipped as the chief brewer of the gods. Of note, there are no lasting images of Ninkasi that survived antiquity, but there are plenty of illustrations from ancient Mesopotamia of beer drinkers enjoying the fermented fruits of her labor as well as a hymn in her honor.[21]

Skipping over a few millennia and a few thousand miles, it wasn't until the modern era in Europe and the United States when brewing transitioned from the home to a regulated and commercialized industry that it became a male-dominated profession. And the men who dominate the industry today are the same ones wrapping their beers in objectifying labels. Blatant sexism is almost expected from Big Beer companies who have long courted male consumers by connecting their products to buxom blondes and masculine hedonism through sports and other *machismo*-touting leisure activities. The culture of craft beer was supposed to be different from the one espoused by its Big Beer adversaries. Yet the inclusion of images that demean women demonstrates the power and ubiquity of sexism in American popular culture and shows that craft beer's most utopian desires have yet to be satiated. Across the supposedly democratic and inclusive grand scene of craft beer, women have been charged with distinction largely based on conventional feminine sexuality above other attributes.

In Las Vegas, billboards that sit above streets and on trucks that move through them use women to sell everything from beer—"I'd Tap That," above a woman draped over a keg, reads an advertisement for local Lee's Discount Liquors—to sexual services by women—"Hot babes, direct to you." It shouldn't be a surprise, then, that some local Las Vegas breweries have succumbed to promoting heteronormative and sexualized depictions of females, thereby enacting the dominant logic of Las Vegas and countering the craft beer scene's presumably oppositional fortitude.

The most egregious perpetrator is the tourist-baiting Sin City Brewing, located on the Strip in three casinos, Planet Hollywood (since 2003), Venetian (since 2009), and Bally's (since 2017), and a stand-alone bar that opened in 2014 on the bustling corner of Harmon Avenue and Las Vegas Boulevard. The name itself capitalizes on the city's most hackneyed and often contested moniker. Coupled with its logo—a red blocked shapely feminine silhouette with a devil's tail—the brewery is positioned to sell the image of lusty women more than the beer it pours.

On a pleasant spring afternoon I ran into a group of young men from Ohio in town for a bachelor party. Leaning against the concrete barrier designed to keep pedestrians safe from the cars on the Strip, each sipped a Sin City beer in a Sin City plastic cup. I approached them casually and with equal aplomb asked one of them what they were drinking. He admitted he didn't know, that he and his buddies bought the beers for the cup itself. "How perfect. A Sin City beer in the heart of Sin City. Awesome!" one of the tank-topped young dudes exclaimed. "This cup's a keeper!" And the beers that filled their cups were not fussed over. Instead, they were drained down their throats with relative ease. The names of those beers are harder to swallow: Weisse (pronounced as "vice") is Nice, Never Pass Up on a Blonde, Say Hello to Amber (described as "full-bodied and proud"), Ale with a Tale, and the Dark Side of Sin. The brewery proudly publicizes onsite photo shoots of Playboy Playmates Holly Madison and Laura Croft gripping phallic tap handles while wearing "I Have Sinned"–emblazed T-shirts and panties.[22]

Even though they're the most blatant and consistent culprit, Sin City isn't the only local craft brewery to adopt the "beer-and-women-are-for-men-to-consume" motif. Tenaya Creek's Red Ryder Ale is adorned with a redheaded woman in a red dress spreading her legs across the edges of a simulacrum of the famed Radio Flyer wagon, revealing her black lingerie. Along with a few other notorious culprits, an online blog devoted to "craft beer's contributions to art" called out Tenaya Creek's label: "Red Ryder! Get it? RYDER! Ride her! And she's got red hair! Label text even talks about the beer like it's a feisty woman who wants to have sex with you (Really, she doesn't. Because she's not real). Seriously, stop it. Your designer, Barret Thomson, is talented. Don't squander good work on a cheap joke."[23] A female craft beer fan alerted me to and pointed the feminist finger at Banger Brewing's name and logo, two complementary *and* complimentary curvy lines that could easily be seen as the outline of a conventionally sexy woman's body. The guys who founded and run Banger don't shy from the ambiguity and the enticement it potentially conjures.[24]

Breweries aren't the only guilty offenders. The symbolic code they reinforce, however, is also sustained by craft beer drinkers themselves, often about breweries and their wares. It's not uncommon to hear people refer to dark beer with high ABVs and the people who can "hold their alcohol" as masculine, while fruit-forward beers, lighter in color and alcohol content, are for the ladies. And even within the supposed egalitarian space of the craft beer scene, gendered claims are casually made without much thought or afterthought. For example, while waiting in line for a pour from local CraftHaus Brewing at a beer festival in Downtown Las Vegas, a white male in his late twenties quipped with a laugh and smirk, "you know how the saying goes, never trust a brewer without a beard."

I make sure to mention this seemingly innocuous yet revealing jibe to the folks responsible for CraftHaus's brews, knowingly putting them in a symbolic predicament between Steve Brockman's rambunctious beard and Steph Cope's dirty blonde femininity.

Steve chuckles and points at Steph with his thumb: "She knows more about brewing than I do. I talk more, sure. But she gets the science more than I do."

Smacking the verbal softball her partner threw, Steph enthusiastically chimes in: "You don't need a dick to mash wort!"

Though there were a few local female homebrewers before she came to Las Vegas in 2014, Steph is the first female *professional* brewer in

Nevada, a label she takes pride in. She is quick to deflect attention from herself despite the fact that local scenesters and media are drawn to her easygoing disposition and brewing acumen. A year into her stint at CraftHaus, she graced the cover of *Vegas Seven*'s annual beer issue (a tradition only a few years in). Pictured standing near the top of a pyramid of kegs holding a slim silver barrel over her shoulder, Steph humbly admits that she wouldn't have been able to climb so high in the scene—though not in the picture, she used a ladder for that—without the support of both local and translocal craft beer folk. She sports pink boots that cover her calves in the picture, as well as on many days she brews, to show her allegiance with the Pink Boots Society.

Started as a blog documenting brewmaster Teri Fahrendorf's road trip to meet and convene with other female brewers, Pink Boots is made up of female beer professionals intent on furthering their education and comradery.[25] The society has about twenty-five hundred members across fifty chapters in the United States and beyond. Though Las Vegas is not home to one of those chapters, Steph gathered local members at CraftHaus for International Women's Collaboration Brew Day (IWCBD), an event sponsored by Pink Boots in honor of May 8's International Women's Day. In 2015 they brewed United Red Ale that Steph and company "tweaked" to reflect their local desert setting by adding a combination of mesquite, cherrywood, and oak smoked malt. The following year, they brewed a gose (pronounced "goes-uh"), a light, tart, and slightly salty German beer. Steph's words of advice on how to make the brew appeared on Pink Boots' website.

From her first day in Las Vegas with the brewery's owners Dave and Wyndee Forrest, Steph felt welcomed and embraced for her brewing abilities, even in the male-dominated world of craft beer and in the male-centric culture of Las Vegas. After Dave and Wyndee lured the brewing duo to Las Vegas from Denver, where they were residing at the time working with folks at Crooked Stave and Upslope, they took them hiking in nearby Red Rock Canyon and then Downtown to the Atomic.

"Dave and Wyndee definitely did their homework," Steve reminisces fondly. "We really didn't know much about the city, only stuff we've seen in movies or TV, really. They went out of their way to show us other stuff. I think we drove down the Strip only once that trip. We weren't interested in gambling and dancing girls. And neither were they."

"The more we learned about the project, the more and more it appealed to us," Steph explains. "All four of us were on the same board thinking about things to do at the brewery. . . . We liked that instead of complaining about the lack of community or culture in Vegas, they wanted to build it. And we wanted to do that with them."

Though they had other job offers, the prospect of building something from the start was appealing to the traveling Aussies. What made it even more appealing was not only that they were going to go against the norms of gaming—you won't find video poker in their taproom—but also that Steph, as noted above, would become the city's and state's first female brewer and Wyndee would become the city's and state's first female brewery owner. Together, they broke through the local craft beer glass ceiling. Within the local Las Vegas scene, there was already a strong cadre of strong women who were influencing the scene by curating nuanced tap lists with Cicerone certifications in hand. But women were still at least an arm's length away from the brewing process.

A little over a year after CraftHaus brewed and canned its first beers and opened its doors to the public, Las Vegas native Amanda Koeller moved back home after graduating from the Master Brewer's program at the University of California, Davis. She landed a position as the lead brewer at Big Dog's Brewing after longtime brewer Dave Otto left to start a brewing program at PT's, a well-established local chain of sports bars. Though Amanda's hire doubled the number of female brewers in Las Vegas to the grand total of two, it signaled at least a minimal degree of progress.

It is worth noting, however, that neither Steph nor Amanda is brewing alone. Both are, in effect, *co*–head brewers, each partnered with a man (Steph has Steve and Amanda has Dave Pascual, who left Chicago

Brewing Company to help fill Otto's shoes with his own batches of award-winning beers). As such, while the status of women in the craft beer scene, locally and translocally, is changing and seemingly gaining value, the subordinate roles that the majority of women play are still at odds with the purported egalitarian and democratic ethos of craft. If craft breweries continue to use women's bodies as sexualized or submissive objects on their beers' labels, the industry and the scene that supports it will appear uninviting to women. Though groups like Pink Boots, Barley's Angels, and the Women's Beer Forum have made strides, the leading male voices need to speak out against both latent and manifest forms of sexism to help provide more space and opportunity for women to come to beer for the same reasons that men do: for the beer and for the comradery, neither of which needs to be gendered.

Intoxicating Possessions and the Value of Exclusivity

Even if gender roles and relations were less divisive, craft breweries and brewers would still find themselves square in the middle of ideological tensions between democracy and distinction. Despite a collective declaration hailing the prospects and pleasures of craft production and consumption, like any business, craft breweries need people to buy their product. The more exclusive the product becomes or, more pointedly, the more exclusive their product *appears* to become, the more likely people are to buy it. Craft beer is no different. Though space is often a constraint that prohibits some breweries from producing some of their beers year-round or in higher quantities, for others it is a part of the game of supply and demand. That game can often lead both brewers and those pining for their beers wondering whether or not either of them will ever grab the carrot on the stick, especially if it's a barrel-aged limited-release carrot.

Some craft breweries have capitalized on the desire and intoxication of exclusivity by offering memberships often at varied levels that correspond to the amount of access to certain beers. And there are plenty of beer geeks waiting to gobble up those memberships that, in turn, add to the perceived value of beer based, in large part, on exclusivity. Captain Ahab's descendants are alive and well, busy hunting brewery-only "white whales" designed to stay off the shelves of stores even though they may end up on a beer hoarder's shelf for years to come, unless it's an IPA "required" to be consumed as close to its canning or bottling as possible.

Worse, it might become available for sale or trade on the craft beer "black market," where values rise well above the original cost. An aged rare release like Lost Abbey's 2012 cherry version of their popular Cable Car wild ale was originally sold at forty-five dollars for a 750-milliliter bottle. Only eighty cases were made. A single bottle sold for eight hundred dollars in 2015. An already expensive twenty-dollar four-pack of a fresh double IPA, which someone waited three hours in line for because it was sold only at the brewery, easily and almost immediately jumps to sixty dollars on unregulated beer-geek-enticing eBay-like websites (e.g., mybeercellar.com, beerauctions.com).

This can be explained easily by theories of taste that view social class as inextricably linked to the things that people like. But painting in broad strokes like sociologist Pierre Bourdieu does when he divides the world between those with a "taste of luxury" and those with a "taste of necessity" leaves important details covered.[26] The finer particulars are necessary, especially because *all* craft beer drinking fits squarely into the luxury category. Yes, workers from ancient Egypt to the farms and monasteries of Belgium were once given beer for sustenance. Today, even the most ardent fan wouldn't declare they need to drink craft beer to live. Well, at least not when they're sober.

The twenty-dollar four-pack might make non-craft-beer drinkers wince; it certainly makes plenty of casual craft beer drinkers do so as they subsequently turn toward far less expensive options at local beer stores and taprooms. Because Las Vegas's local breweries haven't obtained the buzzworthy reputations of "hot" breweries embedded in or near cities with well-established craft beer scenes, their beers remain relatively inexpensive. As such, they become *valued* and *value* options for both neophytes and veterans, for the non-beer-hunting geeks, for those whom the local breweries rely on. As one Las Vegas brewer, asking not to be named, told me, to stay in business they need local regulars who value their inclusive offerings rather than the beer geeks who value only exclusive rarities from elsewhere.

> Our target audience isn't the beer geek. Sure, we want our consumer to be educated about beer, but we want them to care about what's made in their city. To take pride in that. We need those people more than we need the beer geeks who only care about the latest limited release that you can only travel or trade for. I get it. It's cool to be one of a hundred or a thousand people to try a specific beer. But is that really about the beer? Is it really about the scene? The culture? The community? Or is it just about, you know, themselves and being cool or hip, like you're in the know or hooked up or something?

Undoubtedly local craft breweries need a consistent local consumer base in ways that even larger regional craft breweries do not.

Economics and culture butt heads, however, when beer geeks—those hunting, muleing, and trading—believe they can help push the scene by pushing the value of particular beers from particular breweries even if they're not directly feeding the local economy.[27]

"Imagine if a bunch of us got together and just kept posting pics and reviews about one of our local beers," a local self-proclaimed beer geek pondered aloud after I asked him if there were any "white whales" brewed in Las Vegas. "If we really rallied around a beer and all talked it up. I don't mean lie. There are some solid beers brewed here. . . . If we picked one and hyped it. It could buzz. . . . It would be good for everyone here."

Though the relative value of local scenesters in the core versus those on the periphery to the local scene is hard to access, the value of the core object outside of the cost of parts and labor is inevitably symbolic. The core object of any scene is more that its material parts, more than the material labor necessary for crafting it. As a *sacralized* object for purchase, it is part of a system of symbolic exchanges as much as, if not more than, a commercial venture. Such objects have "social lives" and "biographies" whereby their meanings and, consequently, values can change over time and across particular contexts.[28]

Value and the *performance of value* are culturally derived rather than based merely on class-based economic terms and presumed rationality. In his discussion of the culturally bounded and quasi-tribal "relational play of price," sociologist Frederick Wherry notes:

> People establish their personal characterizations in relations with other persons, places, and things. Prices and the monies they represent are more than socially embedded; they are also socially embedding. Not only do prices emerge according to implicit rules of engagement in different social contexts, but prices also constitute, in part, the social characterizations of the individuals who must come to understand how these rules of engagement apply to people like them. *Price signals the equivalence of the social characterizations of persons, not simply of exchangeability of commodities in the modern market economy.*[29]

For what may be a small fraction of the craft beer scene, the symbolic value of certain beers both creates and supports their elevated price. The value of a beer obtained or simply sipped at a bottle share so sippers can "tick" it, proclaiming the consecrated elixir had magically enhanced the sippers' value, becomes entwined with their self-worth if they define themselves as part of a reference group that recognizes the acquisition and experience of the rare and scarce as inherently valuable. Reference groups, at least in the case of craft beer, are not bounded by class, though money or the lack of it can exclude some from freely choosing their peers in taste and beers by taste. A penchant for barrel-aged or sour beers—both of which take considerable time to make—can drain a bank account quicker than it takes to slice through a waxed bottle cap.

Performing value is a matter of status that leads to often unstated assumptions and "implicit rules of engagement," in Wherry's words, about consumption practices and the values performed as part of those practices. In the craft beer scene, two practices that tend to value exclusivity over inclusivity are *hoarding* and *ticking*. Though each might be personally gratifying, such practices uphold the value of exclusivity, and specifically the increased value exclusive objects are endowed with, which remains in tension with the democratically driven ethos that craft beer brewers and consumers so often espouse.

Unlike stamps or records, beer is perishable. Beer, like its sturdier and more status-driven cousin wine, is a living organism that changes as it sits and waits to be consumed. How quickly or slowly it morphs largely depends on temperature; the higher the quicker it begins to morph. Sometimes the waiting can enhance the flavors of a beer. Other times it can turn a perfectly descent brew into liquid cardboard from exposure to oxygen or a malt bomb as hops fade away or unexpected microbes assault the brew, leaving vinegar not fit even for a salad. Because the vast majority of beer is brewed to be drunk shortly after it's bottled, canned, or poured from a keg, hoarders must be extremely selective in what they choose to store away. As a general rule, beer should be aged only if it's strong (i.e., high ABV), smoked, or sour. This means that hoarders inevitably discriminate against certain styles of beers and, by proxy, certain breweries.

Many of the people I spoke to who often buy beer to keep and drink sometimes years later called themselves "hoarders" in jest (the Bruery in Placentia, California, even has an "invite-only" level of membership called the Hoarders Society). Despite the seeming playfulness on the part of both consumers and brewers, the label still holds a pejorative connotation within craft beer scenes and outside of its boundaries.[30] Even self-labeled hoarders tend to exude an emotional matrix of both pleasure and guilt. On a handful of occasions, collectors have taken out their smartphone to give me a virtual stroll through their refrigerator or cellar. For the most organized, and perhaps the most obsessive, this is often followed by a virtual scroll through a spreadsheet that lists the names, breweries, styles, and years of the beers they have at home. The largest one I ever saw from a Las Vegas scenester had almost twenty thousand bottles. Not only did he have quantity, he also had quality. And his quality had variety. Half and full cases of coveted brews sat in his cellar as he beamed with joy about his collection.

On an individual level, hoarding beers, like most types of collecting, can be deeply satisfying. Collecting can turn the ordinary into extraordinary as a means for re-enchantment and as a personal accomplishment. It can also intensify to a "perpetual pursuit of inessential luxury goods. It is a continuing quest for self-completion in the marketplace. And it is a sustained faith that happiness lies only an acquisition away."[31] Possession can serve as an index of success, whereby the thrill of the hunt for material acquisitions can be more intoxicating than the beers themselves. I've been told stories on stories of the somewhat paradoxical rush of rushing to wait in line at a brewery or beer store.

"You hear a lot about a particular beer and then you see three bottles of it and you *have* to buy those three bottles," one self-labeled hoarder, who nonetheless asked to remain anonymous, told me. "And don't drink them. Because if you drink them, then you don't *have* them anymore."

It also means that others can't drink them. Yet, when others can have them, especially after the work of "not drinking of them" is expended, hoarding can certainly lead to eventual sharings of well-kept prizes with others. The novelty of the brew is its longevity. And novelty is as appealing as the beer is for its ability to produce both sensuous pleasure and social status. The hoarded brew's perseverance and persistence is the reflected value of the hoarder, or so it may seem, and often becomes so when cheers of approval greet the now opened beer and its keeper. This shows, again, how taste and value are performed collectively in relation to, and with, the material object, correspondingly nicely with sociologists Colin Jerolmack and Iddo Tavory's argument about the socially significant roles of nonhumans:

> Nonhumans act in surprising ways and organize, rather than merely reflect, social worlds and selves. They do so by molding how one will be

> perceived by others and by constraining the possibilities for alternative presentations of self, as well as by acting as totems that conjure up awareness of, and feelings of deep attachment to, a particular social group.[32]

Hoarding beers constitutes a means for identification through a "deep attachment" to the beers and to others who appreciate both the hoarded wares and the practice of hoarding.

Holding on to ageable beers and holding out to share "verticals" or "horizontals" with friends and other scene members are ways that hoarding can support rather than diminish the dominant ethos of craft beer as objects of reverence and elevated symbolic value. A "vertical" is an offering of the same beer by the same brewery from different years. They can range from a few years to over a decade's worth, dependent upon the hoarders' perseverance and persistence. A "horizontal" is an offering of different variations of the same beer from the same year. Hoarders often try to acquire sets by trading to complete either of these two types of collections. Completed sets—either verticals or horizontals—are the most coveted by the collector and those fortunate enough to reap the benefits of someone else's wanting and waiting.

Acquiring and assembling a collection for the purpose of shared tastings is a way to do "craft consumption," as sociologist Colin Campbell notes. "Collectors actively recontextualize individual products, situating them in a larger creation called 'the collection' and thereby giving them a new meaning and significance. This is a process that not only involves possession and grooming rituals, but also the considerable investment of the 'self' of the collector consumer in this new creation."[33] As a "new creation," the process requires skill and knowledge as well as a certain degree of creative prowess. It also involves willpower to save the beers and a sense of communal comradery when beers are put aside and held onto to share with others at a later date.

Here then is an important distinction between "inner-directed" and "outer-directed" practices that is, in effect and affect, a difference between *having* and *sharing*. The former is about individual ownership and possession. The latter is about collective experiences and giving.

The worst scenario of hoarding—for the sake of craft beer scenes as an oppositional force to either bland or status-driven consumerism—is when coveted beers are sold on the secondary market, the black market of resold beers often enabled and enlivened by internet websites, online forums, and Facebook groups. Despite varying state alcohol regulations that pertain to production and distribution as much as they do to shipping, rare beers are regularly packaged, boxed, and sent off via UPS or FedEx to thirsty recipients. Trading is one thing. But the price gouging of the black market is another. And it's the purest example of asocial or even antisocial consumption whereby beer is no longer an aesthetic ware with enlightening and interactive potential. Instead, beer becomes a mere commodity valued for its monetary gain and assumed status-increasing qualities.

Participation in the black market seems to have increased with the number of breweries and, perhaps more importantly, with the number of rare or "one-off" brews from the newest to the most established breweries. Regardless, the practice seems to be frowned upon by most brewers and consumers alike. When a local Las Vegan proposed setting up a bottle share with a two-hundred-dollar black market price buy-in, many were stunned and balked at or even laughed about the prospect. As I was told by a few locals, many of them never consult the black market listings, so they don't even know where to start thinking about their respective collections and whether or not they have anything that someone might pay a hundred dollars for.

When I asked Dave Moore, a regular trader and bottle sharer, about the black market, he laughed with contempt.

> I could unload my fridge and make a nice chunk of change. But I wouldn't do that. Because I know that if I wanted something how I would feel paying four hundred dollars for a bottle of [Assassin] SR-71 [brewed by

> Toppling Goliath in Decorah, Iowa] and I know some guy went and stood in line for two hours and paid twenty dollars, and they only made a hundred bottles. It's just not right. This isn't about the money. Yeah, I want to try everything I can, but selling or paying that much money just isn't cool.

After Dave and I spoke about this, I went home and looked up SR-71 on a few black market sales sites. Though I was shocked when he said four hundred, I was even more stunned by the handful of bottles for sale ranging from nine to eleven hundred dollars. For one bottle. Of beer.

Black market price gouging and the acquisition of overpriced beers are part of a larger status game that occurs inside and outside of the symbolic boundaries of the scene. One of the motivations for pursuing highly coveted rare beers is to increase one's status by being able to say one has or has had this or that brew. One way of showing this status is through ticking, which is simply recording the beers one has tasted. What was once a game between a group of friends in England, led by Mick the Tick, who wanted to see how many beers listed in the *Good Beer Guide* he and his buddies could try and tick off, has now become a near ubiquitous practice at beer bars, festivals, and bottle shares.

Today's tickers are equipped with smartphones with downloaded apps like Untappd. I've seen tickers peruse beer lists for new beers they haven't tried. I've seen them scurry around barstools and barkeeps to snap a quick pic of a bottle or pour before the bottle moves on to someone else or the pour moves across their palate. I've seen grown men and women sitting four or five to a table, noses aimed at their phones rather than in the glasses holding the beverages they've sipped or are yet to imbibe.

The aesthetic experience of the beer shifts quickly from tasting to ticking, from direct contact to a mediated recording and therefore distanced involvement with it. The recording of the experience becomes the experience itself.

Mike Dominiak has seen all of this too, both at his brewery, Bad Beat, and at the other places that compose the "aesthetic ecology" of the Las Vegas craft beer scene.

> I hear it all the time. "Tickers gotta tick," they say. And it's so true. Untappd has formed this beer culture of where people drink not to try beer but to tick it. I'm not going to fault Untappd . . . but drinking craft beer is about conversation but I don't see enough of it sometimes. The only conversation is people talking to themselves, "hey what is this?" "did I check this in yet." It's like a feeding frenzy. Dropping a beer into a pool of piranhas, piranhas with cell phones and beer apps.

He admits, though, that keeping a record can be fun. To be able to see what you've had and where can perhaps help folks recall a good memory or two, especially beer-soaked memories that exist somewhere in the recesses of a blurry mind. But the main problem, according to Mike and others, is that it can take away from the experience of drinking with others, from the communal rituals of collective tasting.

When I tried using Untappd at the beginning stages of my research, I liked giving beer ratings—on a one-to-five scale with half-point increments—and writing pithy tasting notes. But it became tedious and tiresome. It felt like I was contributing to what journalist Chris Colin calls the life-sucking "Yelpification of the universe" where everyone with internet access becomes an expert regardless of their qualifications or knowledge base.[34] My own frustration with Untappd came from feeling like I was spending more time with my phone than with either the people around me or the beer in front me.

"There are some people out there who don't know about beer but don't know they don't know about beer," Mike continues. "The worst I've seen is when there were people ticking and rating our beers, and JJ's and CraftHaus's, during the Henderson Smackdown at Shakespeare's. It was a blind taste test! How do you check in and rate something when you don't even know what is!"

I was at that event and saw the same thing Mike did. I thought they knew something about the beers that I didn't. Apparently not, especially when someone checked Bad Beat's Bluffing Isn't Weisse and gave it the lowest rating possible, complaining that it was sour and infected. Yes. A sour hefeweizen should deserve a low rating. But this wasn't a hefeweizen. It was a Berliner weisse, which is purposely soured and "infected" with the bacteria lactobacillus. Sometimes the desire to tick combined with the desire to act like an expert can create cringe-worthy results, especially for brewers who, admittedly, read the consumers' ratings and reviews with a mixture of trepidation, excitement, and generalized antipathy.

Like Boy Scouts, video games, and slot machines, Untappd awards badges for so-called achievements and as status-marking participation points. There are badges for the sheer number of beers ticked. There are badges for the number of beers of specific styles. There are badges for drinking on particular days of the week and particular holidays. Tick a beer on your birthday and get a badge. Tick one on the Fourth of July and you get a beer bottle dressed up like a Revolutionary War soldier in front of an American flag and the Statue of Liberty.

As the number of breweries grows, so does the number of beers they produce. This provides tickers more opportunities to compile more badges. A popular way of tasting a brewery's offerings is to buy a flight of beer. A flight usually consists of four-ounce pours of different beers. Doing a flight is a great way to experience the variety a brewery has to offer. It's a great way to get to sensuously apprehend what a brewery excels or, conversely, flounders at producing. It's also a great way to accumulate ticks and badges. Though the pursuit of badges can be fun, when it eclipses engagement with the beer, its producers, and fellow consumers, the scene can lose its cultural fortitude as regressive intoxication eclipses reflexive intoxication. That is, the craft beer experience becomes individualized, atomized, and disenchanting instead of communal, collective, and re-enchanting.

Less Distinction, More Democracy

The continued sexism across the craft beer grand scene along with the practices of hoarding, black market selling, and ticking create status hierarchies within a scene that supposedly prides itself on inclusivity.

Such internal status games not only spoil the fun, but spoil the collective narrative of craft beer as an oppositional site and means of resistance and solidarity against Big Beer. Along with the obvious negative consequences associated with or stemming from drunken behaviors—like intoxicated driving and aggressive actions toward others—and alcoholism and other health risks, there are cultural costs to getting too serious about craft beer.

In his discussions of "serious leisure," a category that most if not all scenes fall under, sociologist Robert E. Stebbins identifies the numerous rewards of engagement with it: personal enrichment, improved self-image, feelings of accomplishment and belonging, and the forging of new and intense social connections and affiliations.[35] The costs of serious leisure remain relatively unexplored beyond the burden of lost time and money. Though without too much consideration, however, Stebbins does note that selfishness and obsessiveness can be laid upon participants by both insiders and outsiders, producing negative effects for participants and for the activity the participants are engaged in.[36] The cumulative effects can lead to a valuing of distinction-driven individual gain and exclusivity over democracy-driven collective commitments and inclusivity.

Instead of allowing the craft beer scene to resist the power of cultural objects *over* individuals and groups, these exclusive practices can reproduce the "tragedy of culture" that defines so much of contemporary urbanism. Becoming too devoted to the core objects of the scene gives those objects too much agency and power over the agency of human beings to freely act and make decisions about themselves and those objects. It subsumes and thwarts the creative capacities of individuals to act and experience the objective world as separate from themselves. The "subjective spirit," as Georg Simmel calls it, becomes inundated by "the objectification of spirit."[37] To become possessed by possessions diminishes the capacity of the scene to promote resistance and social change. A scene drunk on its own goods loses sight of the world around it, the diversity of individuals who are part of it, and its ability to upend inequalities within and outside of itself.

5

#craftbeer

Taking a trip up and down the California coast to sample the fermented offerings of the state's most valorized breweries is a dream for many a craft beer enthusiast. But an eleven-day drive that starts and ends in Las Vegas, with stops in San Diego, Los Angeles, and San Francisco and their surrounding areas where some of the most influential and sought-after brews are produced and housed is a lot of work.

To get input on where she should go, Las Vegas local Chelsea Potts asked her Instagram followers by posting a picture of the state of California with "ISO: Highly Recommended Breweries, Distilleries, Bottle Shops . . ." layered over it. "ISO" is beer trader language for "in search of." Three hundred twenty-eight people liked her post, one hundred fifty commented, and another two hundred sent her direct messages.

"The response was incredible! I was so overwhelmed," Chelsea says while describing the trip. Her eyes and grand smile grow as she laughs with a mix of guilty self-indulgence and prideful self-motivation: "Planning felt like a full-time job!"

This was the first time we met, but I knew about her and this trip beforehand. At the time, Chelsea had a large presence and following on Instagram with over fifteen thousand followers. From "graveyard" bottles (emptied bottles "killed" during bottle shares) to lone sought-after and hard-to-find "whales," the pictures she posts reveal her journey through the craft beer scene. They also reveal the uncompromising visual component of craft, while the hundreds of likes and comments reveal the popularity of craft beer fans' mediated practices. Chelsea's glowing smile tends to dominate every picture she's in, often at a bar, at a brewery, or hiking the mountains that surround the Las Vegas Valley accompanied by her mastiff and a canned beer. Her smile is even brighter in person, especially when she talks about her love of craft beer and the sheer variety of flavors that it allows her to experience, as well as the people it helps her meet. This, along with her vast knowledge of beer—she is a Certified Cicerone—clearly attracts people to her, online or off.

When Chelsea first joined Instagram in late 2013, she searched "#craftbeer" and there were fewer than one million hashtags. Five years later, in mid-2018, there were over seventeen million.[1] "The growth has been incredible," she tells me. "Instagram has been a key tool for learning about breweries, and beer releases, and regional trends. When you're on there flipping around," she wags her thumb, pantomiming the typical Instagram navigation gesture on a smartphone, "you see these things from breweries and other people that you wouldn't see elsewhere. I've learned so much from people on Instagram."

She used the social media tool to reach out to other "craft beer lovers"—the term she prefers—to help navigate her fantastic voyage.

> I needed a little help because I wanted to map it out so I wouldn't back track and I wanted to hit about three breweries a day. I contacted all the breweries ahead of time. They were all really accommodating. Sometimes I would contact them when I was getting close and they would have beers waiting for me when I walked in and they'd give me a tour. We tasted the beers, did a little Q&A, and then I was on my way.

Like so many others who post pictures of the lavishly labeled bottles they're drinking or the towering silos filled with soon-to-be boiled grains outside the breweries they're visiting, Chelsea uses craft beer's "virtual scene" to connect her to specific local scenes and to the key players within them. Each city has its own local scene; social media applications like Instagram allow people like Chelsea to "plug in" and interact with them in ways that define the virtual scene, the translocal scene, and respective local scenes through both the acquisition and distribution of knowledge.

The virtual scene allows individuals to share meaningful information that is internally embodied yet externally represented through artifacts (e.g., pics) and practices (e.g., sharing pics online). The practices of showing and sharing are "culturally patterned and meaningful in themselves," learned by adhering to an emerging "group style" of communication that extends beyond physical borders.[2]

Predating the advent of the so-called web 2.0—the version of the internet defined by software and mobile technologies that facilitate the online sharing of personal information and images—by over thirty years, sociologist John Irwin recognized the importance of in-group communication for the development and maintenance of a scene. The people who responded to Chelsea's virtual inquiry pointed her to places where, as Irwin writes, "there are prominent participants at these locations or occasions, and newcomers know that they can join with them in order to participate in the activities."[3] The virtual leads directly back to the local, the embodied, and the emplaced.

With the rise of social media usage, "insiders" no longer need others to promote their lifestyles, to share insights about who they are and what they do. They are able to show the symbols and rituals of their scene in all of its variations and variants. As expressive entities, scenes necessarily rely on some sort of communication system that "keeps up the interest and commitment to the activity, communicates the meanings of the activity system, and announces the times and places of upcoming situated activities."[4] There is a long history of "subcultural" communication through newsletters and pamphlets that includes everything from indie rock zines to Martin Luther's "Disputation on the Power and Efficacy of Indulgences."[5]

Though far less dramatic than Luther's Ninety-Five Theses, most contemporary scenes and leisure groups, as well as today's most virulent social movements and everyday organizations, depend upon computer-mediated communication.[6] According to sociologist Angela Cora Garcia and her colleagues, "The distinction between online and offline worlds is . . . becoming less useful as activities in these realms become increasingly merged in our society, and as the two spaces interact with and transform each other."[7] The practice of sharing images *via* popular social media programs like Instagram, Facebook, and Twitter as well as beer-centric apps like Untappd has affected the grand scene in a number of significant ways.

First, posting pictures is an "interaction ritual" between the individual, others who are present—face-to-face or virtual—and the significant object (e.g., the beer, bottle, or brewery). All the actors involved in such rituals, sociologist Erving Goffman explains, implicitly or explicitly seek to maintain the legitimacy of the exchange,[8] as well as the aesthetic experience it affords. "If I can't share the beer, at least I can share a pic of it," says Dave Moore, who goes by the handle @beerelevance on Instagram. The pics that Dave and others share are, as Goffman notes, "pictorial artifacts [that] allow for a combination of ritual and relic."[9] They mark an aesthetic engagement with an everyday object that elevates its status as a significant object.[10] Moreover, sharing pics is a ritualized performance in front of or even primarily for unknown audiences who, obviously, view posted pics well beyond the physical proximity of the poster and his or her smartphone. As Irwin notes, "The intended audience may be some group not present or some generalized, real, or imaginary group of others."[11] The audience, however, *feels* and, for all intents and purposes, *is* present when members interact with posts. Members of the virtual audience can respond with likes and comments, creating a reciprocated sense of affiliation, allegiance, and appreciation.

Second, the pics that Chelsea, Dave, and others like them post provide information for other craft beer fans. Taking and posting images quickly—hence the "insta" part of Instagram—along with geotags and reviews show not only *what* people are posting, but *where* and *how* they perceived the beer they're drinking or the brewery they're visiting. This informs locals about new beers that have hit their local market as well as new releases inside or outside of one's physical vicinity. According to a 2016 study, 74 percent of craft beer drinkers use their smartphones to access information before making a purchase and 60 percent use them at the store to help them decide what to buy.[12] Aesthetic judgments are not made in a vacuum, especially when others' assessments can be accessed so easily by touching and swiping a handheld screen.

Another way that the virtual scene has affected the grand scene is by serving as inexpensive consumer-driven marketing for breweries. Having a virtual presence is increasingly important for any small business, and craft brewers are no exception. Whether it's a website, a Facebook page, or a Twitter or Instagram account with a simple hashtag, breweries have relied on others to return the favor of creating a buzz not unlike the one produced by their beers. The buzz on social media can turn almost any brewery into the next hot spot.[13]

When she made it to Santa Rosa during her California #beercation, Chelsea talked with the folks at the renowned Russian River Brewery. Their IPAs have become the standard-bearer for the West Coast style, loaded with hops that smell like pine trees and citrus fruit. Anytime someone opens a Pliny the Elder or a Blind Big during a bottle share, the collective focus of the room shifts toward the 500-milliliter bottles, even for those who have had them before. And the once-a-year release of Pliny the Younger—a stronger version of the Elder—summons hours-long waits outside the brewery or the rare restaurant or bar lucky enough to be allocated a keg of it.

Chelsea tells me that Russian River's founding owners Vinnie and Natalie Cilurzo "credit [their success] all to people on social media. People hyping up the brewery and getting people there. They admit themselves that social media is driving their volume."

She then adds the following insight: "These small craft breweries don't have the money to do any marketing. We're doing the advertising and marketing for them, and sharing their beers!"

Critics of "putting the consumer to work"–type branding are often apt to charge big businesses and corporations with exploiting and controlling "free consumers,"[14] but they tend to overlook how cultural resistance can, in practice, be connected to positive values of businesses that serve oppositional social groupings.[15] Sharing pics of and for small businesses spreads information beyond local vicinities for those who don't have the means to do so. With the rise of high-quality cameras in smartphones, where in some cases the traditional uses of the phone are secondary to its other capabilities, along with the advancement of editing applications that are easy to learn and use, images and the way they are used are growing ever more sophisticated and creative.[16]

Though difficult to measure, fans' posts about an up-and-coming brewery can carry more symbolic and aesthetic weight than a multimillion-dollar commercial that features clomping Clydesdales (Budweiser), a silver-bullet train thrashing through the Rockies to promote super cold beer and temperature-reacting cans (Coors), or odd demands about ways to properly live the High Life (Miller). The word-as-text/image/sound of virtual indie or nonmainstream music scenes has helped keep both devoted fans and sonic wanderers informed of the latest and greatest, though not necessarily the most lucrative.[17] The virtual craft beer scene is similar (I've even heard recorded sounds of cans fizzing open and bottles popping). Fans use small media tactics, as opposed to big media commercials on prime-time networks, to disarm its more fiscally endowed foes. Tangentially connected to the "culture jammers" who use the tools of mass marketing to resist the corporate control of culture, virtual scenesters adopt rhetorical strategies that apply to images as much as they do to words.[18]

The words exchanged by online chatters are the elementary forms of "the ritual of sharing information" necessary for showing both *competence of* and *commitment to* a scene's core object.[19] This has been a routine finding of research on virtual scenes catered to persons' interests in specific musicians or musical genres. Unlike virtual music scenes, however, where the experience of the significant object can be mediated through streaming, the virtual craft beer scene necessarily relies on and always comes back to material objects and embodied and emplaced persons. Beer, like any other physical product, cannot be downloaded. Though you can buy beer online, and many do procure out-of-market brews through the internet, the product—the significant object of desire—must be packaged, shipped, and delivered in order to be experienced beyond its visual representation. Once the beer is obtained, the showing and sharing of beer pics can begin. The act of placing one's chosen beverage in a specified place—lined up across a table at a brewery or bar with the tap list in the background or on a patio with a cityscape behind it—to be photographed and then shared to a virtually present audience can harness and turn the power of a potential fetish into a ritual of aesthetic resistance. Craft beer fans have flexed their creative powers by showing beers in beautiful natural or built environments, with luscious food pairings, or, as Instagrammers @louiebaton and @beerfarts have done, as props accompanied by Lego figures and absurdist tales.[20]

The ritual practice of sharing pics develops and affirms a sense of "being able to apply power to the world to change it—however minutely."[21] Sociologist Paul Willis argues that the symbolic work that people actively engage in and with objects—what he calls "grounded aesthetics"—is a way that the sensuous and emotive qualities of everyday life are experienced and lived. He even draws upon an apt beer-related term when he argues that grounded aesthetics are the "yeast of common culture" where ubiquitous ideas and actions are given new meanings by the sharing of interpretations between individuals.[22] The performance of craft beer fans on Instagram is but one way to create new meanings out of received culture, thereby engendering some form of agency or control over popular culture, on- and offline. Creating and posting pics provides a sense of ownership over the product by turning the object into an experience to be shared with others.

Websites like beeradvocate.com, which has been operating since 1996 and whose producers have been publishing the physical magazine *BeerAdvocate* since 2003, and ratebeer.com, whose "mission is to provide independent, unbiased, consumer-driven information about beer and breweries and to enhance the image and worldwide appreciation of beer," offer forums for discussing all things related to craft beer.[23] There are also specialty websites for specific styles of beers as well as homebrewing forums. Together, they provide a space for the virtual scene to flourish that, consequently, emboldens local scenes through its users who are inherently connected to and work through physical places.

Due to the explicit and necessary practice of showing and sharing visual content, in this chapter I draw from my "observant participation" on Instagram as well as in the local Facebook group Las Vegas Beer & Breweries. Showing and sharing my own pics on Instagram under the handle @intoxicationofcraft—named for the working title of this book—afforded me access into the virtual scene by "performing the phenomenon" and, as sociologist Loïc Wacquant argues, "leverage carnal comprehension by deepening [my] social and symbolic insertion into the universe [I'm] stud[ying]."[24] Participating in the virtual scene was another way I was able to participate in both the local and translocal scenes with visceral aptitude.

The explicit and tacit knowledge from the "carnal comprehension" of actions and interactions that I gained through my own embodied showing and sharing supports digital ethnographers Sarah Pink and Larissa Hjorth's claim that "the camera phone should not be understood only in terms of the visual content of the images it produces, but also in its very use."[25] Like those I followed on Instagram, I found myself carefully placing a bottle next to a snifter of bubbly light amber liquid in a place where the sun wouldn't reflect and create bright white spots or where my reflection would show up in the glass. I found myself playing with colors and angles to highlight the beverage itself, the label on the bottle or can it came in, or the place where I ordered and drank it. I found myself eagerly anticipating comments and likes. My own embodied and emplaced practices were complemented and informed by formal interviews and less formal conversations with prominent local Las Vegas craft beer scene Instagrammers.

Recognizing that participating in a virtual scene requires movements of the body within a physical location further supports the ongoing argument of this book about the necessary connections and blurred boundaries between local, translocal, and virtual scenes. Though some scholars have been drawn to, celebrated, or decried the apocalyptic potential of the internet's power to force us to live a "life on the screen,"[26] what I found is that the virtual scene necessarily depends on, accentuates, and, in turn, reestablishes the importance of place. As such, the virtual scene becomes a conduit to and for both a specific local scene and the multitude of local scenes that make up the grand translocal scene.[27] Local Las Vegans are able to show that the presumed beer desert of Las Vegas is part of the grand craft beer scene by sharing pics of beers brewed, sold, and consumed in the city. In this way, the virtual scene provides an aesthetic antidote to the misperceptions of the city that coalesce as the Las Vegas Syndrome. Moreover, using social media as a way of *doing and being scene* highlights the expressive elements of scenes and further shows that people and the things they use are both active participants in social performances.

#drinklocal

Like both Chelsea and Dave, I knew Frank before I met him. I knew him by his Instagram handle: @fronkled. Now I know him as "the Ambassador." After attending a rare keg tapping at Khoury's Fine Wine & Spirits, where I slowly sipped on an eight-ounce pour of Almanac's Farmers Reserve Blueberry Ale, I stopped at the British-themed Shakespeare's Pub and Grille for a quick bite of fish-and-chips. In between forkfuls of fried haddock covered in freshly squeezed lemon juice and malt vinegar, I posted two pictures to my @intoxicationofcraft Instagram account. The first was of the beer I had at Khoury's earlier, the second was the beer I paired with my food, a 2014 Deschutes Abyss, a chewy imperial stout brewed with licorice, cherry bark, vanilla, and black strap molasses, dry hopped with vanilla beans and cherry bark, and then aged in bourbon, Oregon oak, and pinot noir barrels. By the time I finished my meal I had a number of likes on both pics and a message from @fronkled: "Sorry I missed you at Khoury's, try to find me next time you come by for a beer."

I saw him about two months later at the Locals Only Beer Festival put on by Banger Brewing. Frank stood under the tent for the Nevada Craft Brewers Association (NCBA) giving out information and stickers. The proceeds for the festival went to support the fledgling advocacy group. I recognized Frank from his Instagram pics and walked over to him.

"I didn't know you were involved with NCBA," I say.

"Yeah, I try to help when I can. I've been involved with the Nevada Beer Lovers meet-up group for some time, posting stuff online about this or that event." He hands me a circular sticker with the letters "NBL" above an outline of the state of Nevada. "The goal for both groups is to expand knowledge. When you're growing something as fast as craft beer, it's good to separate fact and fiction. You don't want to give a misperception of craft beer, especially if you're passionate about it."

I nod and smile. We shake hands, set up a time to meet again, and ritualistically clink our small tasting glasses together and then take our respective sips.

When we meet at Khoury's a few weeks later, our conversation picks up where we left off. After sitting down at the big oak table in the corner, he pulls a business card out and hands it to me. Emblazoned with the store's logo in the center, Frank's name is followed by the word "Ambassador." Issa gave it to Frank as sort of a joke, but like most jokes, it has some reality to it since Frank has done a lot of unofficial marketing for the store and, in turn, the local scene.

> I'm always talking to people, either when I meet them at beer festivals or breweries or online, telling them to come here to buy beer or to share some beers with us. . . . I live right behind the shop and have been coming here for the last five years or so. It's a great place where people can get local beers or drink other beers with local people. As Khoury's grew, and craft beer grew, I grew with it. *I think I love the culture of craft beer as much as I enjoy the taste of it!*

Frank initially posted about Khoury's on *BeerAdvocate*'s website but has since turned to Instagram. Frank is a professional videographer with a bachelor's degree in film. Instagram was a natural fit to combine his interests.

"The whole visual aspect of beer is kind of great," Frank tells me. "The beer, the label, all of it. I think it's a cool way to showcase a beer. Seeing it is a whole other thing. You can read about it or see it from afar. But then you see a label and read and examine it and then get to taste it. It's an experience I like having, again and again."

"Is there something in particular about craft beer labels that are different than other labels?" I ask.

"Craft is more personal, and personable. When I hear 'craft' I think of people, I think of local creators of beer, I think of the community that surrounds it. Local, small businesses."

The labels, he says, can help differentiate craft from mass-produced. He then picks up the bottle that we're sharing, Tahoe Mountain's Brett Stout (a unique dark fruit-tasting beer with brettanomyces added to it while sitting in oak barrels), adorned with a decorated medieval sword's hilt. "And for people who don't understand the difference," Frank pauses to chuckle, "I'll show them this label." Lowering his voice, mocking the overt masculinity of Big Beer, "This sword will destroy your Budweiser can!"

We share a laugh and take another sip of the funky tart plum liquid.

When he connects with people through Instagram, it is often a result of a beer, and its label, that he's posted while at home, at a brewery, or at Khoury's. He always adds the location to the post if he's at Khoury's; he says those tend to get the most likes and comments. Locals see what he's posted and often lament that they didn't get a chance to share the beer with him and the rest of the place's regulars. Nonlocals see the posts and often ask about the store and the local scene.

> I always respond telling them to come here. And they learn about what Vegas has to offer when they come here and meet us. Being a travel destination, it's worked out pretty good for craft beer. I think it's going to grow even more now because people can come and visit breweries and bars and stop in here to have some beers and meet some of the people who are a part of the scene. And they can drink some pretty damn good beers too!

Though many of the beers that Frank and other local Instagrammers hanging out at Khoury's or elsewhere post have been brought in to the city through their travels or trades, the emphasis is still on the locality of the place where the beers are being shared and consumed. Such practices, however, beg the question of what it means to #drinklocal. That exact question became a point of contention in the local scene during a discussion on a local social media forum.

In early 2015 when the Las Vegas beer scene was starting to hit its stride, Ken Swanson, an avid beer drinker and beer memorabilia collector, set up a public Facebook group called Las Vegas Beer & Breweries. The description of the group reads as follows: "We all love Las Vegas and we all love beer. This is the site to share what is happening with beer and brewing in the world's most exciting city. This group is the official site for the 777 Chapter of the Brewery Collectibles Club of America. Join us live or online and let's enjoy some great brew!" The description's seeming ambiguity left it open to multiple interpretations about what should be shared with the group. Las Vegas as "the world's most exciting city" is pretty straightforward, but the sharing of "what is happening with beer and brewing" can be read in different ways, which led to some consternation as to the criteria of the group and beers *allowed* to be posted.

Shortly after the group reached one thousand members a few months into its existence, a contentious exchange took place about the description of the group and, in effect, the definition of "local." The exchange, which lasted for three days with over one hundred comments, was prompted by an incendiary post on September 3 written in response to what the poster viewed as too many posts of unavailable and out-of-market beers to the local forum:

> I remember when this group was about Vegas beer and Breweries. Now its [*sic*] just people posting what beer they're drinking. BOOORRIIIINNNGGG!! Looked through 10 posts and only 1 was about a beer FROM Vegas and I post about a Vegas brewery . . . and that's not the

> normal for this group. Try sticking to the original idea of this group. Beer FROM Vegas and news about breweries IN Vegas.

The moderator responded quickly, exerting a form of social control by telling the poster and the rest of the members that he had received "a LOAD of messages about this" and had deleted a number of posts that he felt didn't belong in the group. This was, however, far from the end of it and far from the consensus.

Though there have been plenty of other discussions like it since then featuring some of the same actors, forum members engaged in this particular discussion volleyed back and forth with their interpretations of the group's ultimate purpose. One faction supported the view of the original poster, arguing that "local" meant locally brewed. Another faction saw "local" as both beers brewed in Las Vegas and beer available or soon to be available in the local market (e.g., "If it was [*sic*] not for this group, I would miss out on sooooo many tapping and special releases here in town. From local breweries and those that sell here"). A third faction expanded the definition of "local" to encompass breweries that were within a relatively easy driving distance from Las Vegas since Las Vegas is an island surrounded by desert and, as one poster noted, "Posts of something close by (3–5 hour drive away) is not out of place. Vegas is still a small but growing beer market and if we're going to be having festivals where we bring in these breweries that are close by, why not post and help stimulate business for the local guys." And the last faction, seemingly the folks who regularly posted out-of-town beer hauls, stood by their past posts. Many of them, however, ultimately moved over to a smaller and less used "group for Vegas beer lovers to trade and exchange hard to find beer from around the world." Though that move settled the confrontation for the immediate future, the definition of "local" remains a contested issue both on- and offline.

Somewhat ironically, though, the very discussion of the criteria of "local" is a key practice that helps construct the local scene. That is, claims made by social actors are a necessary part of the "negotiated order" that, in turn, shapes both *who*—the participants in the scene—and *what*—the objects of contention or desire—are allowed to be part of it.[28] The negotiation of the symbolic boundary between what should and should not be considered local is, beyond its content, a form of meaning-making that shapes the cultural contours and interactions online. But it also shapes action offline by prompting actors to, first, acquire and, then, share positively sanctioned products that meet the seemingly fluctuating definition of local.

Even in the virtual realm that primarily consists of written discourse and signs (i.e., the visual representation of objects), the meanings of the objects on display are never too far removed from matters of matter. That is, the physical materiality of the beers—the liquids and the vessels that hold them—are inevitably linked to someone's physical location, hence ostensibly connecting the virtual to the local at some point in the beverage's life course from production to consumption. As such, the virtual scene helps foster both person-to-person connections and person-to-place connections. These connections are the cornerstones of what sociologist Lyn Lofland calls the "parochial realm," urban territories "characterized by a sense of commonality among acquaintances and neighbors who are involved in interpersonal networks."[29] While it has been argued that a virtual scene could itself be considered parochial in Lofland's sense,[30] in our case the commonality necessary for both scene development and affiliation is rooted in physical people, places, and things.

Just like what happens in Vegas doesn't stay there, what happens online doesn't stay there either. The virtual scene in this sense functions as a communicative device to foster action and interaction. For example, Bad Beat Brewing will often show and share a picture of the chalkboard above their bar that lists which beers are on tap along with details of the beer (e.g., style, alcohol content, IBUs) and prices. Or they'll show "behind-the-scenes" shots of the brewery and the brewing process. Tenaya Creek posts similar pics and will often post about their beers and how they might pair with the offerings of the evening's selected food truck. And then when someone else reposts local breweries' pics to the Las Vegas Beer & Breweries group or their personal Instagram account, the intent is to inform scene members about a local happening and urge them to act and move beyond their screen and engage with the local scene.

#beerstagram

If a brewery well outside of Las Vegas, from the rocky eastern coastline of Portland, Maine, to the green streets of Portland, Oregon, and anywhere in between, releases a "hot" beer, plenty of Instagram posts of the beer and the lines of folks waiting to secure it will show up posthaste. For even the most coveted, there's a good chance that beer will show up in Las Vegas, though not through the typical means of sanctioned distribution. With the increase of craft beer traders and travelers, the odds have never been better in Las Vegas to taste a buzzed-about brew. The safe money is on someone popping a bottle, can, or growler at Khoury's, CraftHaus's Thursday night shares, Atomic's Second Saturday shares, 595 Craft and Kitchen's last Saturday shares, or any of the other open-to-anyone-who-brings-a-beer shares around the city. Traders and travelers benefit greatly from social media and the virtual scene. For many of them, it's the main way they learn about new beers and connect with people who can get them.

Scanning through Instagram and searching tags like #craftbeer, #instabeer, and #beerstagram, it's easy to see which beers are trending. The same beer or brewery will start showing up on the accounts of people all over the country. The medium provides a stark visual depiction of the belief in *translocalism*, the desire not only for one's own local products but for local products made elsewhere. And, as discussed in previous chapters, sometimes other people's local products obtain or are endowed with a greater value than those regularly or easily available within a specific market or locale. The search for and eventual attainment of the somewhat exotic wares is part of an in-group status system that can, paradoxically, take away from the experience of the beer itself.

FIGURE 5.1. Pictures of bottle share "graveyards" (#bottleshare #graveyard) are often posted to Instagram to show (off) both translocal knowledge and local sharing. (Photo by author)

That is, the pursuit can become so intoxicating that the beer becomes merely a sign of one's status rather than an object to be tasted and experienced. Obtaining beers for their limited bottle count or merely for their trendiness turns craft beer drinkers into exotic collectors, "ticking" and marking their amount and variety of beer consumption on apps like Untappd, and hoarding bottles and cans in cellars and multiple refrigerators devoted to housing their conquests.

Others use their translocal knowledge to gain more far-reaching aesthetic experiences from products unavailable locally. The virtual scene helps them acquire translocal knowledge—learning about new and highly rated beers—and then, after they obtain their sought-after beer, by showing and sharing them online, transmit that knowledge to locals and nonlocals alike. For about two years, Dave has been trading and traveling to obtain beers he wasn't able to buy locally. He then posts pictures of his beers, either as a collection with the commonly used #beermail and #porchbomb tags (translation: it came in the mail and it arrived at my front door, respectively). Most often though, Dave will put his soon to be drunken beer in a glass next to the opened bottle or can atop the granite countertop in his kitchen. And he always includes his signature declaration: "Life is Craft!"

When Dave invited me to his house to talk about the #craftbeerlife, a bottle of Wicked Weed's White Angel from Asheville, North Carolina, that he recently received through a trade was waiting for me on that same countertop I had seen so many times on Instagram.[31] The sour ale blended with grapes and aged in white wine barrels had a bright cidery taste and a slightly bitter and dry finish, perfect on a late summer day in the desert.

We first sniff then sip from our glasses at the same time. Dave puts his glass back down on the table and looks me in the eyes. "This is what I love about craft beer. I appreciate the depth, the taste, the aromas. I love the experience and I love talking about the experience. And I love trying new beers." His desire for new aesthetic experiences is what motivates his traveling and trading and, subsequently, his virtual sharing.

> When you first get into craft beer, you hear about certain beers. Being on the West Coast, we all hear about Pliny. So that triggered my questions about what other beers were out there. You hear about Heady Topper [from the Alchemist in Waterbury, Vermont], you hear about Zombie Dust [from Three Floyds in Munster, Indiana]. And those are some of the main ones, and you just want to try them. High rated beers. Gotta try it. Just gotta try it. So I looked around the beer stores here and couldn't find any of these beers. I started going to Arizona and California. I'd spend like six hundred dollars and then load up the car and head back to Las Vegas.

Traveling for beer, or at least incorporating beer into their travel plans, is a common practice for those devoted to craft beer translocalism. Again and again I heard tales of trips to different breweries in pursuit of limited releases and, in turn, limited aesthetic experiences.

As Dave learned more about beers available across the country, he used what he was able to purchase locally to trade for beers brewed outside of reasonable driving distances. Dave scoured the internet to increase his knowledge about the grand scene and its delectable offerings. He soon found a Facebook group called I Love Craft Beer. One day, coincidently and fortuitously, someone else named Dave Moore showed up on his newsfeed. The other Dave Moore, who lives on the East Coast, reached out to him and asked if he ever traded.

"He said let's trade. And then it just snowballed. And now I'm like a FedEx company. I just shipped four boxes this morning!"

Trading has increased Dave's and others' translocal knowledge. When he posts his beers on Instagram, he is taking part in a translocal scene through virtual means. When he puts local Las Vegas–brewed beers in the packages he ships, he's helping the local scene play a role in the translocal scene. And when he brings the beers that he posts on Instagram to local bottle shares, he increases the collectively accumulated knowledge of craft beer for locals and, consequently, locals elsewhere when he shows and shares pics of the beer at what sociologist Antoine Hennion calls the "moment of attention." "This moment," writes Hennion, "marks itself by the surge of an intensified contact, provoking a shift between the self toward the object, and a shift of the object towards itself."[32] Though capturing the moment when the experience of taste happens in a photograph is not the same as the experience itself, the posted photograph nevertheless provides at least a minimal point of contact between the local, translocal, and virtual scenes.

#vegascraftbeer

The images that consumers and breweries post on Instagram are micro-narratives, short stories, however abbreviated. Whether showing lime green hops cascading out of a bucket into swirling wort or simply disseminating information about a "Geeks Who Drink" trivia night, they are telling a story about who they are by presenting a part of themselves to an imagined audience. That audience, however, is not a figment of the imagination nor is its presence not felt. The audience is a collective actor within the scene, not a mere passive observer of it. It affects the scene and the story it tells and the story others tell about it. On a social media platform like Instagram, audience members can note their approval of images by touching the heart icon to "like" it, they can comment on a post, or they can even repost it as a virtual retelling.

If we think about images as narratives—pictures are, as they say, worth a thousand words—then it's easy to see how Instagram posts are means for creating a narrative identity for both individual posters and collective scenes. As sociologist Donileen Loseke writes, "What is true about all types of narrative identity is that narratives cannot be understood apart from history and culture—both local and writ large—because the multiple contexts of storytelling define what is, and what is not, evaluated as an acceptable or a good story."[33] The acceptance of a good story, or a good image, shows that one belongs, that one is part of the tribe, the movement, the culture, the scene. And this works on both individual and collective levels for breweries, distributors, bars, restaurants, stores, and consumers.

Telling a good story through a good image shows an allegiance with the grand scene that sets the criteria for affiliation. A brewery's virtual presence is a way to get exposure to both local and translocal scenes. By adopting the rhetorical visual strategies of successful craft breweries, new breweries often mimic their successful predecessors and implicit collaborators. Imitation may be a form of flattery, but it is, first, a way of *showing affiliation*. In the early twentieth century, seminal social theorist Georg Simmel noted the importance of and concomitant ways that groups and individuals oscillated between uniformity and differentiation. Though painting with broad strokes, he nevertheless poignantly writes, "The whole history of society is reflected in the conflict, the compromise, the reconciliations, slowly won and quickly lost, that appear between adaptation to our social group and individual elevation from it."[34] Before elevation can occur, adaptation in the form of imitation must take place to show affiliation to the social group or, in our discussion, the scene.

In a social world and scene where innovation and creativity are praised, imitation might be viewed negatively. Yet, according to Simmel, "imitation gives the individual the assurance of not standing alone in his or her actions."[35] This goes for groups and organizations as well. When a new brewery opens, or has plans to do so, its proprietors need to show their connection with the grand scene as a means for establishing both legitimacy and affiliation. This process played out in the Las Vegas craft beer scene online with the introduction of #vegascraftbeer and offline through the places where narratives come to life.

Before they opened their full-fledged operation for business, folks from the new Las Vegas breweries brought their beers to local craft beer drinkers, either at festivals or at gathering spots like Khoury's. "The guys from Banger and Bad Beat, for example, brought their original homebrews in here, and asked if we like this or this. And we did, for the most part," Frank "the Ambassador" tells me. "And that's how the culture grows. We're kind of like a test market." In physical places, brewers can share their fermented concoctions with embodied and emplaced persons to see what works and what doesn't. While the quality of the beer is the most significant criterion for any brewery, its virtual "presentation of self" is a key means for broadcasting a brewery's affective affiliation to a scene that extends beyond physical borders and boundaries.[36]

Local craft breweries have, either explicitly or implicitly, adopted many of the social media practices of more well-known establishments. By scrolling through the images they post, the viewer is thrust into a visual smorgasbord of shiny silver tanks, freshly poured beers, totemic logos on glasses and growlers, food trucks, and shots of upcoming or recently held events. For example, Banger Brewing often shares beers that are part of their "one-off" series. Followers are presented with beers like their hefeweizen infused with honey, ginger, and lemon. Other local breweries present similar limited versions of their beers. CraftHaus does so almost every week with their "Firkin Fridays," often giving locals a chance to name the beer and use the brewery's sacred hammer to tap it open.

Showing affiliation by sharing pics on social media works for stores catering to and trying to entice craft beer consumers. Instead of tacking a flyer to a light post or corkboard—a common practice for punk bands and small businesses alike in the days of "old media"—every week Khoury's posts a flyer announcing new arrivals and Wednesday night keg tapping parties. Liquor Outlet puts their new beers in a pyramid form, creating an instant mystique around them. Top Shelf Wine & Spirits uses both still photographs and mini videos to promote not only their new arrivals but their increasingly intoxicating promotions. From raffles for bottles of Cantillon to their #beerforapenny and "mystery box" games of chance, Top Shelf has ingratiated itself to local craft beer enthusiasts in a short amount of time. They often follow up the original post with pics of the happy winner holding his or her winnings, providing a form of validation for both the store and the local scene. This type of validation satiates what sociologist Richard Chalfen refers to as "the human desire and need for pictorial evidence."[37] In popular parlance, this comes in the form of the often-stated "pics or it didn't happen" mandate and mantra.

Though the posts from breweries and businesses can be read through the lens of marketing, and they certainly do serve that purpose, the pics are a means for showing and sharing their affiliation. In so doing, they are also actively constructing a visual and virtually narrated sense of place for themselves and for the local scene at large.

#beertography

Regardless of whether it's a dark syrupy imperial stout or a hazy orange New England IPA, or a row of emptied bottles and cans whose labels can be read only by squinting, visual images can elicit a visceral response. You don't have to be Pavlov's dog to feel the tingling sensation on your tongue known as thirst. This is yet another way that the boundary between the virtual and the local is blurred. The online stimuli of visual images can spark a response in the most local entity, the body. And those images were posted by other embodied and emplaced persons. Moreover, the image gains a sense of agency beyond the poster's actions of, first, taking the photograph and, then, posting it to or through a social media app.

In his illuminating analysis of visual culture, art historian W. J. T. Mitchell begins with the question, "What do photographs want?" To challenge the skeptic, quick to offer the commonsensical rebuttal that photographs don't and can't want anything, Mitchell offers the following instruction: "When [people] scoff at the idea of a magical relation between a picture and what it represents, ask them to take a photograph of their mother and cut out the eyes."[38] This is a good way, he argues, to show not only the power of images but, perhaps more importantly, the emotion and desire they provoke from within the viewer. Try it. You'll see what Mitchell's getting at.

Frank connects the visual and the embodied when he tags his pictures with #visualquenchness, simultaneously showing how a visual can quench one's thirst or, more to the point, how a visual can beckon one's desire for one's thirst to be quenched. Dave includes "Life is Craft!" with every pic as a way to connect his pics to a way of life that he claims "appreciates the multisensory aspects of craft beer." Under the name @ beersnobchronicles, Ruby Romero often presents pictures of herself and other "babes" to depict the tantalizing and titillating sights of beautiful beers and bodies. Using a combination of still photos and videos, Sylvia Bravo as @craftylady24_7 shows her frequent travels to and from breweries and bottle shares as well as in-motion pics of her both pouring and drinking the beers she's acquired. Another local Las Vegas craft beer Instagrammer/beertographer, Chris Jacobs, uses social media and his moniker @beerzombies in a way that connects the local, translocal, and virtual by creating what he calls "art experiences" on- and offline.

"In the last few years," Chris says with a smile, "I've been called Beer Zombie more than I've been called my name." His smile opens into a full-on laugh, followed by a sip of Ballast Point's Grapefruit Sculpin IPA. He looks down at the beer in his hand, licks his lips, and gives praise to his beverage. "You know, I used to trade for this and was super excited. Now I can go to the store and grab it. These little steps are making a huge difference helping the local scene grow."

I take a sip of my beverage, the same fruity hop bomb he's drinking, and ask about his presence on Instagram and his @beerzombies virtual nom de plume. He tells me that his love of street art and craft beer go hand and hand, with a bit of postapocalyptic pop culture sprinkled in for good measure. He started doing graffiti-like street art as a teenager, pasting images to walls, street signs, and light posts.

"I had a street art name, We Are Zombies. It was like a Shepard Fairey political thing, you know. Like open your eyes, we're all zombies." As he got older and had kids he moved away from illegal acts toward safer practices but still managed to work with his original real-time avatar.

> So I took the We Are Zombies name and a logo I had been using for a long time. It was a bearded zombie. I took that and transferred it over to a beard made out of hops. And under that umbrella I had all my loves in one. I still do my art as Beer Zombies, but now it's a legitimate business, licenses, taxes, all that. I still do the street art, but now I get paid for it. And I now get to have beer reviews and pics with that too. I merged it all together as the same thing with my motto "Craft Till Death."

The hop-bearded beer zombie is present on everything he produces in both the material and virtual worlds. Whether he started the trend or not is debatable. He does, however, own the trademark for the hopped beard, a relatively common image in a scene composed of many hop-loving men with beards. I saw an outrageous example at the 2014 Great

American Beer Festival in Denver. It wasn't a logo. It was a man who expertly manipulated and shaped his beard to look like the bundled cones of a hop flower. Chris enjoys seeing others experiment with the idea because, to him, it strengthens the visual recognition of beers and beards so much so that, in the summer of 2016, he released a hop-scented beard oil.[39]

Gaining a relative degree of fame from his social media use, he's produced murals for the award-winning local craft-centric bar and restaurant Pizza Rock at both of its locations in the valley. Above the bar at its Green Valley location hangs a Beer Zombies head flanked by slices of dripping pizza ensconced with the words "Respect the Craft." Chris decorated Khoury's patio with a Beer Zombies mural that quickly became a backdrop for pics posted to Instagram. Other key stages of the local scene (e.g., Tacos & Beer and Atomic Liquors) have commissioned his work for display. Chris has also connected to the translocal scene by pasting murals at nonlocal breweries. For example, he hung a huge Beer Zombies head and an "SD #19 Forever" tag—in honor of famed and adored San Diego Padres player Tony Gwynn—inside the tasting room of San Diego's esteemed AleSmith brewery.[40]

What started as a fun project to post pics of his art and the beers he enjoyed drinking while making or planning his artwork has turned into a key source of his identity and an enchanting labor of love. "There's a path that it's on. I don't know where the end is, but it's taking me there. Not that I don't have a choice. Just that it's flowing and I'm going to ride it to see what happens," Chris says enthusiastically. "And taking pics of beers certainly has had its perks!" Due to his #beertography, breweries will send him beers or invite him to festivals so he can show and share his pictures to the over thirty thousand people who follow his account. His postings of beer photos, like those of other prominent beertographers like @hoperature, @aleateur, @brewstills, @goodbeerhunting, the aforementioned @louiebaton, and the sultan of snark @dontdrinkbeers, have not only created a new way of being a craft beer fan but also affected the way viewers relate to and consume beer, stretching it from material good to visual object of desire. And the more enticing the picture—as well as the color of the beer, the shape of its glassware, and physical setting—the more emotional and sensuous response the viewer will have.

There is an obvious disconnect between how we think a beer might taste from looking at a picture of it and how a beer actually tastes when sipping its material form. But that doesn't mean that "virtualization atrophies the senses [and] disconnects the operations from each other and from physical sensation," as some scholars have argued.[41] Instead, following Hennion's notion of taste as something that is collectively enacted and performed, the virtual scene "provides a frame" for viewers to recognize and even *feel* the inferred tastes presented through purposefully curated mediated images.

> Taste closely depends on its situations and material *devices*: time and space frame, tools, circumstances, rules, ways of doing things. It involves a meticulous temporal organization, collective arrangements, objects, and instruments of all kinds, and a wide range of techniques to manage all that. . . . Far from revealing a purely ritual or arbitrary nature of our tastes, the importance of these devices signals the conditional nature of pleasure and effect, the fact that it does not automatically depend on either the products or our preferences.[42]

Hennion italicizes "devices" on purpose, though I'm not sure if he had smartphones in mind. Regardless, social media tools like Instagram are devices that help define and perform taste for the poster and the viewer alike. We don't have to look too far to appreciate the visceral sensations we can get from looking at a photograph, itself a device for communicating ideas, feelings, and emotions. Poking out the eyes of a picture of a loved one, as Mitchell suggests, or even deleting virtual pictures—a different tactile sensation than physical cutting—from our computers of past lovers will certainly bring upon pangs of emotion and likely a spilled tear or two.

The images presented by beertographers are more than simply static entities meant only to represent something else. They are, instead, *living* symbols invested with meanings that tap into the desires and fantasies or "situational emotions" of onlookers.[43] The pics exert a degree of agency by stimulating and prompting both action and interaction beyond the virtual realm. Chris embraces his pics' abilities to tantalize viewers in order to enhance the collectively agreed upon value of the beers he captures and, for the sake of the scene itself, foster connections between people. He occasionally initiates contests or giveaways where people can win stuff with the Beer Zombies logo on it or bottles of beer. "I've given away really good beers, it's not cheap, but I want to let people know that I'm not just some faceless company or some random guy," Chris says with a smile, happy throwing shade at disenchanting corporations. Leaning forward, he declares, "I'm a beer guy, and I love beer, and anyone who loves craft beer can be a friend of mine."

In order to connect with craft beer enthusiasts in the San Diego area, in early 2015 he set up a scavenger hunt. In between his visits to breweries, he would hide beers in inconspicuous places. The breezy SoCal temps kept them cool enough for them to stay outside for a few hours. Chris admits that he was nervous about it.

"I didn't even know if anyone was going to want to do this. But the response was amazing. I was getting all these direct messages saying 'We're looking,' 'We found one,' 'Let us know if others were found.' It was real cool."

During that particular hunt as well as other times he travels, he posts pictures of the beers he's drinking and makes sure to label where he is or where he's going, thereby fostering an affective connection between his picture, his location, and his self. "Folks will see my post and come and say 'Hi' and drink or share a beer with me."

I interrupt him. "No offense, but you're just a dude. What's the appeal? What's motivating you to do this?"

"That's right. I'm just a regular dude who loves good beer. I'm not sure why I do it, but I know that it's about the beer and the lifestyle. And if

FIGURE 5.2. A Beer Zombies glass filled with local Joseph James Brewing Company's Bat Chit Hazy New England–style IPA. (Photo by author)

I'm going to drink good beer with good people, and I have a platform to show it, why not? And people seem to like it."

In this way, Chris connects his sense of self both to craft beer and to others who enjoy and find meaning in it. The aesthetic experience of an image posted to Instagram, then, gives way to the aesthetic experience of selfhood and the aesthetic experience of sociality, both of which are pleasures unto themselves. The self and the socializing between selves connected by shared aesthetic desires and engagements are eventually, if not inevitably, summoned back to material places like those where Chris hid beers or where people found him to meet, greet, and clink glasses together.

An avid beer trader and collector with a separate room in his house devoted to "hoarding" about a thousand beers, excluding the IPAs he gets that are intended to be consumed fresh, Chris is a devotee of not only translocalism but also his local scene. His commitment to the local scene plays out in two separate but related ways. First, his Beer Zombies merchandise—ranging from shirts and hats to beard oil and glassware—is adorned with his either "Craft Till Death" or "Drink Local or Die" moral mandates. As such, he feels the need to purchase and share locally brewed beverages.

> I get that "local" is a little strange, no one here, or most places, is doing "estate beers," kind of the most hardcore type of local. [Estate beers are made of ingredients grown and cultivated from one location.] But I always make sure to pick up some local beers when I go to the store. I always have local beers in my fridge and usually put a few in boxes that I send to people all over the country. I don't want to be a hypocrite. *I really believe that you get behind your local breweries and that helps your scene and you get to be a part of it, you get to be a part of something bigger than yourself.*

In the last line, he alludes to the second way he connects to local scene. Playing a role and being a part of the scene isn't confined to the supply side of the scene. He is part of it as a consumer but, perhaps more importantly, as an intermediary between local and translocal scenes through his role in the virtual scene.

Like other local Las Vegas beertographers, Chris and his Beer Zombies alter ego take on an "iconic" or "totemic" purpose by showing through and with their pics the vast and varied social encounters with craft beer in Las Vegas. Regardless of whether or not beers they show are brewed locally or admired translocally, individually and collectively they show the breadth and depth of the craft beer scene in a city often disparaged or ignored for its participation in the ongoing (r)evolution of taste. Pics of tulip glasses purposely placed next to the bottles or cans that transported the sacred elixirs are practices that bind the local scene, where the pic took place, to viewers connected to the local, translocal, or virtual scenes. Sometimes they connect all three.

Following sociologist Jeffrey Alexander's discussion of "iconic consciousness," we can say that those connections are fostered by contact with the material object even if that object is presented virtually. Alexander contends that "iconic consciousness occurs when an aesthetically shaped materiality signifies social value. Contact with this aesthetic surface, whether by sight, smell, taste, sound or touch, provides a sensual experience that transmits meaning."[44] Because the aesthetic surfaces of pictures are shared virtually, contact with them and the aesthetic experiences they foster can stretch beyond physical boundaries, uniting onlookers who are having, have had, or want to have similar aesthetic experiences with the picture and, in the end, with the content of it. Fostering those emotions and desires is a key contribution that individuals like Chris and other beertographers make to the scene as intermediaries between producers and consumers, between the various levels of the scenes, and between the symbolic and material building blocks of social life.

#craftbeerscene

Studies of "new media" and virtual scenes tend to go in two directions. The first explores the digital realm as an object of inquiry itself. Here, questions about the presentation of selves and the interaction of those selves in virtual spaces take precedent over embodied and emplaced experiences. The second strand attempts to show how embodied and emplaced persons use smartphones and their apps. Here, questions about the effects of such uses, and their gratifications, on the affective demeanor of the people and the places they photograph are of interest. In this chapter, I align with the latter by showing the connections between on- and offline practices and how those practices change the way places are experienced and interpreted through the showing and sharing of craft beer pics.

The virtual craft beer scene doesn't exist without the variety of local craft beer scenes that fuel or, more pointedly, upload it. Yet, without confounding correlation and causation, we can see how local scenes are enhanced by the virtual scenes that connect them to other local scenes that coalesce in a grand translocal scene. Both posting and viewing pics are active ways to promote an aesthetic education and sensibility that can be drawn upon in the local context in embodied and emplaced ways.

6

Beauty in the Eyes of the Beer Holder

"You're not worthy!" the gargoyle declares, smiling mischievously.

The unexpected pronouncement might shock the uninitiated while walking through the growing beer selection at liquor stores, bars, groceries, and gas station convenience marts. The gargoyle's taunt pushes some people to keep moving. Others will stop with surprise, joy, or contempt, or some mixture of those emotions. That seems to be the gargoyle's point, to poke and prod. This becomes clear after picking up the twenty-two-ounce bomber that displays his etched image, turning it to the opposite side, and reading the description of Stone Brewing's Arrogant Bastard Ale.

"It is quite doubtful that you have the taste or sophistication to be able to appreciate an ale of this quality and depth," the label instigates. "We would suggest that you stick to safer and more familiar territory—maybe something with a multi-million dollar ad campaign aimed at convincing you it's made in a little brewery, or one that implies that their tasteless fizzy yellow beverage will give you more sex appeal. Perhaps you think multi-million dollar ad campaigns make things taste better."

The seemingly mundane act of buying beer can double now as an anxiety-provoking assault on one's identity and ability to make "proper" aesthetic judgments.

The desire for pleasurable sensuous experiences is a social value, where aesthetics and values comingle as individuals negotiate the contours of taste. Situations arise in our everyday lives that push us to make evaluative judgments about what we find beautiful or ugly, exciting or dull, agreeable or otherwise. I emphasize our "everyday lives" to highlight the unnecessary boundaries between the art gallery and the liquor store. Ordinary actions and interactions are bound by both the moral and aesthetic orders we adhere to.[1] Ordinary experiences, like buying beer, serve other purposes than simply "displaying aesthetic taste."[2] They are, instead, connected to processes of learning about oneself with others in routine places and familiarized locales.[3]

Moreover, the activities of everyday life and the core objects that those activities support and coproduce are even more significant for the continued maintenance of scenes than those rarefied moments of dictated intensity at museums or other places of sanctioned aesthetic worship. Seeing that beer in the store and having an internal debate about whether to buy it and drink it later are mundane acts that are nonetheless aesthetic experiences. That internal debate, the conversation in our head between what sociologist George Herbert Mead called the "I" and the "me,"[4] is cognitive as much as it is sensuous. And it is often the place where individuals reflect upon and figure out where they stand on pressing cultural issues ranging from the trivial to the most vital.[5]

The conversations we have in our heads about everyday objects and how they *feel* don't often stay there. They play out on the stages of liquor stores, convenience marts, and other places where we make decisions and evaluative judgments, like choosing to take the gargoyle's challenge and buy the bottle bearing his image. Such choices depend, however, not only on our *background* experiences or dispositions but also on the *foreground* factors that make a beer, or another one on the shelf near it, desirable or not. Sociologist Claudio Benzecry focusses on the foreground to uncover the seductive elements of opera.[6] According to Benzecry, "The result of this strategy is to understand what is morally and sensually attractive about a practice as much as how the practice is constitutive of the person who partakes in it."[7] The seduction of a beer label and the potential it holds inside are felt within individuals, yet are still beholden, in part, to past encounters with craft beer.

Still, the interpretation of the gargoyle's instigating decree likely depends upon onlookers' past experiences with the beer, other craft beers like it, and the scene itself. Neophytes or the uninitiated might be turned off or, conversely, intrigued by the blatant proclamation. More experienced craft beer aficionados will likely be familiar with Stone Brewing and their other popular offerings like their Enjoy By IPA series or their more limited barrel-aged beers like Bastards Midnight Brunch, a ramped-up version of Arrogant Bastard brewed with espresso beans and then aged in both bourbon and maple syrup barrels. Because of Stone's relative longevity (founded in 1996) and availability (across the United States and abroad), they are well known and respected across the grand translocal scene. Many people I talked to noted that a Stone beer, usually either their classic IPA or the provocative Arrogant Bastard, was their first craft beer. It was, as we will see, their "epiphany object," changing the way they drank, who they drank with, and what they did to spread their newfound joy to others.[8]

Like with most issues of taste, no one is born with an innate appreciation of craft beer. Learning to taste is a process that is far from passively or automatically conferred by one's social position. The skills and knowledge to perform taste are acquired *with* others rather than ascribed *by* others. And the learning process to acquire tasting techniques and skills requires action.[9] The *types* of action one engages in vary depending on one's *experiential* position along a pliable pathway of aesthetic appreciation. The shifts and turning points in the ways individuals relate to a particular object are part of what sociologists Iddo Tavory and Daniel Winchester call "experiential careers." As they note, tracking these types of changes in the way a "cared for" object is understood through embodied practices reveals a trajectory of "learning-through-doing," a learning that is both inherently embodied and inherently social.[10]

By taking this idea and focusing thoroughly on the social side of embodied experiences, we can say that scenes rely on individuals at various levels of their experiential career. Because scenes are publicly available and open and voluntarily joined and enacted, they are necessarily home to individuals with varying levels of experience and knowledge of the binding object of desire. This type of diversity offers a necessary degree of dynamism to a scene. Without such differences in "experiential careers" among participants, contemporary scenes are likely to grow stagnant and lose their flavor like bygone scenes of old.[11]

The reality of experiential careers was summed up nicely by Nick Tribulato, the Las Vegas craft beer scene staple we met earlier in the book. Having worked behind a few bars, helped some festivals curate their offerings, and handed out hundreds of samples at supermarkets across the valley, Nick has learned to negotiate his varying roles as an intermediary between the beer and tasters. He quickly surmises their level of experience in order to foster the most enjoyable encounter for those waiting for him to hand them a beverage. He then provides them with a "frame" to approach and taste the beer through, a "frame" that is necessarily "coproduced" by virtue of their past experiences, the beer itself, and other particularities of the occasion.[12]

"Everyone is at a different place in their craft beer journey. Our job is to meet them where they're at and help move them along the path." Nick's insight was echoed by other interviewees from both sides of the bar; I heard stories of first beers and first loves from those at all places in "their craft beer journey." Expert brewers, brewery reps, distributors, and bartenders, as well as self-described or accredited beer geeks—the folks whom Nick is referring to when he says "our job"—are in positions to offer knowledge along with a cold brew (though *never* pouring into a frosted pint glass because the cold dulls the beer's flavor, as the craft beer neophyte learns quickly at the beginning of the path).

In his analysis of the rock 'n' roll scene in Austin before its attention-grabbing scene helped define the city as an island in the middle of Texas, American studies scholar Barry Shank writes, "Spectators become fans, fans become musicians, musicians are always already fans."[13] This easily translates to the craft beer scene as: *Drinkers become fans, fans become brewers, brewers are always already fans.*

Though roles can shift depending upon intensities of knowledge, skills, and interest in craft beer, individuals can play multiple roles in a scene during various stages of their experiential career as well as on various stages of the scene. Turned on or "plugged in" to craft beer, some fans may feel the nudge of their entrepreneurial spirit and open a new brewery or beer bar or push a new brand into the local market for scene participants—from the beginner to the connoisseur—to taste, evaluate, and discuss. Scenes rely on a flow of individuals to push and pull the scene, and the core object it encapsulates, in new and novel "unscripted" directions.

For a scene to work, people need to be attracted to it and, more importantly, to the core object that defines the scene and holds it together. That attraction isn't simply given, granted, or gained without a degree of reflexivity. "If one stops even for a fraction of a second, to observe oneself tasting, the gesture is installed," writes sociologist Antoine Hennion. "From a fortuitous, isolated event that happens to you, one moves into the continuity of an ongoing interest."[14] The initial point of sensuous contact becomes a revelation, an epiphany, an affective conversion from one of way of being in the world to another. This is an *aesthetic awakening.*

Awoken to the possibilities of new aesthetic experiences, a person may choose to explore those possibilities further by seeking out means for both formal and informal learning about the object of desire and the activities that account for its existence, namely its production and consumption, as well as the documented histories of such acts. Both the acquisition of this specified knowledge and the attachment to it are paramount to the process of *aesthetic connoisseurship*. Though levels of expertise are assumed, it is a reluctantly cumulative process because learning is as continuous as forgetting and relearning are certain.

Whether obtained through formal means like classes or from casual conversations during informal drinking sessions is beside the point. The main point is that a scene relies on its knowledge holders and keepers to, looking one way, help awaken the unaware or seemingly uninterested and, looking the other way, help change the social environment that the core object resides within and emerges from. Regarding the latter, people who use their sensuous knowledge to change a scene's aesthetic ecology engage in acts of *aesthetic entrepreneurship*. In the same way that taste as a coproduction is "formed and deformed by its social environment,"[15] so too can a social environment be "formed and deformed" by new objects to taste and ways of tasting. Aesthetic entrepreneurs actively change the somatic order of social life.[16]

All three of these actions are forms of socialization that require the adoption and use of sensuous knowledge. The first two—awakenings and connoisseurship—are inward-facing or inner-directed, which imply personal growth and development. The third—entrepreneurship—is other-facing or outward-directed, whereby sensuous knowledge is used to change or aid the growth and development of other persons' sensuous knowledge. And that knowledge derives from local, translocal, and virtual sources, albeit in various combinations to provide a scene that functions as a mechanism for re-enchanting local culture through shared experiences and expressions. And they are all mediated or afforded by the sensuous character of the significant object that binds people together into a scene rather than merely a random assortment of like-minded or like-*bodied* individuals.

Aesthetic Awakenings, or How Tastes Change

Except for the most experimental forms of theater, actors need to know their lines. Such knowledge is necessary for a scene to work, for a scene to express its intended meaning, for a scene to make an impact on both actors and audience members. A cultural scene requires its own type of knowledge and requires people to learn it and, for it to survive beyond its initial articulation, people to teach others about it and how to "plug in" to it. To act on a stage with familiar friends or live in a city with unfamiliar strangers, and make it work, the acquisition of meanings and skills is paramount on both individual and collective levels.[17] But education is meaningless if there isn't an initial spark to pique the interest of newcomers and neophytes.

That spark was of great interest to sociologist Howard Becker in his seminal article about people learning to smoke marijuana in the early

1950s, before it was commonly used and well before it became legal in certain states. Regardless, his findings still apply to first-time users of just about anything. Becker convincingly argues against psychological studies that focus on individual traits as the reasons or motivations for engaging in so-called deviant behavior. Instead, he shows how any "given kind of behavior is the result of a sequence of social experiences during which the person acquires a conception of the meaning of the behavior, and perceptions and judgments of objects and situations, all of which make the activity possible and desirable."[18] The focus, then, is on the process of the change rather than some particular psychological or socially determined disposition.

First, the novice must learn how to use the product. Then, the novice must learn, often from clues and cues given by experienced users, to recognize the feelings of "getting high." Next, after recognizing the drug's effects, the user must be able to identify them as pleasurable. Like the taste for other things, the taste for marijuana is socially acquired, though not in a simple unreflexive way. That is, the user relies on others to *help* him or her articulate the effects and determine if it feels good or not. I emphasize the word "help" here to de-emphasize the need for others and to move the analysis toward the corporeal affects of the object of desire and attraction on the user. Like the passionate opera fans studied by Benzecry, craft beer drinkers don't approach beer as an ambiguous entity at first and then rely solely on others to teach them "how to consume and enjoy it properly."[19] Others help, especially since a shared awareness is necessary for sustained engagement. And those others don't always have to be physically copresent, as is the case with virtual scenes. More to the point, like the powerful sensuality of opera, craft beer—with its cadre of smells and flavors and styles and alcohol content—compels and seduces some to explore further.

Becker notes that most marijuana users will not get high their first time and might even find the effects physically disagreeable (e.g., dry mouth, paranoia, hunger). Yet if they choose to continue using and eventually find pleasure from marijuana, they've crossed some sort of experiential threshold. They've shifted what the object means and how they relate to it. They've taken the first step along the path of their "experiential career" with the significant object. At that point, we can say they've gone through an *aesthetic awakening*. New meanings of both the object and their bodies have been acquired and established and, as sociologist Thomas DeGloma shows, become "storied forms of social interaction."[20] Such stories rely on the interplay of selves, other selves, and "epiphany objects."

DeGloma's narrative analysis of "awakening stories" adds depth and dimension to our understanding of personal change. He provides us with a language to explore the ways that individuals' aesthetic dispositions morph in relation to aesthetic experiences. Negotiating aesthetic choices—at and across varying levels of social strata—coincides with negotiating what defines the good life.[21] DeGloma's exhaustive study of "awakening stories" reveals a common, socially pattered story formula that transcends genre and standard sociological variables.

"Individuals who are in otherwise different situations," writes DeGloma, "use the same story formula to emplot their lives around a transformative realization of 'truth,' whatever the storyteller understands truth to be at the time the story is told."[22] Regardless of whether they're talking about religious conversion or deconversion, changes in political ideologies, or repressed past traumatic experiences, storytellers tend to see the past as a state of "darkness" followed by an "experience of discovery and personal transformation" that helped them "see the light."[23]

If we apply, at the very least, DeGloma's insights about "awakening stories" as a form of social knowledge that allows individuals to express and make claims about both personal changes *and* social allegiances, then we can advance studies of taste and tasting beyond those that see preferences and somatic acts as mechanically determined by socioeconomic background. Instead, taste and tasting are activities that are deeply embedded into the practices of *becoming* a self at the micro level, or a scene at the meso level, neither of which is inevitable. Narratives of "seeing the light" can be applied to moments of aesthetic contact and evaluation, whereby the object of taste, according to Hennion, "acts and moves . . . [and] transforms those who take possession of it and do something else with it."[24] As we will see, the intoxication of craft can lead to a new aesthetic perspective and new social relationships through direct contact with the newfound significant object of desire.

"I Think This Is What Beer Is Supposed to Taste Like"

If everyone is at different stages on their craft beer journey, then that journey has to begin somewhere and somehow. Many people were eager to tell me their "first craft beer" story, whether I asked or not. Each story followed a similar trajectory. Those stories, as common among "awakening stories," were defining features of their transition to an aesthetically aware self, which was often presented in juxtaposition to or as a negation of their former self.[25] Jake's "aesthetic awakening" story is a good example.

Jake moved to Las Vegas in 2003. Until recently, he worked for one of the local off-Strip casinos. Like many transplants turned locals, it took a little bit of time for Jake to develop an attachment to Las Vegas. The impetus for the change in his feelings about the city came through his taste buds, and, in effect, through a change in his overall taste preferences and ritually learned and practiced tasting. It led him to people he bonded with, to a collective, to a scene where his tasting coincided with the tasting of aligned others.[26] Following sociologist Bruno Latour, craft beer is a participant that can "authorize, allow, afford, encourage, permit, suggest, influence, block, render possible, [or] forbid" particular practices.[27]

By his own admission, Jake was a pretty standard beer drinker. "Throughout most of my twenties I was a Coors Light drinker, a Bud Light drinker, a Corona drinker." He pauses and smiles with anticipation.

"And then." He pauses again. "So, I was really into gargoyles," he begins.

I smile.

Jake points at me. "You already see where I'm going with this." We share a moment of shared recognition of shared sensuous knowledge.

He adjusts his backward black baseball cap slightly and shifts in his seat to lean forward. "One year for my birthday my brother gave me a bomber of Arrogant Bastard because it had the gargoyle on it. He was like 'it has a gargoyle and a cool label and you drink beer so I got this for you.'"

"So I remember the day," Jake reminisces, shifting atop his stool. "We were going into a four-day weekend for Thanksgiving break, it was a Wednesday, and I was like, I'm going to pop this sucker open and see what it's all about. I was reading the back, and I was like this is too much to read . . . it just didn't make sense to me at the time."

This is actually a common practice that craft breweries have adopted to set their beers apart from their Big Beer adversaries. While there are some that still have sleek and minimal labels, many offer both quirky illustrations and detailed information about the product. Beyond naming the style, labels list the types of hops, malted barley, and yeast used in the brewing process. Some note the SRM, which indicates the color of the liquid sealed in the can or dark bottle. Some may even include potential food pairings. And others will provide narratives that are sometimes tales of how the brewery decided to brew this particular beer, and sometimes they present local folklore of fantastical origins and creatures.[28] The wax-sealed bombers for Tenaya Creek's Old Jackalope, a highly regarded piney and caramel-tasting barleywine, are adorned with a mythical jackrabbit with antelope horns sitting in a snowy wilderness. With equal parts snark and enchanted allure, the label tells us that "this bottle is only heard of in myths. It's so rare in fact, we have used a magical seal that only opens with an 'Abracadabra,' or the bottle opener hanging from your keys." A mounted taxidermied jackalope, a symbol of the American Mountain West, proudly hangs above the bar at the brewery's taproom, creating even more mystique for visitors, locals and tourists alike.

Jake continues, "I poured it, tasted it, and it was super bitter. I didn't hate it, so I took a few more sips, and a few more sips. And not even that much through, I was like, man, I'm kind of feeling this. I didn't even look at the ABV on the bottle."

"It's about 7 percent, right?"

"Yeah, a little over that. This definitely wasn't your silver bullet in a can," he smirks, making clear reference to Coors Light. Most macro-brewed light lagers have a lower alcoholic content, usually around 4.2 percent ABV. Jake went online to look up information about Stone. At Thanksgiving dinner, the next day, he thanked his brother for the beer and told him, "*I think this is what beer is supposed to taste like. I think I've been doing something wrong all these years.*"

Jake's story, and especially this last line, fits in nicely with DeGloma's model of awakening narratives. It indicates a change whereby something was "wrong" that has now been fixed, or at least perceived as such. And Jake's fix was subsequently reinforced by communing with others who also made a similar transition.

Shortly after his "aesthetic awakening," he downloaded the social media app Untappd. The app allows users to "check in" various beers and provide ratings and minimal comments. They can also note where they found or drank said beverages. Not only did using Untappd increase Jake's knowledge of beer—"I saw how many different types of great beers there are in the world"—but it also connected him to people locally whom he met and eventually started traveling to breweries with in Las Vegas and elsewhere. The virtual merges with the local as mediated names turn into flesh and blood people.

"I met really cool people in the beer world. Started friending folks, started meeting up, drinking, talking about beer. And, kind of unexpectedly, I ended up beer traveling, kind of on a regular basis right now." At the time of our conversation, Jake had recently returned from a "beer-cation" in San Francisco and its surrounding area. He happily stood in line with friends, and strangers, for nine hours to get a chance to drink Russian River's Pliny the Younger, a triple IPA that's available for only two weeks out of the year.

In a matter of a few years, Jake had gone from a "common" beer drinker to a craft beer aficionado. His first Stone Arrogant Bastard opened up new aesthetic possibilities for him that, in turn, led him to a scene that he now identifies with and supports by attending local events, posting beer pics on Instagram, and traveling to other cities and towns to experience their aesthetic offerings. Others have followed a similar path and tell a similar story with the nuances and wrinkles in time of all personal narratives. Steve Wright is one such person.

"I Was Twenty-Seven but Drinking Like a Sixteen-Year-Old"

Before a typical and ritualized Wednesday night bottle share at Khoury's, Steve and I sat across from one another at the big oak table near the far wall. The wall holds the lone television that stays off most of the time, except for a seemingly random soccer match or Nintendo 64 Mario Kart tournament. Khoury's is a regular spot for Steve to meet up with friends, including his roommate Jameson, who works behind the bar and register. It's a ritual site for gatherings of local craft beer drinkers, a place that brings about a religious fervor among its patrons. It's a place where Steve feels more comfortable than he does in church. Now at least.

Steve was a Mormon, emphasis on *was*. He grew up in Southern California, went on his mission to Idaho, and then stayed for college. Shortly after graduating, he married and moved to Austin with his now ex-wife. He credits Austin for doing two things: helping him further question his faith and instilling a love for "local" that he brought with him to Las Vegas after his divorce.

"I didn't have an alcoholic beverage until I was twenty-seven. Twenty-seven! The first drink I had was a Jack and Coke because the guy in front of me ordered it. I didn't even know how to order a drink at a bar," Steve laughs.

"So you can say I gave up religion and started drinking alcohol, shit alcohol, and started drinking craft beer and now I drive people around to breweries." He laughs again. Reminiscing about his awakenings—religious and aesthetic—seems to bring him some joy as if he were going through them again. The retelling of a story, tale, or anecdote, sociologist Erving Goffman notes, is a *replaying* of an event: "A replaying . . .

recounts a personal experience, not merely reports the event."[29] Steve's replaying is visible in both his visceral reactions to his own narrative and the words he uses to tell it.

Las Vegas has a relatively large Mormon population, about 5 percent, over double the national percentage per capita.[30] But Steve was not counted among them. Along with getting used to the heat and dry air while going back to school for a second degree, he had to learn the city. And he was interested in finding a way to connect to the city's local culture or learn if there even was such a thing in Las Vegas. So when he received a message from an old friend's older brother to meet at a local brewery, he saw it as a way to learn about the city and, more importantly, how to be in it.

At the time, Ellis Island Brewery & Casino—a block off the Strip, family owned and brewing since 1998—offered their beers for one dollar every day. New to drinking, Steve liked the price and thought it would be good to meet up with at least a somewhat familiar face. That it was at local spot that brewed their own beer made it even more enticing for Steve.

"I was drinking Bud Light Lime. Shitty vanilla vodka and Cokes. *I was twenty-seven but drinking like a sixteen-year-old.* I tell you, I was waaay behind. Then I had a hefeweizen at Ellis Island. Hadn't tasted anything like it before. And it was local, which was cool. I drank everything they made. And then I just started buying and trying new beers."

He pauses. His smile fades.

Then it comes back.

"Huh. I hadn't thought of that in a long time. That's well done, man. You should bottle that."

Then we laugh about the odd symbolism of Ellis Island as a gateway, a threshold, a turning point from one stage to the next. "Yes! I descended upon Ellis Island. It was dirty. There were strangers everywhere. But when I left, I had a new life."

Where Steve's story differs from Jake's, and from those of many other scene members in the core and on the periphery alike, is that it encompasses the full trajectory from aesthetic awakening to connoisseurship to entrepreneurship. Steve and his business partner Travis started Sin City Brew Tours in 2015. They bought a van and started taking about eight to twelve people per tour to the city's craft breweries. Steve had an aesthetic awakening, continued to pursue it, and, in a short time, turned it into an opportunity for both himself and the local scene. The rise of supplemental businesses like Steve's represents an aesthetic awakening of sorts for the local scene as it has matured as well as for visitors previously unfamiliar with Las Vegas's local craft beer scene. Visitors have only recently been awakened to the possibilities the city has to offer beyond the Strip, and Steve is happy to talk to them about the beers and the breweries that define the aesthetic ecology of the scene.

Aesthetic Connoisseurship, or Growing the Knowing Palate

The history of beer has many twists and turns and a crushing vastness that stretches to humans' earliest civilized days. With neither hyperbole nor hesitation, writers with various intents have told the "history of the world according to beer."[31] To delve into such a history or, more pointedly, to have the *desire* to delve into that history is to take further steps along one's craft beer journey. As those who have "seen the light" purposefully seek new information and a new vocabulary, they in turn uncover new ways of drinking and tasting. Sense, sensibility, and skill can be acquired and fostered as a means for encountering the world and making aesthetic judgments.[32]

Scenes depend on connoisseurs, regardless of whether they're self-proclaimed, credentialed, or otherwise. All scenes have their specialized language to talk about the core object that binds them together. And all scenes need their connoisseurs to keep that language alive. But when it comes to the actual knowledge and skills necessary for changing and perhaps even enhancing aesthetic experiences, discourse is merely an indicator. It is the signifier rather than the signified. It doesn't show how newcomers and casual consumers convert into connoisseurs. Such conversion rituals require more than talk. They require the action and interaction of bodies in motion.[33]

Studies that remain at the level of talk can tell us a lot about what people say about their taste preferences and what they know about the stated rules and rituals of a scene. But they tend to stop there. For example, in their extensive analysis of "foodies," sociologists Josée Johnston and Shyon Baumann focus on culinary discourse because they start with the premise that "human tastes and determinations of food's aesthetic qualities must necessarily be social constructions."[34] Perceptions of what is delicious or disgusting are based on criteria that "elevate certain foods and denigrate others" and, as they argue, "only through an examination of discourse" can "justifications for aesthetic evaluations . . . be observed."[35]

Though Johnston and Baumann's focus serves their mission well, it nevertheless leaves out two important aspects of aesthetic knowledge acquisition. First, because the core object is displaced, visceral embodied reactions to food are neither observed nor felt. Their study of foodies oddly leaves out any actual contact with food. In contrast, my focus here on aesthetic connoisseurship as part of one's "experiential career" brings objects of desire back into play. Moreover, objects are perceived not merely through one sense.[36] Perceptions of objects are connected to the embodied practices necessary for acquiring sensuous knowledge. As Hennion notes, "music lovers"—"active practitioners of a love for music, whether it involves playing, being part of a group, attending concerts or listening to records or the radio"[37]—make particular physical arrangements to listen to music in order to obtain the optimal experience offered by the sensuous auditory stimuli of the summoned tunes.

> Listening is a precise and highly organized activity, but its aim is not to control something or to achieve a specific goal: on the contrary, its objective is to bring about a loss of control, an act of surrender. . . . We must allow ourselves to be carried away, moved, so that something can take place. I have done everything necessary to make something happen but

> it is imperative that I do not try to control what does happen. My little actions, my idiosyncrasies, my rituals, even if they are very active, are "meta-actions," they affect my environment, my mood, but they cannot help me control what music can make me feel, which would be the very negation of my passion.[38]

The type of passion that active listening demands and facilitates belongs to the connoisseur's mind and body. Showing this again with the example of a wine drinker whose lips part to receive the liquid, again, to obtain an optimal experience, Hennion writes, "He has not simply drunk, he has drunk a wine."[39] Wine, in this instance, is the consecrated object of desire, treated with attention and appreciation not as a display of status but as a target for attention and appreciation waiting to be attended to and appreciated. Such consecrated objects are necessary components of scenes and, consequently, for their efficacy as social mechanisms to spark re-enchantment and pursuits of local culture.

Second, Johnston and Baumann view a person's quest to learn how to approach the core object "as a topic for serious aesthetic consideration, deliberation, and appreciation" primarily done for the sake of acquiring status.[40] Status is a part of the craft beer scene, especially through the means of institutionalized classification systems and rankings as well as informal rules of exclusion discussed in the last chapter. But knowledge acquisition serves another purpose. Like tribal elders, craft beer connoisseurs function as stewards for the beverages themselves and the sensuous knowledge they elicit and require to enhance their varied levels of desirability beyond the nominal charges of "good" or "bad."

These knowledge holders, I found, are eager to share information. Closeting information only hurts the craft beer scene, leaving consumers open to Big Beer's slick advertising campaigns and phantom "crafty" crafts. Education about beer is one of the few defenses craft beer brewers, distributors, and consumers have against Big Beer's continued "craftwashing" tactics to mimic or buy craft breweries.[41] Many of the people I talked to who work at brewery taprooms, at bars, or as brewery reps gleefully told me that newcomers to the scene were their favorite people to talk to, and not because it gave them an elevated sense of self-worth but because it can elevate the cultural value of craft beer and, in turn, the scene.

"The pickiest beer drinkers," according to Rose Signor, Certified Cicerone and general manager of Atomic Liquors, "are your Bud Light drinkers and Coors Light drinkers." Some of these folks just want what they've always had. Some even actively turn their nose away from the presumed pretentiousness of craft beer and the people who drink it. Especially those who talk about it, and then talk about it some more. The stereotypical and oft-lampooned beer geek looking for an invitation to show off his or her knowledge can certainly turn people off from trying new beers and expanding their sensory knowledge.

Nick Tribulato recognizes the challenges for the uninitiated. "It can be intimidating for a novice because some can see the beer menu, and *everyone* wants to have the biggest menu in town, and they have no idea where to begin." And when they're surrounded by beer geeks, Nick says, who are talking about beer in great detail at a level the novice didn't even know existed, it can easily overwhelm them, potentially turning them away from, or even against, the scene. Nick sympathizes with the uninitiated.

During his time behind the bars at Freakin' Frog and Money Plays, two bars that were relatively early adopters of craft beer in Las Vegas, Nick used his aesthetic connoisseurship to introduce novices to new ways of tasting.

> The most challenging yet most fulfilling thing for me was to walk them in from where they're at [on their craft beer journey]. If they normally drank Blue Moon [a "crafty" wheat-based beer brewed by Coors], I'd show them Belgian wits [light and lemony with pleasant aromas]. I'm not going to give them an IPA off the bat because they'll probably hate it, all those hops can traumatize them for sure. That's a sure way to turn them off of craft beer.

A beer with a high bitter content like an IPA certainly wouldn't jive with the palate of someone accustomed to drinking more floral or sweeter brews. The objective is to match what a bar has with what a customer brings with them in terms of aesthetic experience. Exposing neophytes to the varieties of craft beer is a key tactic for using one's connoisseur status to foster aesthetic awakenings and, in turn, enhance both the physical size and aesthetic demeanor of the scene.

> That was something that Adam [Carmer, the owner of the now defunct Freakin' Frog] was always pretty dang good at. *You curate their experience, and walk them through the styles and history of beer.* There are craft beer bars in town that can do that, but there are others that might have a great list but they won't walk you through it. They'll just plop the menu down and you have to navigate it yourself.

Leaving the customer wondering about the different beers on the list without guiding them through the available variations doesn't do anyone any good. The customers, the bars, *and* the breweries that made the beers suffer, and so does the scene they're all a part of, especially a young scene.

When people walk into a craft brewery's taproom, unless they've been reluctantly dragged in by a friend, they are likely not looking for a Big Beer light lager. They're likely further along in their craft beer journey. Again, those stations along craft beer's varied paths are unequally populated. So it takes some work by the connoisseur to, as Nick said, "meet them where they're at." This is brewer Steve Brockman's goal when a new face appears in CraftHaus's taproom. If he's not too busy with brewing duties, he'll peek through the plexiglass that separates the brewery from the bar area. Not only does he like to know what people think about their beers, he takes his role as an educator seriously.[42] Steve explicitly connects his desire to educate consumers about beer to the very essence of what makes craft beer "craft."

FIGURE 6.1. Brewer Steve Brockman explains to the crowd gathered to celebrate CraftHaus's Comrade Day the process of brewing their Russian imperial stout. (Photo by author)

> All beer has a story, a story that comes before brewing the beer, and extends on after it. I think it's important to educate people about it and that's an important aspect of craft. That's one of the things that separates us from the big boys [i.e., Big Beer]. So I see people come in here and I want to tell the story. I'll ask them what they think and say "Hey, let's talk about it." We'll drink some more and carry on from there.

When they first opened, CraftHaus offered only two beer styles, an IPA and a saison. Though saisons have become more popular in recent years, they were fairly new to the Las Vegas scene when CraftHaus opened in 2014. As such, Steve and his co-brewer Steph Cope had to explain where saisons' earthy umami flavors, neither bitter nor sweet, come from and what to look for when tasting them.

"Telling the story of the beers, the brewers, the breweries, and how things go," Steve explains, "that's a big part of being craft. So is connecting with the people drinking our beers that we made right over there [points to the bright tanks filled with fresh brew]." People can learn those stories and others informally at a bar or a brewery, as we've just seen. Or people can learn those stories through formal training by taking classes that range from one-off seminars by connoisseurs to full-on semesters geared toward industry-sanctioned certification. The scene relies on both forms of education to both bring new participants within the fold and push those already intoxicated by craft to expand their aesthetic knowledge.

Informal Education

Whether at a bar, restaurant, or taproom, it has become customary for consumers to ask for and receive a sample before ordering. Because most consumers don't abuse this by asking for too many samples, the practice becomes a way to informally test your own palate and how much a particular beer interacts with it. Bartenders and brewers tend to support this, though many of them provide a reasonable test taste in the name of the "flight": usually five or so five-ounce pours of their draft offerings.

Informal learning can also happen during expected encounters, or what sociologist Erving Goffman called "focused gatherings," where "people effectively agree to sustain for a time a single focus of cognitive and visual attention."[43] Of course, for our discussion, we would add other senses to Goffman's limited scope. Regardless, as Goffman notes, the gathering depends upon an "official focus of activity" whereby "official" does not mean formal or institutionalized. Instead, it refers to the defined or understood activity at hand, like a board game (a favored example of Goffman's) or a bottle share (as in our case).[44] And that focus often requires a commitment of individuals' bodies, whether they're sitting hunched over a multicolored and patterned board ready to roll a twelve-sided die or doling out pours of the beer they've been hoarding in their cellar for the last four years to mellow the sharp alcohol bite of a particular imperial stout they brought to share.

Bottle shares are ritualized "focused gatherings" where the various bottles and cans of craft beers are opened, usually one by one, in

FIGURE 6.2. Ritualized bottle shares give participants chances to share beverages and knowledge, drinking with and learning from one another. (Photo by author)

a continuous manner that supports participants' "continuous engrossment" in the encounter with the beer and with the others taking part in the same activity.[45] The collectively sustained focus provides a ripe opportunity to learn about craft beer for newbies and geeks alike. Though some might not explicitly express that learning is the intended outcome of their involvement, their eyes certainly light up when they get a chance to try beers or styles they've only heard of from others or through websites and social media accounts aimed at following the latest trends in craft beer. As such, we can say that there is a latent informal learning aspect to bottle shares for most attendees.

"Wow, that's incredible!" says Darren during one of the Atomic's Second Saturday bottle shares. He had just sipped a dark brown liquid that smelled and tasted like "every breakfast I ever want to have," he shares with a smile as wide as his mouth would stretch. This was his first time trying Funky Buddha's Maple Bacon Coffee Porter. He brought it to the share that day after recently receiving two bottles from a friend in Florida, where Funky Buddha brews its creations. Darren's grin was a permanent fixture as he doled out small pours into the glasses thrusted in front of him by eager soon-to-be sippers. This ritual sharing enhances the collective's assemblage of aesthetic experiences.

A somewhat scattered conversation begins between a few people as they took breaks from talking to swirl the beer in their glasses to bring out all of its aromas and gently let the sweet and roasty brew cover their tongues and slide down their throats. Engaged in this moment of sensuous delight together, a small group of four or five, including Darren, begin discussing the differences and merits between porters and stouts.

"They're really the same; porters originally came from England and stouts came from Ireland."

"Isn't it really about ABV though? Stouts are higher, right?"

"Sometimes. There's a lot of variation within the categories. A Guinness ain't the same stout as a Bomb [brewed by Prairie Artisan Ales]. One's like 4 percent and the other's like 13 percent. Both stouts, but totally different."

"Yeah, but Bomb's got like chocolate and vanilla and chilies packed into it. Of course they're different."

"The real difference," another voice chimes in, "is that stouts and porters are made from different types of malts. Stouts use dark roasted malts that give off a slightly bitter coffee taste. That's why there are so many stouts made with coffee, they complement each other, and not that many coffee porters."

"Okay, but this is a coffee porter. And it's fucking amazing!"

"For sure. And it's brewed with bacon and maple syrup. Incredible!"

The conversation went on like this for a while, shifting from topic to topic as different people came in and out of the conversation and as different beers were poured into emptied glasses. The informality of the talk was palpable, as was the exchange of shared knowledge that accompanied the exchange of shared beers. As many scholars of group behavior note,[46] this type of interaction helps reinforce scene members' identities *as* scene members. Craft beer drinkers become *craft* beer drinkers beyond the obvious fact that they're drinking craft beer. Conversations expand the knowledge base of participants and are the most effective at doing so in focused gatherings where the sensuous activity of tasting is shared. Discourse *about* and embodied experiences *of* the scene's "core object" work to reinforce both aesthetic solidarity and authority through "learning-by-doing." This type of knowledge exists beyond the sheer pragmatic or mechanical habit. It is knowledge that, as the philosopher Maurice Merleau-Ponty wrote, is "forthcoming only when bodily effort is made."[47] Embodied knowledge through visceral contact with an object is foundational knowledge for producers and consumers of other craft wares like cheese, blown glass, and cocktails.[48]

Homebrewing has a long history as an informal means of "learning-by-doing."[49] Its popularity has resurged steadily since the ban against it (an oddly resilient holdover from the days of Prohibition) was overturned and legalized nationally by President Jimmy Carter in 1976, prompting both large suppliers and local shops to serve an interest-driven base. It doesn't take a great leap of the imagination to see how homebrewing led to the first boom in what were only then called "microbreweries."[50] It's also easy to connect the recession to homebrewing and, then, to the meteoric rise of craft breweries in the years that followed.[51]

Homebrewing is a form of "serious leisure" for those pursuing it to achieve recognition at competitions or as a means to a potential career.[52] The practice itself opens up an opportunity to acquire a set of skills and enhance the homebrewer's aesthetic knowledge of the scene's core object. It's a way to bridge the gap between production and consumption. Homebrewers often note the cost of drinking craft beer regularly. One of the reasons many of them started brewing their own beer was because it costs less than craft beer and is better—usually in terms of both flavor and alcohol content—than the Big Beer brews they can buy for the same price.

"I didn't have any money. I was trying to get through college on loans and small jobs. But I wanted to drink, so I just started to make my own beer," says a former homebrewer who turned his hobby into a job at one of the local breweries. "It took a while to figure it out but eventually I started making some stuff that tasted good and then I just kept experimenting with different styles and stuff." After the initial expense of equipment for about a hundred dollars, ingredients to brew five gallons worth of beer can be as low as thirty-five dollars. Prices vary depending upon both the types of materials needed for particular types of beers as well as the different levels of satisfaction and sophistication.

In order to embrace the learning process through homebrewing, I decided to give it a go during the early stages of my research. At least, I thought, I would learn something about the way beer emerges from a combination of boiled sugar water, hops, and yeast that, depending on the strain, eats the sugars with varied amounts of gusto. The amount of sugar eaten creates the alcohol content in beer. I already had a few things needed for brewing in my kitchen: a stove, a few pots, funnels, and wooden spoons. There are, however, some specific objects needed to brew beer, like a fermenter or carboy, typically a five-gallon glass or plastic container used for fermentation. It has a rubber stopper with a plastic "air lock" that allows excess carbon dioxide to escape without exposing the fermenting liquid to unwanted bacteria. When you hear and see the bubbles, you know that the yeast is eating the sugar and turning your barley tea or "wort" (pronounced "wert") into alcohol, a first sign of at least minimal success.

Beginners will often use malt extracts to ensure the proper amount of sugar that more advanced brewers get from boiling grains. Cans of sticky malt extract helped me move along in the process by skipping a few steps. The boiled tea made my house smell like a brewery, which I thought was a good sign. My wife didn't necessarily agree, though she was happy that I had to clean the kitchen and surrounding rooms meticulously before, during, and after the brewing process to avoid contamination and the off-flavors it breeds. Sanitizing everything is one of the most important parts of brewing at any level.

"Relax, don't worry, have a homebrew." Nuclear engineer, founder of the Association of Brewers, the American Homebrewers Association, and the Great American Beer Festival, and Brewers Association president Charlie Papazian repeats this mantra habitually throughout his homebrew bible *The Complete Joy of Homebrewing*.[53] Relaxing. Not worrying. That's great advice. It is; it really is. But beyond a sense of zen that would've kept that mantra from becoming an impenetrable koan, a person must possess the following two characteristics to become a *successful* homebrewer: the patience of stone and compulsive cleanliness. I possess neither of these. Yet I've made some beers that are, well, drinkable, at least. That's something I suppose.

I relied on the advice of current and former homebrewers and didn't pursue any formal training. Along with Papazian's book, I also read articles on websites and gained comforting guidance from internet forums devoted to homebrewing. After a not-so-successful first try using a kit I bought online—it was an IPA that turned out way too sweet and more metallic than was acceptable by any rating system—I sought out the two homebrew shops in Las Vegas. In fact, I was surprised that more than one homebrew shop existed. But as the scene has grown, both shops have shifted from surviving to thriving. Oregon native Steve Berg, the owner of Vegas Homebrew & Winemaking, not only is willing to share advice but described himself as a "cheerleader" of craft beer and of the scene.[54] He often gives demonstrations at local beer festivals, giving the outdoor environment aromatic hints of malted barley stemming from and steaming in his kettles.

Pennsylvania native Gary Hails runs the valley's other shop, U Bottle It, where he sells the necessary ingredients for brewing and teaches classes to brewing neophytes. He regularly hires notable advanced homebrewers to work at the store and to help with his classes as well as to give informal lessons to nervous customers like myself. Of note, some of them have gone on to run their own breweries or work at already well-established ones.[55] Each time I entered U Bottle It, Gary and his crew were always welcoming and willing to listen to what I wanted to brew but were also willing to tell me what I should and shouldn't do. They

FIGURE 6.3. After fermenting in one bucket, a not terrible homebrew is transferred to another bucket for bottling. Notice the sanitizer nearby. (Photo by author)

acted less like judgmental gatekeepers and more like patient guides. For instance, if I wanted to brew a high ABV imperial stout (which I did), I needed to ensure I added enough malts to provide enough sugar for an aggressive yeast strain to eat and produce alcohol. And if I wanted to mimic a bourbon-barrel-aged flavor without investing in an actual used wooden barrel (which costs about two hundred dollars depending on size and former occupant), I should soak oak chips in a mason jar with the bourbon of my choice for about a month (I went with Buffalo Trace). The bourbon seeps into the chips and, in effect, sanitizes them so I would be able to throw them in my carboy after fermentation so the young brew won't become infected by microscopic bacteria from the previously fresh wood chips.

They also warned me not to put too much added sugar when bottling the beer because it could lead to too much carbonation that could produce unwanted outcomes. On one brew, apparently I hadn't been conservative enough at the time of bottling. One bottle gave me a black eye when I opened it and the cap propelled by the gas inside flew with a vengeance at my face. A few months later, another bottle that I was going to serve to friends exploded while sitting on the table in my dining room. Luckily no one was in the room when it happened. Shattered glass and dark syrupy liquid aren't the best ways to greet even the worst dinner guest. If I wanted to keep brewing, maybe I needed to take some classes. And those formal classes exist, for both brewing *and* tasting.

Formal Education

Accompanying the national rise of interest in craft beer, over twenty universities and community colleges have followed the leads of the University of California, Davis and Oregon State University (two schools located in craft "beervanas") by offering various degrees in brewing or fermentation science. There has been some push-back against these programs by those who see them as irrelevant niche or as a way to justify drinking. But like with any craft, technical know-how is necessary for maintaining both high-quality production and consumption.

The connection between brewer and beer drinker, just like the connection between any artisanal craftsperson and those who engage with the products of their labor, is an important part of the success of craft-based economies and the continued desire for re-enchantment through crafted wares.[56] If that connection could be strengthened by ramping up the aesthetic knowledge of industry intermediaries, those responsible for overseeing and enacting the transition from craft producer to craft consumer, both the symbolic and material values of craft beer would grow, as recent history affirms. Interest in craft has changed industries and markets because of the growing affinities between craft production *and* consumption. "Just as craft production is significant . . . for the opportunity it offers for human self-expression and creativity," writes sociologist Colin Campbell, "so too is craft consumption important because of the opportunity it presents for the manifestation of similar valued human qualities."[57] The only thing missing from Campbell's statement is the role of the intermediary, whose actions can be craft-centric rather than merely a device subservient to the not-so-invisible hands of the market.[58]

Ray Daniels, a Harvard Business School grad turned pharmaceutical marketer turned homebrewer and homebrewing author, has a love of beer that has grown the more he has learned about it. After a failed attempt at opening his own brewery in Chicago, he put his marketing skills to work for the Brewers Association in 1996. While editing the association's publications and continuing to travel and drink beers across the United States and elsewhere, the idea of a certification program emerged. Wine experts—sommeliers—have been an accepted and revered part of the food and beverage world. They mediate the void between producers and consumers, endowed with status by both a thankful industry and a knowledge-thirsty public.[59] Why couldn't the same happen for beer?

Daniels knew he needed to get the name right. He didn't want to settle for "beer sommelier," because beer, he and others maintained, deserved an identity of its own. Scouring the pages of dictionaries and thesauruses, he mulled over many terms that were often quickly discarded: Sereveur, Savant de Beer, Marquis de Cerevisiae. Then he found the Italian word, "Cicerone," which roughly translates as "tour guide." Perfect. Daniels wanted would-be Cicerones to be experts. But even more so, he wanted them to act as facilitators guiding consumers through memorable beer experiences along their respective craft beer journeys. As a guide himself, he created a syllabus and made it available online for anyone who wanted to study and then pay forty-nine dollars to take a multiple-choice exam to test their knowledge of beer flavors, history, styles, and proper care.

What began as a fairly simple and inexpensive test burgeoned into a full-blown craft expertise industry. The Cicerone program, in alignment with the Court of Master Sommeliers program, has four distinct rankings within the program. Level 1 is the Certified Beer Server (CBS), followed by Certified Cicerone, Advanced Cicerone, and Master Cicerone. Similar to the mandates of the Sommelier program, those who pass Level 1 can move forward but cannot call themselves Cicerones. The CBS exam is administered online, while the advanced certifications require in-person testing that includes a tasting portion that requires test takers to identify not differences between styles but also off-flavors as well. Each level requires greater degrees of technical knowledge and skill to determine the causes of infections as well as proper food pairings. Though there are other programs to learn the craft of beer brewing, serving, and drinking, including the Beer Judge Certification Program, the Cicerone program has accrued the highest status despite anecdotal claims that exams are too subjectively graded. This led to a low percentage of passes (about 25–30 percent), which meant that those who failed and wanted to take the exam again would have to pay again for the chance to do so. The first-time exam is $395, and those who choose to retake it pay $100 for the tasting portion and/or $175 for the written exam.

At the beginning of 2018, over fifteen hundred Certified Beer Servers worked in Las Vegas, as did forty-two Certified Cicerones and one Advanced Cicerone. No local connoisseur has reached the Master level; there are only thirteen in the world.

What Daniels didn't anticipate, I imagine, is that after the certification program took hold throughout the industry, it would spill over into the craft beer *consuming* public. Or at least the *idea* of it would, the idea that advanced knowledge could and would help foster advanced aesthetic experiences. I didn't anticipate this either when I enrolled in a formal class.

Toward the beginning stages of my fieldwork, serendipitously, I noticed that UNLV's cooperative extension program was offering a course titled "Beer Connoisseurship and Certificate Program." Hmmm. And it was going to be taught by Alex Graham. Hmmm again. I know that name. A well-known staple throughout the scene, Alex was the former head brewer of local Joseph James and, at the time of the class, the Beer Mercenary for local Tenaya Creek. That Alex was a Certified Cicerone wasn't surprising. What was surprising was that he was the only person in the class who worked in the industry. Of the seven students who enrolled in the course, only one had any occupational relation to the food and beverage world. He sold glassware. With the exception of one woman who proudly declared the first day that she "collects certificates" and wasn't "really much of a beer drinker," the others were craft consumers eager to learn more about the ins and outs of their desired beverage.

Guided by Randy Mosher's *Tasting Beer* (which also serves as the core text for the Cicerone program), the Beer Judge Certification Program's seventy-nine-page style guide, and small glasses to serve as temporary homes for our beers, Alex directed us through the entire process of beer: the history, ingredients, brewing process, tasting notes, and so forth.[60] In the small yet brightly lit classroom where we met every Wednesday evening for ten weeks, we spent the first half of each class learning about the designated style of the week. The second half of each class was devoted to sipping examples of the style, often with cheese or food to be paired with the brews, as we discussed their respective flavor profile, color, and mouthfeel. One week, Alex asked us to take out a sheet of paper from our notebooks and draw a grid of sixteen boxes. Looking around at each other, we were unsure what we were about to encounter until Alex walked around placing grains ranging from pale off-white to deep dark brown on our papers. The grains were separated and placed in each box, where we wrote the name of each. Then we chewed them. A pinch from each box. One by one. From sweet rice to the skillfully charred and purposely burnt.

We tasted beer from the inside out.

Another week, Alex brought in a case with small vials of liquid. He bought the case from the Cicerone program. Each vial contained a non-toxic liquid that could be applied to each beer to give it undesirable off-flavor such as cardboard or skunk. If your beer tastes like cardboard, that's a sign of oxidation, meaning air had gotten into the beer during the bottling or canning process, while it was in the bottle or can, or at some other point between production and consumption. If your beer tastes skunky, it means that the hops were exposed to UV rays from sunlight or florescent lights at some point during or after fermentation. Light creates the same chemical—mercaptan—that exists in skunks' secreted spray. This can happen easily to beer in clear bottles, like a Corona or Miller Genuine Draft, because they don't block any light. Hence, most if not all craft brewers use dark bottles that block 98 percent of light or cans that keep their brews completely safe from invading rays.

The issue about light is important throughout the grand craft beer scene, but it takes on heightened importance in Nevada, where the sun shines brightly most days of the year. Irrespective of environmental context, however, Alex's lesson about off-flavors brought home an important point about the aesthetics of beer and perhaps about aesthetics in general. That is, sensuous knowledge of any cultural product is not just about recognizing beauty. It's about knowing what is flawed, why, and how to fix it. That type of knowledge is indispensable for brewers but has become almost equally important to consumers making well-informed evaluative judgments about the significant objects that define the scene they're participating in.

Aesthetic Entrepreneurship, or How to Change Others' Tastes

"We don't necessarily need more good beers in Las Vegas," one brewery rep tells me. "We need more good beer drinkers." For a scene to form and become recognized throughout a city, and even beyond its borders, it needs others willing to connect knowledge to action and, in effect, connect those in the know to those at the beginning of their path toward "beervana." These barrel-aged bodhisattvas and evangelists of hops, people individually and collectively trying to use craft beer to help others taste what they deem as the good life, are *aesthetic entrepreneurs*. Sociologists Dennis Waskul and Phillip Vannini write that when individuals interpret and give meaning to sensory stimuli in everyday practices and interactions, they are doing "somatic work."[61] They note that "somatic work implicates aesthetic and moral dimensions of sense-making and impression management." Aesthetic entrepreneurs engage in somatic work but take their labor one step further by actively trying to change the available sensory stimuli in a particular context in order to affect others' embodied experiences.

To make such changes, to purposely resense, or reassemble, the city,[62] is the crux of aesthetic entrepreneurialism. The idea of entrepreneurship, however, is often marred by its conventional connections to the business sector. The qualities of being entrepreneurial are often connected to making new products or services that will yield a profit. This is how "conventional entrepreneurship" is often defined, stemming from economist Joseph Schumpeter's classic theories of development of wealth under capitalism.[63] His ideas have provided justification for focusing on individual traits rather than social circumstances or relations to predict or explain economic successes.[64] Of course many in the craft beer business want to make money, but they often talk about trying to keep the lights on rather than getting bigger lights.

The inclusion of *aesthetic* as a qualifier for entrepreneurship is intended to demarcate the sensuous side of creativity that reaches beyond the dollars and cents of economics and moves toward the emotions and senses of embodied and emplaced persons.

The aesthetic entrepreneur shouldn't be confused with the "cultural entrepreneur." The qualifier "cultural" has been used to discuss the roles of the entrepreneur in the "culture industries" and the arts, the cultural context of entrepreneurship, the entrepreneurial practices like storytelling that conventional entrepreneurs use to mobilize resources, and the claims-making practices of leaders of public debates over cultural symbols.[65]

In his work on cultural entrepreneurship, sociologist Paul DiMaggio shows how, in the mid-nineteenth century, Boston's elite—the Boston Brahmins—actively resisted the perceived debasement of culture that they viewed was caused by growing working-class/popular sentiments in their city. In order to "save" high culture, elites institutionalized the distinctions between the categories of "true art" and popular entertainments by creating the Boston Symphony Orchestra and the Museum of Fine Arts. Because they were working in the realm of the arts, DiMaggio defines them as cultural entrepreneurs. This limits the qualifier "cultural" and overestimates their differences from conventional entrepreneurs. In fact, urban developers have often relied on the "cultural" qualifier to connect with yet ultimately *use* the arts as a means for massaging public perceptions of often socially hazardous "upscaling" and gentrification-inducing renewal projects.[66] Sociologist David Grazian likens cultural entrepreneurs to "con men" trying to swindle the young and hip into partaking in the consumer pleasures offered by entertainment zones with velvet-roped clubs and high-concept restaurants.[67]

A narrow view of cultural entrepreneurs like DiMaggio's sees them as *only* patrons of the arts who are involved with economic exchanges. And a critical view like Grazian's risks seeing cultural entrepreneurs as *only* master manipulators. Sociologist Richard Swedberg presents a more inclusive view based on his reading of Schumpeter's ideas.

> I argue (in Schumpeter's spirit) that economic entrepreneurship primarily aims at creating something new (and profitable) in the area of the economy, while cultural entrepreneurship aims at creating something new (and appreciated) in the area of culture. While moneymaking is often a crucial component of cultural entrepreneurship, it does not constitute

> its primary focus. Cultural entrepreneurship, as I see it, may therefore be defined as *the carrying out of a novel combination that results in something new and appreciated in the cultural sphere.*[68]

Swedberg's definition helps us connect practice and product. He does not, however, help us incorporate the sensuous aspects of local culture and of those who are trying to do "somatic work" in cities. This is precisely where using "aesthetic" as a qualifier comes into play for the sake of analytic and empirical precision when we acknowledge that "somatic work" exists in and through *all* arenas of the cultural sphere.

Aesthetic entrepreneurs equipped with sensuous knowledge of their product and the city they work within come in a few forms within the craft beer scene. The most obvious candidates are brewery owners and their support personnel who engage in acts of "place making."[69] In postindustrial cities, old and sometimes abandoned buildings have often been refurbished as a means for connecting to the heritage of local culture.[70] Critics often connect repurposed renovations to issues of gentrification, but those discussions usually stop there without fully uncovering the aesthetic affordances of breweries beyond the commodification of "authenticity." When a brewery opens in a neighborhood or even in a nondescript industrial park, it brings with it a certain aesthetic regardless of the presence of brick walls and exposed beams. Even from the outside, the smells of brewing beer can flood the air. Silos filled with grains can often be seen upon approach. Many people, including myself, assumed that the white tower outside the original Tenaya Creek location was just for show. Nope. There were grains sitting in there ready to be milled and boiled.

Las Vegas has never been an industrial city. Its products have always been experiences and services. So there aren't many old buildings for breweries to take over. And "old" is relative. For better and for worse, with the exception of Tenaya Creek's new location in an uninhibited plumbing supply store built in the late 1960s in Downtown's Historic Westside, local breweries have primarily had to either build their own places (e.g., Big Dog's, Lovelady) or move into bland, monochromic tan office parks spotted with uninviting dark-tinted windows (e.g., Bad Beat, CraftHaus).

When Dave and Wyndee Forrest decided to open CraftHaus in an office park, they were overly aware of the need to make their taproom a comfortable place for people to gather. It needed to be a place that reflected the aesthetic sensibility of their beers. And because craft beer was still relatively new in Las Vegas in 2014 when they opened, the pressure was greater than it might have been if they had been entering an already established scene rather than helping pioneer something that had yet to exist. So they carried out a "novel combination" of the bland outside and a bright colorful inside to create a place where craft beer geeks, casual drinkers, and neophytes would want to come from all over the valley and drink their beer, rather than simply come, pick up beer, and go home.

Their signature style is based on a modern reworking of German cuckoo clocks. "We have cuckoo clocks on our wall set to each time zone we're originally from," says Wyndee, who is responsible for the taproom's decor. "These craftsmen devoted a lot of time in making these one-of-a-kind clocks, and we thought, 'That's what we're doing with our beers.'" The clocks aren't only on the walls though. Their logo on the shirts, hats, and glassware that welcome you after walking through the tinted glass doors is a two-dimensional neon green clock with a tulip glass on top of it, an ode to both the burgeoning craft beer scene in Las Vegas and Germany's revered traditional brewing legacy. A large metal version of the logo is back lit and bookended by six-foot cutouts of cans of their two original brews, Evocation Saison and Resinate IPA, each emblazoned with CraftHaus's name and logo.

CraftHaus's co–head brewers, Steve Brockman and Steph Cope, praise Wyndee's attention to detail. "I love the bright logo and the colors around the taproom," Steph places her hand on the slick glass that sits atop used wood pallets and holds both our beers and potted succulents, "and even this cool table works so nicely with our bright and flavorful beers."

According to sociologist Richard Sennett, "The good craftsman is a poor salesman, absorbed in doing something well, unable to explain the value of what he or she is doing."[71] This seems to ring true at CraftHaus, where Steve and Steph can devote their time to the "art and science of brewing"—a phrase they both use often—leaving the outward presentation to the other couple. Because Steve and Steph have traveled and worked in breweries in major craft beer hubs (e.g., Denver, Portland, San Diego), they are quite aware that their beers don't exist in a cultural vacuum. Influencing the aesthetic demeanor of the city beyond their taproom nevertheless starts with the taproom. And a taproom in Las Vegas, says Steve, has challenges that others in more craft-beer-centric cities don't have to face.

> It's not like San Diego where you can get away with a jockey box in a shed. People here want a nice comfortable place to take a break and enjoy their beer. In San Diego, for example, the interest [in craft beer] is already so high. But to get people into craft beer here, where people are surrounded by some of the most lavish stuff in the world on the Strip, a few couches in a warehouse isn't going to cut it.

Steve's comment speaks to the influence of geographical context on the work of local aesthetic entrepreneurs. In order to attract new demographics to new sensuous experiences, aesthetic entrepreneurs cannot operate on the assumption of universal, decontextualized, and disembodied aesthetic principles. This is similar to the underdeveloped and underappreciated point Lofland makes about the pleasures derived from cities' built environments. In order to understand such pleasures, it's better to observe how people react and interact rather than fall back on assumptions about "pan-human . . . prescribed designs."[72] It also recalls sociologist Paul Willis's call for a "grounded aesthetics" that is indebted to the common culture of everyday life.[73] We can see this in Steve's next statement:

> We love how Wyndee went out of her way to step up the scenery. . . . A guy who's become a bit of a regular once said to me, "You guys are the

> best fucking coffee shop ever." I was like that's pretty much the vibe we're going for. He's like, "Yeah this is a cool place to hang out, and I can have a good beer here too. Feels good."

Without aesthetic entrepreneurs to design comfortable places for people to drink craft beer with other craft beer drinkers, the scene would go flat.

Making our way through and across the scene's widely dispersed aesthetic ecology, it's easy to notice the growing presence of such persons and the places they've established. That list includes CraftHaus's brewing neighbors—Bad Beat and the newest addition to the scene, Astronomy Aleworks (who are using space themes for their beers' names and their taproom's decor)—and other local breweries trying to survive without gaming, as well as non-gaming craft-centric places like Tacos & Beer and relative newcomer 595 Craft and Kitchen. Owner and manager Van-Alan Nguyen of 595 moved from craft-beer-soaked San Diego to Las Vegas, in part to help the city's beer scene move closer in the direction of craft. His aesthetic entrepreneurship has been quickly awarded by a loyal local following that devours the restaurant's banh mi sandwiches as much as its twenty-plus rotating draft selections.

While members of the Nevada Craft Brewers Association have sought to connect the dots between the scene's various places as an umbrella organization, Steve Wright physically connects the dots by driving people to multiple spots during his beer tours. I noted earlier that Steve's "experiential career" moved through the three paths outlined in this chapter—from awakening to connoisseurship to entrepreneurship—all of which came from a desire to connect to and be a part of local culture.

"I'm not a brewer. I'm not a bartender. But I love craft beer and the people," says Steve. "I wanted to give something back. So we started Sin City Brew Tours as a way to show off the cool beer in Las Vegas." Steve's entrepreneurship is evidence of the scene's maturation. And it comes full circle when, in his position as tour guide, he gets to introduce neophytes to the world of craft beer as they taste the city's various offerings, potentially awakened to the aesthetic realities they didn't think were even possible or available in Las Vegas.

Aesthetic Knowledge and the Rise of Scenes

Local scenes don't emerge by themselves, nor are they the province of traditional urban boosters. They exist in a more organic, albeit more haphazard way than traditional communities. Instead of being based on relatively fixed social attributes, they require voluntary membership that accommodates a variety of roles and levels of knowledge. And the levels of knowledge of persons within a scene are the result of contact with the local, translocal, and virtual manifestations of scenes.

We've seen how the local aids the development of awakened palates through direct contact between individuals, material products, and other persons. The translocal provides knowledge that surpasses or at least can outlive the local context. And the virtual can provide new forms of knowledge for the connoisseur and can also be a means for connecting the locally awakened to one another. The aesthetic entrepreneur draws from all three levels of the scene to bring it back home, to the local level, to affect the local scene itself. Sociologists Daniel Silver and Terry Nichols Clark note that highlighting urban scenes "directs our focus not at 'common values' or 'ways of life' that are hermetically sealed from 'other cultures' but rather at multiple, loosely binding, more flexible arrays of local meanings."[74] The various roles of scene participants and their varying degrees of knowledge acquisition and usage coalesce into a continuous yet paradoxically stable and malleable definable collective entity that exists outside of any one particular individual. As much as learning to taste feels like a personal endeavor, it isn't. It is a social act and a social practice. Learning to taste, through either informal or formal means, is dependent upon others, including the aesthetic qualities of material objects and physical places.

So while sipping on a beer while sitting on my patio might feel like a personal act, it is connected to a multitude of others who brewed the beer, who had the knowledge that they gained from others to brew the beer, who made the beer available, and who taught me how to sip and savor it. It's not about me. It's about them and the scene they made happen and keep making happen.

Conclusion

Whose Beer? Whose City?

The stories that make up our lives are ever unfolding, with multiple ends and beginnings and broken narratives and convoluted plot lines that are both stranger *and* more ordinary than fiction. Lucky is the ethnographer who, regardless of time spent in the field, is able to observe and participate in a flow of events as they occur naturally that satisfies the key characteristics of a story. I don't want to put myself in the lucky category. That would be too self-congratulatory and narcissistic. Yet I am lucky. I'm lucky that my family and I were safe at home, three miles down the road from Mandalay Bay Resort and Casino, on the night a gunman aimed and fired his rigged automatic rifles at an unsuspecting crowd. A sea of bullets designed to rip through armor and bones rained down from the thirty-second floor of the hotel. They flew through the cool desert air across the Strip and into the crowd for ten minutes, taking the lives of fifty-eight people and injuring hundreds of others attending the last night of the Route 91 country music festival.

On October 1, 2017—now dubbed One October—Las Vegas was home to the largest mass shooting in US history. It will forever remain in the collective memory of Las Vegas locals, many of whom at least knew someone who knew someone who was at the concert that night.[1] And many more knew someone who knew someone who helped out by donating blood or cooking meals for first responders and victims or getting a Las Vegas–themed tattoo whose proceeds were donated to the Las Vegas Victim's Fund.

Like other cities that have experienced traumatic events in recent years, such as the Boston Marathon bombing of 2003 or Orlando's Pulse nightclub shooting in 2016, Las Vegas locals quickly adopted the Vegas Strong moniker as a social media hashtag and local source of recovery and recuperation.

But what does this have to do with craft beer besides the fact that, for better and for worse, people often turn to alcohol to help ease their pain after a tragedy occurs? First, members of the food and beverage industry were present the night of the concert serving attendees. Many of those people had connections to or were full participants in the local craft beer scene. Second, regardless of how temporary or fleeting moments of association often are between scene members, the shooting and the collective trauma it instigated compelled the scene to act more like a traditional community, or at least in the ways we tend to think of them. The connective tissue of the collective had been damaged, but as sociologist Kai Erikson writes, "It is the *community* that cushions pain, the *community* that provides a context for intimacy, the *community* that serves as repository for binding traditions."[2] Scenes often face outward to express what they are to newcomers and the uninitiated. Here, the scene turned inward to help heal its own.

A few days after the shooting, I stopped in at Office Bar on my way home from a day of teaching. Actually, I did a lot more listening than speaking in my classes that day. I wanted to open the floor to anyone who wanted to talk about what we all just went through. I heard stories of graduate students huddled in offices as they watched UNLV become a temporary trauma center and a gathering place for people who couldn't get home or back to their hotel rooms. I heard stories of people fleeing to find their friends lost in the scrambling crowd. And I heard stories of voluntary heroism, like one of my undergraduate students who was driving in the area as the shooting was happening and used her truck to shuttle people to safety.

My students' stories were still swirling in my head as I found a seat at the bar. Even though his shift was over, Tony was still hanging around while Matt served me a beer. Both bartenders usually welcome me with a smile, a fist bump, and a rundown of the new beers they just got in. Though we were surrounded by alcohol, the mood was noticeably sober that day.

I wanted something local. Matt gave me a twelve-ounce snifter of Able Baker's Honey Dip Stout. I smelled it, sipped it, and then took a photo to post on Instagram that included #vegasstrong. We didn't talk much about the beer that afternoon. We exchanged stories about people we knew who were at Route 91, about media reports and conspiracy theories, and about all the pizza Chris Palmeri made for people at hospitals across the valley. Naked City Pizza is connected to Office Bar, separated only by a wall and small window for bartenders to place orders and receive food. As if on cue, Chris, the owner of Naked City, walked in and up to the bar. I leaned over and thanked him for what he had done. He looked exhausted.

"We cooked over eight thousand slices," Chris muttered. "Eight thousand! But I'm just thankful for all the people who volunteered to drive to the people who needed to eat." He then ordered the same beer I did.

"To Vegas!" we said as we clinked glasses.

Days turned into weeks and sorrow mixed with local pride.[3] Tired of the sadness and fear that engulfed his city in the weeks after that fateful night, head brewer Kyle Weniger gathered his team at Joseph James and a few other industry friends to help celebrate the myriad ways locals dealt with the tragedy. And he did what he does best. He brewed a beer. With other local brewers. With local ingredients.

And they called it Vegas Strong Ale.

The beer was born as a true partnership with other breweries and businesses. It was brewed with chocolate courtesy of Hexx Kitchen+Bar, the coffee beans were donated by Mothership Coffee Roasters, and the honey came from Pahrump Honey Company and was paid for by Motley Brews, the group behind local beer festivals and other events. The Brewers Supply Group and Tenaya Creek Brewery donated the malt and PT's Brewing lent the hops. The thirty-six 15-gallon kegs landed at most

FIGURE C.1. Not long after the tragedy of One October, local brewers collaborated to make a beer that represented Las Vegas and could help their city heal.

of the scene's key nodes, where they were purchased at full price. *All* of the proceeds from the limited brew were donated, as was the normal margin from distributor Nevada Beverage. The collaborative brew clocked in at about 8.5 percent ABV and was both bold and sweet. Because the Vegas Strong Ale, which wasn't bottled or canned, could be found only on tap, it forced scene members of all types to leave their homes and enjoy the beer in public. Together.

Regardless of how trivial brewing a beer might be when compared to the grueling work of first responders and hospital workers, it still shows a way that people relate to the world with and through other people and cultural objects alike. The Vegas Strong Ale served as a rallying point, as a totem, that both *showed* and *shaped* the bonds of belonging and social solidarity.[4] In this way, even those who weren't involved in brewing the beer could still take ownership of it as the beer's mere existence and presence speaks for the scene's values of local lore and attachment. The beer takes on the attitude of the scene and the scene takes on the attitude of the beer. Vegas Strong Ale, then, is more than a symbol. Rather, it acts on and is "entangled" with the scene, its members, and all others who encounter it.[5]

It took time, effort, and a higher degree of aesthetic maturation for the local scene to be in a position to offer something like Vegas Strong Ale. Indeed, much has changed in the Las Vegas craft beer scene since I started studying it. Once sought-after beers now sit on shelves at bottle shops and liquor stores. Craft beer can be found and consumed while watching minor league baseball or college basketball or eating ramen or pho in Chinatown or attending a concert at the Brooklyn Bowl on the Strip. Social and cultural change doesn't happen on its own. A scene, as a mechanism of and for change, is an interactive and interactional accomplishment brought to life by the labor and love of passionate producers and consumers, as well as those intermediaries who bridge the gap between the two.

The passion of the local scene's core participants has elevated it beyond a mere niche subculture or market. With ever increasing options from the over six thousand breweries nationwide, craft beer has moved from the fringe onto the menus and into the glasses of respective mainstream places and persons, pushing the boundaries of its original oppositional fortitude as new initiates are brought into the expanding fold. Is a bigger scene a better scene? The answer is "no" for exclusive status mongers. But it's an unquestionable "yes" for both those who want to spread the gospel of craft with evangelical zeal and those who simply want a greater selection of crafted wares and related happenings within their local confines. And it certainly helps out the local breweries trying to keep lights on and, for the sake of the scene, master their craft.

The scene has grown a great deal since I began my fieldwork in earnest in 2014. Some stages have grown, emerged, shifted, and disappeared. Some actors have exited and their roles have been filled by dutiful understudies or newcomers or recent transplants. I observed. I listened. And I participated in the key aesthetic practices that, along with its significant objects, breathe life into the scene.

So, after many conversations, many of which were over craft beers from here and elsewhere, what did I "untap" in Las Vegas, and what does it reveal about the expressive and sensuous experiences of and in contemporary cities? What have we gleaned about the multiple levels of scale that local scenes work on, through, and with? How do scenes work as necessary forms of associations by providing social settings for social interactions with others and with mutually desired significant objects? And how do they do so in the face of the paradoxically coupled social forces of homogenization and individuation?

To answer these questions and others, let's recall the three main components of a scene that have shaped the analysis presented throughout this book. First, it is an *expressive* entity. It is a collective claims-making tool, a social mechanism that both shapes and is shaped by participants' ideas and ideals of the core thing, the significant object, that summons participants to and participation in the scene itself. More than a mere value-neutral collectivity, as if there could even be such a thing, a scene provides stability beyond individual preferences for making evaluative judgments about taste and tasting.

Second, participation in a scene is *voluntary*. Unlike other more common social attributes, becoming a member of a scene is the result of choices rather than inherited demands. Here then is taste as sense and sensibility, a learned activity of embodied knowledge that participants often have to go out of their way to acquire. And third, scenes are *public*. Though they may function more like parochial realms populated with acquaintances with common interests, they exist in the public realm.[6] They are available in and through publicly open places for both hardcore members to congregate and reinforce their aesthetic disposition and for newcomers to enter and become acquainted with the people and places and the things that foster the scene. And as a public entity, it forms an "aesthetic ecology" as a stage for the "visceral politics" of taste and tasting that can influence the power dynamics in and reputation of a city for both insiders and outsiders.[7]

The Las Vegas craft beer scene satisfies all three dimensions. More importantly, using the three dimensions as an analytical and heuristic device allows us to see the ways that each is accomplished through the embodied practices of emplaced persons in local settings, albeit with connections to a translocal grand scene often facilitated by the social-media-driven virtual scene.

What Does the Scene Say?

As the scene is an expressive entity, claims about it come in verbal, textual, visual, and behavioral forms.[8] From the yeast that eats the sugar necessary for alcohol that creates gurgling bubbles of oxygen to the clinking of snifters with freshly poured elixirs and the focused attention paid to each sip thereafter, we can hear, see, and taste the decisive cries of the "ethos of craft."[9] This ethos traverses the boundaries of work and leisure and is embodied by brewers, distributors, bartenders, and drinkers alike. It is an aesthetic disposition that takes a normative stance that values the creative processes of production and consumption. Though mechanical equipment is necessary for modern-day brewing at any scale, craft brewers pride themselves on using both their hands and their minds in opposition to the presumed perils of automation used by Big Beer macrobreweries. And consumers are happy to pay higher prices for the fermented fruits of their labor.

Craft is small-scale, whereby small implies a sense of humanity while large assumes the impersonal. Craft is the creative blending of art and science in the search not for truth or beauty but rather for an aura of authenticity. Though the values associated with authenticity are paradoxical—summoning the appeal to either tradition or novelty, or both—the desire for it nevertheless propels the ethos of craft as an oppositional force against the impinging power of Big Beer and its Big Contracts with Big Casinos.[10] The ethos of craft espouses a postindustrial nostalgia for the preindustrial coupled with a forward-looking creative impulse. "Craft encourages sensitivity and empathy for one's medium" whereby the core medium or object of a scene is an active participant who "determines, develops, and changes throughout a process, requiring minute, subtle reactions and decisions by the craftsperson."[11]

Craft beer is as much an arena for the master technician as it is for the playful artist. As such, creativity and innovation are rewarded despite the reputational and economic risks of experimentation. From CraftHaus's "tweaks" of their core beers (e.g., brewing their Evocation Saison with hibiscus flowers) to Tenaya Creek's off-line series of one-time experiments (e.g., blending their imperial stout with their brown ale and resting it on toasted coconut, vanilla, and cocoa nibs) to Bad Beat's limited-release hazy IPAs with inventive names and nuanced combinations of hops (e.g., Ja Boi Can Handle His Hops brewed with Amarillo, Hallertau Blanc, and Waimea hops), locals flood these breweries' respective taprooms to try something new and, counterintuitively, on trend beyond the local.

Creativity in the craft beer scene is often born out of collaboration, as the aforementioned Vegas Strong Ale suggests. But creativity and collaboration aren't confined to brewing. They happen in, and often in concert with, the realms of distribution and consumption. The first two Beer Zombies Festivals, in 2017 and 2018, for example, would not have happened if collaboration weren't a part of the craft ethos. Working under that same aesthetic umbrella, Beer Zombies—the equally virtual and embodied persona of Chris Jacobs—combined forces with boutique distributor Dave Bowers—who moved from Tacos & Beer to help local craft distribution at Vin Sauvage—and Rose Signor—the general manager and craft curator at Atomic Liquors in Downtown Las Vegas. We've heard from all three of these local actors in previous chapters. Chris used his increasingly popular online identity to connect with new up-and-coming breweries outside of Las Vegas and worked with Dave to bring their wares to the city for a festival hosted by Rose's famed bar. All three have achieved a quasi–local celebrity status for their work in, with, and on the scene and created a festival that not only sold out each year, but became a source of pride for locals to both embrace and enable. Through the organizers' actions and those of the festival's attendees, a collective pronouncement was made about Las Vegas: forget what you've heard, this desert city is no longer a beer desert.

Herein lies perhaps the most resounding aspect and effect of the scene's expressivity. It has conjured a renewed and redefined *feeling* about the city. The scene engenders a collective sentiment and sentimentality that fosters re-enchanted local "place attachment" and gratification. Across the United States, "neolocalism" has emerged as an antidote to mass feelings of unrooted or even uprooted placelessness. In their analysis of the first big jump in American microbreweries—when there were only around one thousand nationwide and it was mostly a coastal phenomenon—geographers Steven Schnell and Joseph Reese saw it as a response to "the smothering homogeneity of popular, national culture" and as a means for people to "reestablish connections with local communities, settings, and economies."[12] This scenario has played out on the local Las Vegas stage with an intoxicating amount of gusto as part of a complex and melodramatic play between local residents and their city.

Craft beer is not only a symbol of the local scene; its physical presence and sensuous effects act as a key character in the counternarrative to the dominant stories of and about Las Vegas. Though Las Vegas and the "Vegas Baby" tales of debauchery shown throughout popular media and repeated after tourists' blurry weekend trips are no strangers to alcohol, the combined practices of aesthetic discernment by scene participants present a more refined and rarefied engagement with intoxicating wares and, in turn, with each other.

Schnell and Reese, and others who have followed their lead, focused their attention on locally brewed craft beers and how they support local place attachment. I found that beers from elsewhere also play substantial roles in the local scene. A vibrant beer scene is made up of a mix of local and translocal products, not unlike the mix of local natives and newcomers who produce the scene itself through their practice of, and not just belief in, an ethos of craft. Origins of the brews aside, the drinking of them by embodied and emplaced persons facilitates collective and communal bonding with and through the desired and desirable beers. The scene, then, can be said to express taste as a way of being in the world that necessarily depends on other people as both producers and consumers of crafted goods and services.

Whose Scene Is It?

Either as an individual contemplative act of discerning the various smells, colors, flavors, and mouthfeel of a beer or as a social activity where the facets of various beverages are debated and celebrated, craft beer drinking is admittedly fun. And so are brewing, serving, and distributing it. If there was one thing that all my field experiences had in common, besides beer, it was the pervasive presence of smiles. And it wasn't just the beer talking. Smiles were indicators of ownership, an ownership of experiences and voluntary actions within a scene that was theirs, though not theirs alone.

Instead of thinking of fun as merely a psychological state or as something only individuals have, we're better off understanding fun as a social activity and phenomenon.[13] Fun is not embedded within individual acts themselves. It is a consequence, and effect (and affect), of social relations that are voluntarily *chosen*. Part of what makes scenes fun in and of themselves is that, unlike more relatively static and binding attributes like race, class, and gender, participation is voluntary. The power to choose to be a part of a scene, and how much to be a part of it, provides a looseness and flexibility that many find endearing and uplifting. Following sociologist Michel Maffesoli, this type of "elective sociality" can serve as a means for the re-enchantment of social life.[14] As simple as it might seem, the acts of choosing to be with others who have similar aesthetic affinities and gathering around a shared object of desire are fun.

Moments of fun express and are enhanced by two significant aspects of scene participation that are distinct but related: engagement with the scene and engagement with the scene's core object. First, levels of participation necessarily vary. In the local scene, there is a continuum of participation from the hardcore members who hold up the center (e.g., the "beer geeks," the brewers, the distributors, the bartenders) to those on the periphery who benefit from the core while also supporting it by buying and imbibing craft beer instead of Big Beer. There are no small roles. All participants play roles that add to the stability of the scene beyond any single actor's status or charisma. Over the course of my research, I've seen plenty of people leave Las Vegas and then watched others take their place or at least one adjacent to the spot they left open. This type of flexibility aides in the stability of a scene as it survives after losing core members. The forms of engagement and interaction remain the same despite the turnover. And such turnover also adds to the scene's dynamism.

As a dynamic entity, the scene is composed of smaller groups. There's the northwest valley crowd that frequents Big Dog's and the one that held regular bottle shares at the old Tenaya Creek location. There's the Khoury's crowd whose regular Wednesday, and often Friday, bottle shares provide shared experiences on the southern end. There's the Beer Zombies bunch that shift between Downtown's Atomic and Spring Valley's 595 Craft and Kitchen for festivals, bottle shares, and tap offerings. CraftHaus, Bad Beat, and Lovelady breweries—all in the southeastern corner of the valley—all have their devotees. And there are also the "traveling packs" not beholden to any specific geography. In fact, most of the individuals in the various small groups often overlap for particular events to form a grand "traveling pack" that, in turn, morphs into a citywide scene with porous boundaries. The scene is open enough to include wavering levels of participation and commitment between and within individuals in a way that an inclusive group's "style" might constrict the rules of engagement.[15]

Moreover, the flexible boundaries of a scene allow for *pluralism without consensus*. That is, the ethos of craft might be adopted when it comes to beer, but that doesn't necessarily or automatically translate to other areas of one's social life. There isn't a clear "homology" between taste preferences and other social attributes, though social class, race, and gender obviously affect access and experience. But assuming that aesthetic choices are primarily subconscious and predetermined modes of reception is highly problematic because social actors are afforded little or no power to endow the things they consume with significance or meaning. I found fewer affinities between aesthetic dispositions and, say, political leanings than I expected when I started my research. I've met craft beer enthusiasts who voted for Hillary Clinton, voted for Donald Trump, or didn't vote at all. I've met gun-loving and gun-fearing men and women who equally and forcefully defend their right to craft beer. Even in other arenas of the cultural sphere, some like heavy metal and punk, others like noodling jam bands, while others lean toward top-forty hits or hip-hop bangers.

As a means for pleasure-seeking social behavior, the scene allows for a variety of ideologies and pop culture preferences to exist with in it, yet can minimize differences in relation to the scene's core object. A certain "moral minimalism"[16] both provides stability beyond individual preferences and gives rise to a taste etiquette that supports the desire or goal of living an authentic, sacred, or "good life," however defined. In this way, scene is both a more powerful conceptual tool and a more honest reflection of urban culture than small groups, however valuable they are for studying interpersonal dynamics. As an aesthetic umbrella under which small groups gather, scenes have a greater spatial reach, both locally and beyond.[17] Scenes highlight the important parts of a city's civic culture that promote inclusivity and heterogeneity in ways that small groups by themselves cannot.

To assume that any scene is entirely open would be foolish. But I found that the Las Vegas craft beer scene allows enough room for both the neophyte and the connoisseur to coexist within it and feel comfortable. Regardless of sanctioned credentials or years of craft beer experience, the connoisseurs I met, and learned from, are eager to educate newcomers. They're eager to pass along a specific form of knowledge, a sensuous embodied knowledge that helps individuals connect through a common language and a host of common activities around a core object. Tasting is a learned activity. Understanding the different styles of beers is best acquired through an active and attentive engagement with them. For some, this comes through brewing. But for most, even those who brew for a profession or as a hobby, engagement comes through the main thing people do with beer. They drink it.

The ways that individuals engage with the significant object of desire provide an answer to who "owns" the scene. Instead of thinking of cultural amenities as determined by those controlling a city's purse strings, scenes belong to those who *choose* to use them to exercise their taste preferences through learned ways of tasting that bring people and objects together. Such acts of tasting require modes of evaluation and discernment for their own sake and not necessarily or automatically as symbolic markers of social position. "Fussing over" craft beer is a type of "serious leisure" that connects fussers to one another via a shared consecration of an object that is deemed worthwhile to fuss over. Though for some the joy of craft beer can come from hunting and gathering a rare limited release, the vast majority find joy through drinking, especially with others. They can then experience the beers together, discuss their nuances, and drink some more. This type of ritualistic intoxication results both from the alcohol and from moments of pure sociability, providing us with keen examples of the necessarily collective coproduction of taste, tasting, and fun.

Where Does the Scene Happen?

Like any other form of association—from the family to the nation—a scene is an idea. But that doesn't mean it exists only in people's heads. It is not a purely cognitive or mental formation. For a scene to exist, it must be publicly available, or "retrievable" as sociologist Michael Schudson would put.[18] Scenes are, according to cultural studies scholar Will Straw, "publicly observable clusters of urban sociability. . . . Scenes make cultural activity visible and decipherable by rendering it public, taking it from acts of private production and consumption into public contexts of sociability, conviviality, and interaction."[19] There is a physical and material component to *all* scenes. Even virtual scenes that happen through social media depend on physical devices to access others and physical places, like a desk with a computer or a park bench to sit on while scrolling with a smartphone. Local scenes are settled within places as people move in, through, and with them to participate in the scene's ritualized practices.

From the breweries to the bars and bottles shops, all of those places where beers are brewed, exchanged, or consumed in public provide a physical presence for and of the scene. Together, they are the conduits that the aura of the scene's "aesthetic ecology" flows through. Though most of these places, except for city- or county-owned plots where festivals are occasionally held, are commercial and, in turn, privately owned; they are essentially public because they are shared. And necessarily so.

Businesses need publics to survive. And publics—especially those that revolve around a core object of desire—need businesses for their scenes to survive. On a very basic level, these places supply the scene with significant objects to imbibe and languish over, even for homebrewers who rely on others to make malts, hops, and yeast cultures available. Though the consumption of brewed goods can happen in private, the movement from inception to distribution to consumption is a thoroughly public affair. The legal requirements of the three-tiered system reinforce it. A beer brewed at Joseph James is picked up by someone from Nevada Beverage, who then drops the bottles, cans, or kegs at bars, restaurants, liquor stores, and supermarkets across the Las Vegas Valley. Or on the rare occasions that a few cases of Cantillon make it to Las Vegas, they need to cross the Atlantic Ocean from Belgium and land at Shelton Brothers in Massachusetts, to then make their way into the eagerly waiting hands of Dave Bowers at Vin Sauvage. Dave might share a picture of the goodies on social media to make sour beer fans salivate. Then he'll drop them at a few of the scene's key nodes, where they're picked out of coolers, purchased, and taken home or, as is often the case at a place like Khoury's Fine Wine & Spirits, opened to share with fellow beer geeks and curious strangers.

The places where people *do* scene and *be* scene are the essential building blocks of local culture. Their outward appearances—from the silos filled with grains at breweries to stores advertising "craft beer sold here" or bars with signs from craft breweries hanging in their windows—provide a collective public face for the scene, announcing to those inside and outside of the scene that the ethos of craft is welcomed and supported. Like street names, graffiti, or lush green parks, such visual pronouncements are woven into the ongoing narratives of urban cultures.[20]

The scene's "magnet places" quite literally ground participants' actions and interactions in a definable way by providing stages for positively sanctioned behaviors that might seem odd elsewhere, like letting, or even encouraging, strangers to put their lips on your glass so they can try the beer you're drinking. This type of sharing provides a level of public intimacy that is rarely seen or acknowledged. But this particular practice is part of the craft beer scene's script, acted out on local and translocal stages. Today's urban scenes are often characterized by "less tightly written" scripts than those of the past so that "actors are freer to engage in somewhat spontaneous acting with others in particular social settings. . . . Even in the case of the more spontaneous, new urban scenes, there is a general outline of a script and roles, but these are loosely sketched . . . creating drama in interaction with other actors."[21] Dramatic moments aren't necessarily contentious moments. They are simply moments of heightened awareness of significant objects and the others who share in their significance.

Public dramas take form as public rituals that aide both the scripted stability and spontaneous fluidity of the scene. Seminal sociologist Émile Durkheim's ideas about rituals as binding mechanisms that generate *collective effervescence*—a motivating warm feeling within and between participants that signals solidarity and togetherness—are as relevant today as they were when he first wrote about them in 1912. For as Durkheim writes, "There are no immortal gospels, and there is no reason to believe that humanity is incapable of conceiving new ones."[22] The craft beer scene's gospels are enacted through the rituals of festivals, bottle shares, tap takeovers, beer dinners, and other moments when collective and individual attention is focused on the scene's consecrated object. Following Durkheim's argument that through rituals people in effect worship themselves because their sacred objects embody the ideals and values that they themselves hold, we can make the same argument about the craft beer scene and its public events. Drinking and sharing beers with others are public displays of affection and affiliation.

As the number of ritualized craft beer events increases across the Las Vegas Valley, they actively butt up against the dominant cultural logic that the city has operated under for decades. The publicness of such rituals forces through the *reputational constraints* of the city's prevailing image and helps redefine with happens in Vegas. Instead of withdrawing to the privacy of their own homes, local participants come to these events to be with others who, in variable and varying ways, have used craft beer to find their city and change the way it tastes.

Crafting Re-enchantment

Have you ever tried to take a picture of something in motion? Maybe a train as it rumbles through the desert. Maybe a plane straightening its wings for a soft landing. Or a kid, maybe your kid, jumping through sprinklers to cool off in the summer. Whatever the subject may be, the photo usually ends up blurry and never seems to capture the *feeling* of the moment. At many times I felt that way while researching and writing this book. From the time I started my research on the scene in 2014 to my last typed words about it in 2018, a lot has changed. More beers have been brewed. More beers are available at more places, including the

Strip. And more and more people are turning away from Big Beer and embracing the ethos of craft.

In order to do justice to Las Vegas (neon warts and all), craft beer (and its overwhelming variety of intoxicating versions), and the people who care about both, I set out to capture what this scene feels like, even as it twists and turns, with as much depth and clarity as I could. Popular culture is contested terrain, and writing about it is often harder than it may seem, especially when attending to the people, places, and things that people hold near and dear.

What happens to the scene from here on out will be of interest to those in it, to those near it, and to anyone interested in the ways that contemporary urbanites attempt to carve new ways to confront growing feelings of apathy, indifference, and alienation. At a time when many Americans distrust or even fear our most sacred social institutions, knowing that people are still actively trying to re-enchant the world they live in provides at least some sense of solace and hope for the future. That scenes can cross over and through more conventional social boundaries and allegiances for the sake of collective leisure and sensuous pleasure shows their importance both for living in or near contemporary American cities and for studying and learning from them. And if the craft beer scene can live up to its ideals of inclusivity, bringing greater diversity on the sides of both production and consumption, then the scene—in its local, translocal, and virtual manifestations—can serve as a model of and for living a well-crafted life. Cheers to that.

ACKNOWLEDGMENTS

Acclaimed British novelist and cultural critic Zadie Smith advises authors to "protect the time and space in which you write. Keep everybody away from it, even the people who are most important to you." This sage warning rang true as I wrote most of this book during the dark hours of night with the glare of a computer screen lighting my fingers as they jerked across the keys in front of me. The lamp staring at the books on my desk and the hundred or so squared notes stuck to the walls of my office were my only company while my most important people slept upstairs. Even my old black lab Greta knew to stay out and sleep on the living room couch while I was working.

But writing alone doesn't mean you're alone. It might feel like a solitary act, but when writing ethnography, the words and actions of others are not simply the qualitative fodder of analysis. They populate the book. And necessarily so. As a "professional stranger," I would sometimes catch myself at a beer festival or bottle share wondering if the people there had any idea how much time I spent listening to their words repeated through recordings or through rereading my scribbled field notes. I spent much more time with them than they did with me, achieving a level of intimacy that wasn't, and couldn't, be reciprocated.

It is to them, the people who make the local craft beer scene happen, the people who populate this book, that I owe the greatest debt and gratitude. I am deeply thankful to and for the folks who shared their time, their stories, and, for a good many, their beers with me. Whether through casual conversations or formal interviews, they welcomed me into their lives and revealed the intricacies of their passions. And many of them welcomed me into events they hosted so I could participate in the scene along with them. Though there are too many to name in full, the following individuals often went out of their way to answer my questions and point me to others for answers to other questions: Carl Askew, Dave Bowers, Steve Brockman, Steph Cope, Frank DiNicola, Mike Dominiak, Mike Gaddy, Alex Graham, Tom Harwood, Chris Jacobs, Sarah Johnson, Issa Khoury, Dave Moore, Michael Shetler, Rose Signor, Nick Tribulato, and Kyle Weniger. And to fellow local beer writers, Jim Begley and Pat Evans, cheers!

Outside the geographic confines of the local scene, I'm grateful to Julia Herz, Paul Gatza, and the Brewers Association for providing me with access to the Great American Beer Festival as well as to the Media Luncheon where I got to meet and hear from some of the most influential people in the world of craft beer.

I am lucky to have a position in a department where my colleagues, with varying degrees of interest in craft beer and local culture, are supportive of and interested in my work. I am sure that my increasing knowledge about beer both benefitted and bored them during happy hours and other get-togethers. To my UNLV folks down the hall and around the way, thanks go to Christie Batson, Barb Brents, Georgiann Davis, David Dickens, Robert Futrell, and Ranita Ray for your continued support, encouragement, and insights throughout the various stages of this project. Tyler Schafer was my research assistant and companion when I began my fieldwork and Maddie Jo Evans helped with her photography skills while the book was taking shape. And Celine Ayala served as a great conversation partner as we were both trying to understand various scenes in Las Vegas.

The University of Nevada, Las Vegas granted me a semester sabbatical leave that afforded me the time to fully immerse myself in the scene. I'm thankful for the Black Mountain Institute and its director, Joshua Wolf Shenk, for honoring me with a Faculty Fellowship that allowed me to spend even more time in the field and then a platform to talk about my work. My work also benefitted from travel funds from the university, the College of Liberal Arts, and the Department of Sociology.

I had a number of opportunities to present small portions of this book at conferences, including an invitation to give the George Herbert

Mead Lecture at the National Communication Association's annual meeting. Whether during formal panels and sessions or afterward during informal chats (often at bars or breweries near conference hotels), a number of scholars acted as springboards for my ideas and offered valuable feedback that strengthened the interpretations offered throughout this book. On this front, grateful thanks go to Tom DeGloma, Gary Alan Fine, William Ryan Force, Daina Cheyenne Harvey, Yuki Kato, Joe Kotarba, Maggie Kusenbach, Richard Lloyd, Melinda Milligan, Richard Ocejo, Dennis Waskul, and Jonathan Wynn.

I give special thanks to my longtime childhood friends Dan Smalheiser and Kris Nelson, both of whom work in the food and beverage industry in two of the greatest craft beer meccas, Denver, Colorado, and Burlington, Vermont, respectively. Their insights and support helped during every stage of my research and writing.

Ilene Kalish is a masterful editor. Her keen aesthetic eye and gracious wit, along with the continuous support and attention she gives to my ideas and writing, have made me a better scholar than I would be otherwise. Ilene and her team at NYU Press are incredible assets to writers and, without too much hyperbole, to the written word. And I have to acknowledge copy editor Joseph Dahm. His keen attention to detail and gentle nudges have implicitly taught me about my own writing quirks.

My father, Alan Borer, deserves credit for unknowingly introducing me to "good" beer when I stole some of his Brooklyn Brewery beers when I was too young to buy them myself. But as we both got older, I've tried my best to pay him back, for the beer and for his unconditional support.

This book is dedicated to my wife, Katrina, whose unwavering and unrivaled love made it possible. Thank you for keeping me from getting lost in either my work or my head. You're the best. And thank you to my beautiful sons, Silas and Julian, who, as an unintended consequence of this book, have visited far more breweries than any six- or two-year-old should.

APPENDIX A

Local Craft Breweries[a]

Name and Opening Year	Address and Area	Representative Beers
Big Dog's Brewing (est. 1993/2003)[b,c]	4543 N. Rancho Drive, Northwest	Red Hydrant Ale—English-style brown Tripel Dog Dare—Belgian-style tripel
Triple 7 Restaurant & Brewery (est. 1996)	200 N. Main St., Downtown	Carlsbad—IPA Black Chip—English porter
Ellis Island Casino & Brewery (est. 1998)[b,c]	4178 Koval Ln., the Strip	Light—light lager Amber—amber ale
Chicago Brewing Company (est. 1999)[b,c]	2201 S. Fort Apache Rd., Summerlin	Old Town Brown—brown ale Quad Damn It—Belgian-style quadrupel ale
Tenaya Creek Brewery (est. 2002)	831 W. Bonanza Rd., Downtown	Hop Ride—IPA Ol' Jackalope—barleywine
Barley's Casino & Brewing Co. (est. 2004)[b,c]	4500 E. Sunset Rd., Henderson	Blue Diamond—German Helles-style lager Black Mountain—dark lager
Sin City Brewing Co. (est. 2005)	3717 Las Vegas Blvd., the Strip	Never Pass Up on a Blonde—light lager Say Hello to Amber—amber ale
Boulder Dam Brewing (est. 2007)	453 Nevada Hwy., Boulder City	Hell's Hole—hefeweizen Black Canyon—American stout
Joseph James Brewing Co. (est. 2008)	155 N. Gibson Rd., Henderson (no taproom)	Citra Rye—pale ale Imperial smoked porter with cacao nibs
Banger Brewing (est. 2013)	450 Fremont St. #135, Downtown	El Heffe—jalapeño hefeweizen Morning Joe—coffee Kölsch
Able Baker Brewing (est. 2014)	155 N. Gibson Rd., Henderson (no taproom)	Honey Dip—imperial stout with honey and Madagascar vanilla beans then aged on American oak Chris Kael Impale'd Ale—imperial brown ale
Bad Beat Brewing (est. 2014)	7380 Eastgate Rd. #110, Henderson	Queen of Hearts—Berliner Weisse with pink guava and ginger BBA Morning Payoff—imperial breakfast stout aged in bourbon barrels

Local Craft Breweries *cont.*

Name and Opening Year	Address and Area	Representative Beers
CraftHaus Brewery (est. 2014)	7350 Eastgate Rd. #110, Henderson	Evocation—saison Amigo—Mexican imperial stout with Mexican vanilla, cocoa nibs, cinnamon, dried chilies
Hop Nuts Brewing (est. 2015)	1120 S Main St. #150, Downtown	18b—pale ale The Golden Knight—Belgian golden strong ale
Old School Brewing Co. (2015–17)[b,c]	8410 W. Desert Inn Rd., Spring Valley	Homeroom—hefeweizen Varsity—vanilla porter
Lovelady Brewing (est. 2016)	20 S. Water St., Downtown Henderson	Love Juice—New England–style IPA Outbock—bock/IPA hybrid
PT's Brewing Company (est. 2016)[c]	3101 N. Tenaya Way, Northwest	Hualapai—IPA Boulder—Irish-style nitro stout
Astronomy Aleworks (est. 2018)	7350 Eastgate Rd. #170, Henderson	Pluto IS A Planet—West Coast IPA Pluto IS NOT A Planet—New England–style IPA

a. Gordon Biersch, BJ's, and Yard House are not included because they are national chains.

b. Indicates that smoking is permitted inside.

c. Indicates presence of video poker at the bar.

APPENDIX B

Notable Local Craft Beer Bars and Restaurants[a]

Name and Opening Year	Address and Area	Craft Offerings
Atomic Liquors (est. 1945/2012)[b]	917 Fremont St., Downtown	18 rotating taps (one dedicated to Busch, style listed as "Crappy Lager") bottle and can list
The Sand Dollar Lounge (est. 1976/2009)	3355 Spring Mountain Rd., Chinatown	10 rotating taps bottle and can list
Office Bar (est. 1985)[b,c]	4608 Paradise Rd., East of Strip	14 rotating taps "Beer Zombies" Craft Beer Pop-Up Shop for bottles and cans
Money Plays (est. 1989)[b,c]	474 W. Flamingo Rd., West of Strip	24 rotating taps (about half are "crafty") Bottle and can list
Burger Bar (est. 2004)	3930 S. Las Vegas Blvd., the Strip (inside Mandalay Bay)	28 rotating taps Bottle and can list
Khoury's Fine Wine & Spirts (est. 2006)	9915 S. Eastern Ave. #110, Henderson	11 rotating taps Bottles and cans for sale plus cork-age fee for on-premise consumption
Aces & Ales—Nellis (est. 2009)[b,c]	3740 S. Nellis Blvd., Eastside	20 rotating taps Bottle list (offers rare and aged beers)
Holsteins (est. 2011)	3708 S. Las Vegas Blvd., the Strip (inside the Cosmopolitan)	20 rotating taps Bottle and can list
Public House (est. 2012)	3355 S Las Vegas Blvd., the Strip (inside the Venetian)	24 rotating taps; 3 casks Bottle and can list
Aces & Ales—Tenaya (est. 2013)[b,c]	2801 N. Tenaya Way, Northwest	50 rotating taps Bottle list
Tacos & Beer (est. 2013)	3900 Paradise Rd., East of Strip	20 rotating taps Bottle and can list
Pizza Rock—DTLV (est. 2013)	201 N. 3rd St., Downtown	23 rotating taps Bottle and can list
Rx Boiler Room (est. 2013)	3930 S. Las Vegas Blvd., the Strip (inside Mandalay Bay)	6 rotating taps including collabora-tion with local brewery CraftHaus
Velveteen Rabbit (est. 2013)	1218 S. Main St., Downtown	12 rotating taps Bottle and can list

Notable Local Craft Beer Bars and Restaurants *cont.*

Name and Opening Year	Address and Area	Representative Beers
District One (est. 2014)	3400 S. Jones Blvd. #8, Chinatown	8 rotating taps Bottle and can list
Public School 702 (est. 2015)	1850 Festival Plaza Dr., Summerlin	24 rotating taps Bottle and can list
Pizza Rock—GVR (est. 2015)	2300 Paseo Verde Pkwy., Henderson (inside Green Valley Ranch)	40 rotating taps Bottle and can list
PKWY Tavern (est. 2015)[b,c]	9820 W. Flamingo Rd.	120 rotating taps Bottle and can list
BeerHaus (est. 2016)	3784 S. Las Vegas Blvd., the Strip (at the Park MGM)	21 rotating taps Bottle and can list
Pub 365 (est. 2016)	255 E. Flamingo Rd., East of Strip (in the Tuscany)	60 rotating taps Bottle and can list (and the Unicorn list of rare and aged beers)
Rebel Republic (est. 2016)[b,c]	3540 W. Sahara Ave., West of Strip	26 rotating taps Bottle and can list
595 Craft and Kitchen (est. 2017)	4950 S. Rainbow Blvd., Spring Valley	24 rotating taps Bottle and can list
The Kitchen at Atomic (est. 2017)	927 Fremont St., Downtown	9 rotating taps Bottle and can list
Nevada Taste Site (est. 2018)	1221 S. Main St., Downtown	20 rotating taps (all Nevada beers)
Three Sheets Craft Beer Bar (est. 2018)	1115 S. Casino Center Blvd., Downtown	30 rotating taps Bottle and can list
Beers, Burgers, and Desserts (est. 2018)	2411 W. Sahara Ave., West of Strip (inside Palace Station)	35 rotating taps, 3 casks Bottle and can list

a. World of Beer and Yard House are not included because they are national chains.

b. Indicates that smoking is permitted inside.

c. Indicates presence of video poker at the bar.

NOTES

INTRODUCTION

1 Sociologist Melinda Milligan's influential work on "place attachment" juxtaposes a place's "interactional past" (persons' memories of it) with its "interactional potential" (persons' imagined expectations of it). I'm using her term here to connect expectations with the embodied experiences of individuals moving in and through the places that constitute the local ecology of a scene and, in turn, the city it's embedded within. See Melinda J. Milligan, "Interactional Past and Potential: The Social Construction of Place Attachment," *Symbolic Interaction* 21 (1998): 1–33.

2 See Richard Sennett, *The Craftsman* (New Haven, CT: Yale University Press, 2008).

3 Brewers Association, "National Beer Sales and Production" (2017), www.brewers association.org.

4 For example, in 2017, a distributor in Massachusetts backed by AB InBev was fined by the state's Alcohol Beverage Control Commission for giving nearly a million dollars' worth of refrigeration and beer-dispensing equipment to over four hundred Boston-area bars and liquor stores to stock Budweiser and other AB InBev beers. Dan Adams, "Anheuser-Busch Disputes Charge of $1 Million 'Pay-to-Play' Scheme," *Boston Globe*, November 28, 2017.

5 William L. Fox, *In the Desert of Desire: Las Vegas and the Culture of Spectacle* (Reno: University of Nevada Press, 2007).

6 When I asked Beth, the artist of the label, about this, she told me that locals often ask her about it. Like a magician, she chooses not to reveal the "behind-the-scenes" answer.

7 Sociologist Richard Ocejo notes that the vast majority of people he studied within various crafted occupations—bartenders, distillers, barbers, and butchers—across New York City didn't view what they were doing as a resistance to a dominant culture, though a number of his interviewees discussed career changes motivated by a quest for meaning. Richard E. Ocejo, *Masters of Craft: Old Jobs in the New Urban Economy* (Princeton, NJ: Princeton University Press, 2017). Similarly, sociologists Daina Harvey and Ellis Jones found that the brewers they interviewed in New England were less concerned about battling Big Beer than they were interested in issues of environment sustainability. Daina Harvey and Ellis Jones, "Ethical Brews: New England, Networked Ecologies, and a New Craft Beer Movement," in

Untapped: Exploring the Cultural Dimensions of the Craft Beer Revolution, ed. Nathaniel G. Chapman, J. Slade Lellock, and Cameron D. Lippard (Morgantown: University of West Virginia Press, 2017). The fact that "craft" was already a part of the culture of the Northeast in places that have traditionally valued both creativity and localism highlights the importance of context for understanding the role of craft and strengthens my argument that craft beer has been used to oppose Las Vegas's dominant culture and image as solely imported kitsch.

8 R. Richard Wohl and Anselm L. Strauss, "Symbolic Representation and the Urban Milieu," *American Journal of Sociology* 63 (1958): 526.

9 Ibid., 529.

10 See, respectively, Jerome Krase, *Seeing Cities Change: Local Culture and Class* (Aldershot, UK: Ashgate, 2012); David Grazian, *Blue Chicago: The Search for Authenticity in Urban Blues Clubs* (Chicago: University of Chicago Press, 2003); and Kevin Fox Gotham, *Authentic New Orleans: Tourism, Culture, and Race in the Big Easy* (New York: New York University Press, 2007).

11 Dennis Judd and Susan Fainstein, eds., *The Tourist City* (New Haven, CT: Yale University Press, 1999), 9–10.

12 Mark Gottdiener, Claudia Collins, and David R. Dickens, *Las Vegas: The Social Production of an All-American City* (Oxford: Blackwell, 1999); Hal Rothman and Mike Davis, "Introduction: The Many Faces of Las Vegas," in *The Grit Beneath the Glitter: Tales from the Real Las Vegas*, ed. Hal Rothman and Mike Davis (Berkeley: University of California Press, 2002).

13 Marc Cooper, *The Last Honest Place in America: Paradise and Perdition in the New Las Vegas* (New York: Nation Books, 2004).

14 Russell Belk, "May the Farce Be with You: On Las Vegas and Consumer Infantalization," *Consumption, Markets, and Culture* 4 (2000): 107.

15 See Juliet Flower MacCannell, "Las Vegas: The Post-Cinematic City," *Performance Research* 6 (2001): 46–64.

16 Stanley Fish, *Is There a Text in This Class? The Authority of Interpretive Communities* (Cambridge, MA: Harvard University Press, 1980); Neil Reid, Ralph B. McLaughlin, and Michael S. Moore, "From Yellow Fizz to Big Biz: American Craft Beer Comes of Age," *Focus on Geography* 57 (2014): 114–25; Kathleen J. Fitzgerald, "Thinking Globally, Acting Locally: Locavorism and Humanist Sociology," *Humanity & Society* 40 (2016): 3–21; Colin Campbell, "The Craft Consumer: Culture, Craft, and Consumption in a Postmodern Society," *Journal of Consumer Culture* 5 (2005): 23–44; and Phillip Vannini and Jonathan Taggart, "Do-It-Yourself or Do-It-With? The Regenerative Life Skills of Off-Grid Home Builders," *Cultural Geographies* 21 (2014): 267–85.

17 Clifford Geertz, "Afterword," in *Senses of Place*, ed. Steven Feld and Keith H. Basso (Santa Fe, NM: School of American Research Press, 1996), 262.

18 Steven M. Schnell and Joseph F. Reese, "Microbreweries as Tools of Local Identity," *Journal of Cultural Geography* 21 (2003): 46.

19 Charles Heying, ed., *Brew to Bikes: Portland's Artisan Economy* (Portland, OR: Ooligan Press, 2010); Ocejo, *Masters of Craft.*

20 Richard E. Ocejo, *Upscaling Downtown: From Bowery Saloons to Cocktail Bars in New York City* (Princeton, NJ: Princeton University Press, 2014); Chloe Fox Miller, "The Contemporary Geographies of Craft-Based Manufacturing," *Geography Compass* 11 (2017): 1–13.

21 William A. Douglass and Pauliina Raento, "The Tradition of Invention: Conceiving Las Vegas," *Annals of Tourism Research* 31 (2004): 12.

22 Gottdiener, Collins, and Dickens, *Las Vegas.*

23 For extended discussions of the notion of "tastescape," see J. Douglas Porteous, *Landscapes of the Mind: Worlds of Sense and Metaphor* (Toronto: University of Toronto Press, 1990), and Michael Ian Borer, "Being in the City: The Sociology of Urban Experiences," *Sociology Compass* 7 (2013): 965–83.

24 As of the time of this writing, there are at least four books and hundreds of news articles and blog posts published since 2011 that use the phrase "Craft Beer Revolution" in their titles or subtitles. Two of the books are by journalists, Joshua M. Bernstein, *Brewed Awakening: Behind the Beers and Brewers Leading the World's Craft Brewing Revolution* (New York: Steriling Epicure, 2011) and Tom Acitelli, *The Audacity of Hops: The History of America's Craft Beer Revolution* (Chicago: Chicago Review Press, 2013); one is an edited academic book, Chapman, Lellock, and Lippard, *Untapped*; and the other is by the cofounder of Brooklyn Brewery, one of the most successful and longest running craft breweries in the United States, Steve Hindy, *The Craft Beer Revolution: How a Band of Microbrewers Is Transforming the World's Favorite Drink* (New York: Palgrave Macmillan, 2014). At a discussion of the "state of craft beer" during the first craft beer festival at Mandalay Bay Resort and Casino in 2014, Certified Cicerone Sarah M. Johnson, the food and beverage manager of MGM Resorts, asked a panel of craft brewers what their "desert island" beer would be: if they could have only one beer for the rest of their life, what would it be? Hindy was the only one who named a beer from his own brewery. The audience took the response in stride, though they would have cringed at such pomposity if Hindy's longevity in and advocacy of craft beer wasn't so well known and respected and if the dry-hopped Saison Sorachi Ace, the beer he named, weren't regarded as a top-notch beverage.

25 Diane M. Rodgers and Ryan Taves, "The Epistemic Culture of Homebrewers and Microbrewers," *Sociological Spectrum* 37 (2017): 129.

26 Christine Harold, *Ourspace: Resisting the Corporate Control of Culture* (Minneapolis: University of Minnesota Press, 2007), 162.

27 Brewers Association, "Number of Breweries" (2017), www.brewersassociation.org.

28 Howard S. Becker, *Art Worlds* (Berkeley: University of California Press, 1982), chap. 9.

29 Campbell, "Craft Consumer," 25.

30 Acitelli, *Audacity of Hops*, 179.

31 Douglas Holt and Douglas Cameron, *Cultural Strategy: Using Innovative Ideologies to Build Breakthrough Brands* (Oxford: Oxford University Press, 2010), 232.

32 Ibid., 238.

33 Ibid., 240.

34 Not only has New Belgium taken the lead with their innovative and relatively inexpensive beer—from, depending on state, about $7 a six-pack to only $15 for their 22-ounce experimental and genre-bending/pushing brews—they are "employee owned" and have a fairly progressive business structure and model.

35 Acitelli, *Audacity of Hops*, 313.

36 The association amended the definition in 2010—changing "small" from annual production of two million barrels or less to six million barrels or less—to allow growing craft brewers not to be penalized for their success, to reflect the realities of doing business in a marketplace dominated by multinational corporations brewing over a hundred million barrels, and to align with the association's excise tax recalibration efforts.

37 Brewers Association, "Craft vs. Crafty" (2012), www.brewersassociation.org.

38 Brewers Association, "Brewers Association Launches Independent Craft Brewer Seal Retail Program" (2018), www.brewersassociation.org.

39 Here, sociologist Claude Fischer's arguments about cities' need for a critical mass to support various subcultures can be applied to a type of popular culture itself. See Claude S. Fischer, "Toward a Subcultural Theory of Urbanism," *American Journal of Sociology* 80 (1975): 1319–41.

40 Laura Grindstaff, "Culture and Popular Culture: A Case for Sociology," *Annals of the American Academy of Political and Social Science* 619 (2008): 208, 212.

41 Georg Simmel, "The Concept and Tragedy of Culture," in *Simmel on Culture: Selected Writings*, ed. David Frisby and Mike Featherstone (London: SAGE, 1997).

42 Andrea Fontana and Frederick Preston, "Postmodern Neon Architecture: From Signs to Icons," *Studies in Symbolic Interactionism* 11 (1990): 3–24.

43 See Umberto Eco, *Travels in Hyperreality* (San Diego, CA: Harcourt Brace Jovanovich, 1986); MacCannell, "Las Vegas," 46–64; George Ritzer and Todd Stillman, "The Modern Las Vegas Casino-Hotel: The Paradigmatic New Means of Consumption," *M@n@gement* 4 (2001): 83–99; John Hannigan, *Fantasy City: Pleasure and Profit in the Postmodern Metropolis* (New York: Routledge, 2005); Charles Soukup, "The Postmodern Ethnographic Flaneur and the Study of Hyper-Mediated Everyday Life," *Journal of Contemporary Ethnography* 42 (2013): 226–54; Simon Gottschalk and Marko Salvaggio, "Stuck Inside of Mobile: Ethnography in Non-places," *Journal of Contemporary Ethnography* 44 (2015): 3–33; and Stacy M. Jameson, Karen Klugman, Jane Kuenz, and Susan Willis, *Strip Cultures: Finding America in Las Vegas* (Durham, NC: Duke University Press, 2015).

44 Douglass and Raento, "Tradition of Invention," 20–21.

45 See Gottdiener, Collins, and Dickens, *Las Vegas*.

46 Heather Paxson, "The 'Art' and 'Science' of Handcrafting Cheese in the United States," *Endeavour* 35 (2011): 116.

47 Most states, including Nevada, are tied to a post–World War II three-tiered system that keeps producers (i.e., brewers) from distributors or wholesalers and from retailers (both "off premises" like supermarkets and "on premises" like bars).

48 I say "about" twelve because the status of breweries connected to and run by casinos puts both their independence and craft nature in question throughout the local scene and beyond.

49 Ashley Mears, "Seeing Culture through the Eye of the Beholder: Four Methods in Pursuit of Taste," *Theory and Society* 43 (2014): 306.

50 Clifford Geertz, *The Interpretation of Cultures* (New York: Basic Books, 1973), 14.

51 See Joseph R. Gusfield, *Contested Meanings: The Construction of Alcohol Problems* (Madison: University of Wisconsin Press, 1996).

52 Philip A. Mellor and Chris Shilling, *Sociology of the Sacred: Religion, Embodiment and Social Change* (Thousand Oaks, CA: SAGE, 2014), 51.

53 Daniel J. Monti, Michael Ian Borer, and Lyn C. Macgregor, *Urban People and Places: The Sociology of Cities, Suburbs, and Towns* (Thousand Oaks, CA: SAGE, 2014).

54 Gary Alan Fine, "The Sociology of the Local: Action and Its Publics," *Sociological Theory* 28 (2010): 372.

55 Ken Miller, "Home Brewer Eric Villareal Is an Engineer by Day—and a Confessed Beer Geek at Night," *Las Vegas Weekly*, October 2010, 18, emphasis added.

56 Ken Miller, "Drink What's Next: The Coming Year Could Bring a Craft Brew Explosion to Southern Nevada," *Las Vegas Weekly*, April 25, 2013, 20–21.

57 David Hesmondhalgh, "Subcultures, Scenes or Tribes? None of the Above," *Journal of Youth Studies* 8 (2005): 29.

58 Martyn Hammersley and Paul Atkinson, *Ethnography: Principles in Practice* (London: Routledge, 2007), 145.

59 Roberta Sassatelli, "A Serial Ethnographer: An Interview with Gary Alan Fine," *Qualitative Sociology* 33 (2010): 91.

60 See Andy Bennett and Keith Kahn-Harris, eds., *After Subculture: Critical Studies in Contemporary Youth Culture* (Basingstoke, UK: Palgrave, 2004).

61 Hesmondhalgh, "Subcultures, Scenes or Tribes?," 24.

62 Will Straw, "Scenes and Sensibilities," *Public* 22/23 (2001): 248, emphasis added. Even as Straw's work supports and has influenced or has been influenced by many of these studies, he doesn't shy away from asking an important interrogative question: "How useful is a term which designates both the effervescence of our favourite bar and the sum total of all global phenomena surrounding a subgenre of Heavy Metal music?"

63 Andy Bennett and Richard A. Peterson, eds., *Music Scenes: Local, Translocal, and Virtual* (Nashville: Vanderbilt University Press, 2004).

64 "Idioculture consists of a system of knowledge, beliefs, behaviors, and customs shared by members of an interacting group to which members can refer and

employ as the basis of further interaction." Gary Alan Fine, "Small Groups and Culture Creation: The Idioculture of Little League Baseball Teams," *American Sociological Review* 44 (1979): 735.

65 See Richard Lloyd, *Neo-Bohemia: Art and Commerce in the Postindustrial City* (New York: Routledge, 2005); Andrew Deener, *Venice: A Contested Bohemia in Los Angeles* (Chicago: University of Chicago Press, 2012); and Ocejo, *Upscaling Downtown.*

66 See, respectively, Barry Shank, *Dissonant Identities: The Rock 'N' Roll Scene in Austin, Texas* (Hanover, NH: Wesleyan University Press, 1994); Joseph A. Kotarba, *Baby Boomer Rock 'n' Roll Fans: The Music Never Ends* (Lanham, MD: Scarecrow Press, 2013); Keith Harris, "'Roots'? The Relationship between the Global and the Local within the Extreme Metal Scene," *Popular Music* 19 (2000): 13–30; Kristin Schilt, "'Riot Grrrl Is . . .': Contestation over Meaning in a Music Scene," in Bennett and Peterson, *Music Scenes*; Tammy Anderson, *Rave Culture: The Alteration and Decline of a Philadelphia Music Scene* (Philadelphia: Temple University Press, 2009); and Jooyoung Lee, *Blowin' Up: Rap Dreams in South Central* (Chicago: University of Chicago Press, 2016).

67 Harvey Molotch and Mark Treskon, "Changing Art: Soho, Chelsea and the Dynamic Geography of Galleries in New York City," *International Journal of Urban and Regional Research* 33 (2009): 517–41; and Benjamin Woo, "Alpha Nerds: Cultural Intermediaries in a Subcultural Scene," *European Journal of Cultural Studies* 15 (2012): 659–76.

68 "Scene thinking ought to animate every stage of research: alerting researchers to possible sites of inquiry; helping us pose questions that bring into focus the unseen or overlooked in everyday life; and suggesting categories based on the meaning of circulation and flow, rather than what presents itself as permanent and thus somehow more significant." Benjamin Woo, Jamie Rennie, and Stuart R. Poyntz, "Scene Thinking: Introduction," *Cultural Studies* 29 (2015): 292.

69 Daniel Aaron Silver and Terry Nichols Clark, *Scenescapes: How Qualities of Place Shape Social Life* (Chicago: University of Chicago Press, 2016), 52–69.

70 Ibid., chap. 3.

71 John Irwin, *Scenes* (Beverly Hills, CA: SAGE, 1977).

72 Erving Goffman, *The Presentation of Self in Everyday Life* (Garden City, NY: Doubleday, 1959).

73 Irwin, *Scenes*, 66.

74 Ibid., 23.

75 Herbert J. Gans, *Popular Culture & High Culture: An Analysis and Evaluation of Taste* (New York: Basic Books, 1999), 4.

76 See Antoine Hennion, "Those Things That Hold Us Together: Taste and Sociology," *Cultural Sociology* 1 (2007): 97–114.

77 Irwin, *Scenes*, 31.

78 Ibid., 45.

79 "The domain of mesostructure does not deny the institutional structures of social orders, but it does deny that those structures can be understood without understanding how they are enacted. Nor does it deny the importance of interaction processes. Indeed, it is through interaction that structures are enacted, but in that process, interaction becomes conditional interaction. In terms of classical theory, mesostructure portrays freedom as possible through constraint and constraint as a consequence of freedom. The center of that domain thus consists of mediating processes and the webs of significance and group affiliation that form the interstitial arenas of social life." David R. Maines, "In Search of Mesostructure: Studies in the Negotiated Order," *Urban Life* 11 (1982): 276.

80 John Irwin, "Notes on the Status of the Concept Subculture," in *The Subcultures Reader*, ed. Ken Gelder and Sarah Thornton (New York: Routledge, 1997), 66–67.

81 See Scott R. Harris, *What Is Constructionism? Navigating Its Use in Sociology* (Boulder, CO: Lynne Rienner, 2010).

82 Tia DeNora, *Music in Everyday Life* (Cambridge: Cambridge University Press, 2000), 6.

83 Gary Alan Fine, *Everyday Genius: Self-Taught Art and the Culture of Authenticity* (Chicago: University of Chicago Press, 2006), 35.

84 Terry Eagleton, *The Ideology of the Aesthetic* (Oxford: Basil Blackwell, 1990), 75–77.

85 Maurice Merleau-Ponty, *Phenomenology of Perception* (London: Routledge, 1962).

86 Pierre Bourdieu, *Distinction: A Social Critique of the Judgement of Taste* (Cambridge, MA: Harvard University Press, 1984).

87 Michael Ian Borer, *Faithful to Fenway: Believing in Boston, Baseball, and America's Most Beloved Ballpark* (New York: New York University Press, 2008), chap. 4.

88 Goffman argued that when doing participant observation of and with a "set of individuals," it was necessary to subject "your own body and your personality . . . so that you are close to them while they are responding to what life does to them . . . to pick up their minor grunts and groans as they respond to their situation." And even though you can leave their situation "you act as if you can't and you try to accept all of the desirable and undesirable things that are a feature of their life. That 'tunes your body up' and with your 'tuned-up' body . . . you're empathetic enough to sense what is that they're responding to." Erving Goffman, "On Fieldwork," *Journal of Contemporary Ethnography* 18 (1989): 125–26. Goffman's focus on the body trained or "tuned-up" to sense and respond to the situations and objects uncannily anticipated the recent recognition and rise of "sensuous scholarship."

89 My use of the term "significant object" is a nod to sociologists Colin Jerolmack and Iddo Tavory's discussion of George Herbert Mead's "implicit thesis about

nonhumans and the social self." Colin Jerolmack and Iddo Tavory, "Molds and Totems: Nonhumans and the Constitution of the Social Self," *Sociological Theory* 32 (2014): 64–77.

90 Jean Anthelme Brillat-Savarin, *The Physiology of Taste: Or Meditations on Transcendental Gastronomy* (New York: Knopf, 2009), 49.

91 Antoine Hennion, "The Pragmatics of Taste," in *The Blackwell Companion to the Sociology of Culture*, ed. Mark D. Jacobs and Nancy Weiss Hanrahan (Malden, MA: Blackwell, 2005), 136.

92 Michael Ian Borer, "The Location of Culture: The Urban Culturalist Perspective," *City & Community* 5 (2006): 175–76.

93 Geertz, *Interpretation of Cultures*, chap. 1.

94 For a discussion of "objectivity as fairness," see Sherri Grasmuck, *Protecting Home: Class, Race, and Masculinity in Boys' Baseball* (New Brunswick, NJ: Rutgers University Press, 2005), 220–22; and for an extended discussion of transparency in ethnographic research, see Victoria Reyes, "Three Models of Transparency in Ethnographic Research: Naming Places, Naming People, and Sharing Data," *Ethnography* 19 (2018): 204–22.

95 In response to a few recent trends in qualitative research, sociologist Paul Atkinson writes, "When we refer to *social actors* that is not a synonym for 'people.' The emphasis is on the social, and a recognition that selfhood and personhood are emergent processes. One of the most important acts of recuperation that we can perform is to reaffirm that the interactionist tradition is not a reductionist emphasis on the individual, and that research is not just about persons, personal experience or the self of the author." Paul Atkinson, "Rescuing Interactionism from Qualitative Research," *Symbolic Interaction* 38 (2015): 473.

96 According to Fine, the "seven pillars" of a peopled ethnography are that it (1) is theoretical, (2) builds on other ethnographies and research studies, (3) examines interacting small groups, (4) relies on multiple research sites, (5) is based on extensive observation, (6) is richly ethnographic, and (7) distances researcher and researched. Gary Alan Fine, "Towards a Peopled Ethnography: Developing Theory from Group Life," *Ethnography* 4 (2003): 41–60. Of note, Fine's last point about the distance and detachment from our research participants should be taken as a guiding light rather than a steadfast rule simply because spending time with others requires mutual levels of respect, even when it doesn't correspond to reciprocated levels of intimacy. I see people out at events or while eating dinner with my wife and kids and we exchange pleasantries. I often wonder if they have any idea of how much time and energy I've spent hearing their words repeated through recordings or through rereading my scribbled field notes. It's a curious dynamic, and one that seems inevitable when studying local cultures with the intent to understand its embodied and emplaced sensuousness. As anthropologist Sarah Pink argues, "We acknowledge how the researcher her or himself becomes part of a place, as she or

he is involved in a locality, encounters the social, sensory, and material elements other environment, and her or his trajectory become temporarily intertwined with the people and things that also constitute the place." Sarah Pink, *Situating Everyday Life: Practices and Places* (London: SAGE, 2012), 38.

97 Anthony Giddens, *Modernity and Self-Identity: Self and Society in the Late Modern Age* (Stanford, CA: Stanford University Press, 1991), 46–47.

CHAPTER 1: ONCE UPON A BEER DESERT

1 In many American cities, craft breweries have received both praise and admonishment for opening in former industrial buildings. At best, they can foster needed redevelopment of blighted areas (see Stephan Weiler, "Pioneers and Settlers in Lo-Do Denver: Private Risk and Public Benefits in Urban Redevelopment," *Urban Studies* 37 [2000]: 167–79), boost local cultural heritage (see Alison E. Feeney, "Cultural Heritage, Sustainable Development, and the Impacts of Craft Breweries in Pennsylvania," *City, Culture and Society* 9 [2017]: 21–30), or even help establish a local place identity to supplant a nondescript one (see Krista E. Paulsen and Hayley E. Tuller, "Crafting Place: Craft Beer and Authenticity in Jacksonville, Florida," in *Untapped: Exploring the Cultural Dimensions of the Craft Beer Revolution*, ed. Nathaniel G. Chapman, J. Slade Lellock, and Cameron D. Lippard [Morgantown: West Virginia University 2017]). But at worst, moving to former industrial buildings can aid in the gentrification-driven displacement of existing residents (see Vanessa Mathews and Roger M. Picton, "Intoxifying Gentrification: Brew Pubs and the Geography of Post-industrial Heritage," *Urban Geography* 35 [2014]: 337–56).

2 For recent cultural analyses that show the life course of products, especially food and drink, that have developed as cultural trends, see Sarah Bowen, *Divided Spirits: Tequila, Mezcal, and the Politics of Production* (Oakland: University of California Press, 2015); Jennifer A. Jordan, *Edible Memory: The Lure of Heirloom Tomatoes and Other Forgotten Foods* (Chicago: University of Chicago Press, 2015); Michaela DeSoucey, *Contested Tastes: Foie Gras and the Politics of Food* (Princeton, NJ: Princeton University Press, 2016); Mark Padoongpatt, *Flavors of Empire: Food and the Making of Thai America* (Oakland: University of California Press, 2017); and Richard E. Ocejo, *Masters of Craft: Old Jobs in the New Urban Economy* (Princeton, NJ: Princeton University Press, 2017).

3 Dave moved to the distribution side of the craft beer scene, working first for Cepage and then for Vin Sauvage, companies known for their extensive wine portfolios but willing to dabble in the fast-growing market of craft beers. Dave oversees the international and American brands of esteemed importer and distributor Shelton Brothers Inc. Through their partnership, Dave has expanded local offerings and consequently locals' palates with European brews from the likes of Denmark's Mikkeller, Belgium's 3 Fonteinen, and Canada's Dieu du Ciel and American-based beers from Ale Apothecary, Jester King, and Jolly Pumpkin.

4 These artworks were created by local artist Donovan Fitzgerald for Tacos & Beer. A few years later, Chris Jacobs (aka Beer Zombies) plastered his collage-style murals over much of the remaining wall space.

5 See Michael Ian Borer, "Re-sensing Las Vegas: Aesthetic Entrepreneurship and Local Urban Culture," *Journal of Urbanism: International Research on Placemaking and Urban Sustainability* 10 (2017): 111–24.The Master Cicerone and Beer Judge Certification Program designations were developed in recent years as the craft beer boom was launching to help ensure that craft beer maintained the highest of qualities. At the 2014 Craft Brewers Conference, Brewers Association president Paul Gatza voiced concerns that with many new brewers entering the market with little experience and inferior product, quality might dip. "With so many brewery openings, the potential is there for things to start to degrade on the quality side, and we wouldn't want that to color the willingness of the beer drinker to try new brands," Gatza said. "If a beer drinker has a bad experience, they are just going to go back to companies they know and trust." Dave echoed a similar philosophy about the attention he gives to both customers and brewers as the "middle man" between them.

6 Though this isn't a hard statistic, this is the number I was given by three prominent craft beers specialists who work at the biggest distributors in the city.

7 This is a slight paraphrase of the powerful lesson handed down to us from W. I. Thomas and Dorothy Swain Thomas. Their well-known sociological dictum, labeled the "Thomas Theorem," states, "If [persons] define situations as real, they are real in their consequences."

8 See Graeme Evans, "Hard-Branding the Cultural City—From Prado to Prada," *International Journal of Urban and Regional Research* 27 (2003): 417–40; Miriam Greenberg, *Branding New York: How a City in Crisis Was Sold to the World* (New York: Routledge, 2009); and Daniel Silver and Terry Nichols Clark, "Buzz as an Urban Resource," *Canadian Journal of Sociology* 38 (2013): 1–32.

9 John Hannigan, *Fantasy City: Pleasure and Profit in the Postmodern Metropolis* (New York: Routledge, 2005), 71.

10 Mark Gottdiener, Claudia Collins, and David R. Dickens, *Las Vegas: The Social Production of an All-American City* (Oxford: Blackwell, 1999), 68.

11 Richard D. Lloyd and Terry Nichols Clark, "The City as an Entertainment Machine," in *Critical Perspectives on Urban Redevelopment* (Research in Urban Sociology vol. 6), ed. Kevin Fox Gotham (Bingley, UK: Emerald, 2001).

12 The idea of a city as some type of machine—from one that's built by humans to one that controls them—has been a prominent metaphor in urban sociology. See Peter Langer, "Sociology—Four Images of Organized Diversity," in *Cities of the Mind: Images and Themes of the City in the Social Sciences*, ed. Lloyd Rodwin and Robert M. Hollister (New York: Plenum, 1984).

13 Las Vegas Convention and Visitors Authority, Clark County Department of Comprehensive Planning, "Las Vegas Metropolitan Population Trends: 1980–2016."

14 US Census Bureau, "Selected Social Characteristics in the United States: 2008–2012" (American Community Survey 5-Year Estimates).

15 The Las Vegas/Vegas distinction has tempered since the 2017–18 "impossible" inaugural season of the city's first professional sports team, the NHL's Vegas Golden Knights. Locals were hesitant at first but embraced both the team and its name after the October 1 Massacre on the Strip. As the team kept winning, all the way to the fifth game of the Stanley Cup Finals, chants of "Go Knights Go!" thundered inside T-Mobile Arena and throughout the valley.

16 I first wrote about the Las Vegas Syndrome as part of a collection of essays published in *Contexts*, a purportedly nonacademic-friendly magazine published by the American Sociological Association. The essays were commissioned, in part, as a rebuttal to comments made by fellow sociologists who attended the organization's annual meeting in 2011. (The conference location changed from Chicago to Las Vegas due to labor disputes at one of the designated hotels in Chicago.) Of particular note, urban sociologist Sharon Zukin offered her take on Las Vegas during the conference in a two-minute video produced by Norton Publishing. The first words she utters are, "I really hate Las Vegas," and then she goes on to declare that no one is actually having fun. Suffering from the Las Vegas Syndrome, her gaze only leers upon the Strip, and like so many others before and after her, she conflates the Strip with the rest of Las Vegas, where *real* people live and actually have fun from time to time in their homes and within the myriad of non-Strip places across the valley. And it should be noted that *real* people engage with the Strip too, which is, despite some commentator's insistence, a *real* place.

17 This is true for all scenes that run counter to a city's dominant cultural logic. Craft beer producers, distributors, and consumers aren't the only ones doing this in Las Vegas. They are joined by artists, gardeners, and runners, among others.

18 The role of storytelling as part of the human condition has been well documented. For ways that it applies to sociological analyses, see David R. Maines, "Narrative's Moment and Sociology's Phenomena: Toward a Narrative Sociology," *Sociological Quarterly* 34 (1993): 17–38; and Donileen R. Loseke, "The Study of Identity as Cultural, Institutional, Organizational, and Personal Narratives: Theoretical and Empirical Integrations," *Sociological Quarterly* 48 (2007): 661–88.

19 See Shan Nelson-Rowe, "The Moral Drama of Multicultural Education," in *Images of Issues: Typifying Contemporary Social Problems*, ed. Joel Best (New York: Aldine de Gruyter, 1995); and Elisabeth Anker, "Villains, Victims and Heroes: Melodrama, Media, and September 11," *Journal of Communication* 55 (2005): 22–37.

20 Michael Schudson, "How Culture Works: Perspectives from Media Studies on the Efficacy of Symbols," *Theory & Society* 18 (1989): 170.

21 Harvey Molotch, William Freudenburg, and Krista E. Paulsen, "History Repeats Itself, but How? City Character, Urban Tradition, and the Accomplishment of Place," *American Sociological Review* 65 (2000): 791–823.

22 Gerald Suttles, "The Cumulative Texture of Local Urban Culture," *American Journal of Sociology* 90 (1984): 283–304.

23 Harvey Molotch, *Where Stuff Comes From: How Toasters, Toilets, Cars, Computers and Many Other Things Come to Be as They Are* (New York: Routledge, 2004), 162.

24 Similar claims can be, and have been, made about the smaller parts of cities like neighborhoods and the larger regions that cities are embedded within. For the former, see Japonica Brown-Saracino, *A Neighborhood That Never Changes: Gentrification, Social Preservation, and the Search for Authenticity* (Chicago: University of Chicago Press, 2010), Frederick F. Wherry, *The Philadelphia Barrio: The Arts, Branding, and Neighborhood Transformation* (Chicago: University of Chicago Press, 2011), and Sarah Zelner, "The Perpetuation of Neighborhood Reputation: An Interactionist Approach," *Symbolic Interaction* 38 (2015): 575–93. For the latter, see Zandria F. Robinson, *This Ain't Chicago: Race, Class, and Regional Identity in the Post-Soul South* (Chapel Hill: University of North Carolina Press, 2014).

25 Gary Alan Fine, *Difficult Reputations: Collective Memories of the Evil, Inept, and Controversial* (Chicago: University of Chicago Press, 2001).

26 The individual and collective search and desire for authenticity is a defining feature of our contemporary era and can be seen across a multitude of cultural spheres. See David Grazian, *Blue Chicago: The Search for Authenticity in Urban Blues Clubs* (Chicago: University of Chicago Press, 2003); Michael Ian Borer, *Faithful to Fenway: Believing in Boston, Baseball, and America's Most Beloved Ballpark* (New York: New York University Press, 2008); William Ryan Force, "Consumption Styles and the Fluid Complexity of Punk Authenticity," *Symbolic Interaction* 32 (2009): 289–309; Sharon Zukin, *Naked City: The Death and Life of Authentic Urban Places* (Oxford: Oxford University Press, 2009); Amanda Koontz, "Constructing Authenticity: A Review of Trends and Influences in the Process of Authentication in Consumption," *Sociology Compass* 4 (2010): 977–88; Michaela DeSoucey, "Gastronationalism: Food Traditions and Authenticity Politics in the European Union," *American Sociological Review* 75 (2010): 432–55; Jonathan R. Wynn, *Music/City: American Festivals and Placemaking in Austin, Nashville, and Newport* (Chicago: University of Chicago Press, 2015); Phillip Vannini and J. Patrick Williams, eds., *Authenticity in Culture, Self, and Society* (New York: Routledge, 2016); Ocejo, *Masters of Craft*.

27 Bruce Bégout, *Zeropolis: The Experience of Las Vegas* (London: Reaktion Books, 2003), 23.

28 See Donileen R. Loseke and Margarethe Kusenbach, "The Social Construction of Emotion," in *Handbook of Constructionist Research*, ed. James A. Holstein and Jaber F. Gubrium (New York: Guilford, 2008).

29 Georg Simmel, "The Metropolis and the Mental Life," in *On Individuality and Social Forms*, ed. Donald Levine (Chicago: University of Chicago Press, 1971), 325.

30 See Anne Lorentzen, "Cities in the Experience Economy," *European Planning Studies* 17 (2009): 829–45.

31 Simmel notes that in the modern world of urban life the eye is "destined for a completely sociological unique achievement: the connection and interaction of individuals that lies in the act of individuals looking at one another." The eye's "completely unique sociological achievement" is connected to the expressiveness of the face and the equally comforting and disturbing movements of mutual recognition between strangers looking at one another. Simmel declares that "one cannot take through the eye without giving at the same time." The eye produces the "most complete reciprocity" between strangers, while the ear and the nose can only take without giving. Georg Simmel, "Sociology of the Senses," in *Simmel on Culture: Selected Writings*, ed. David Frisby and Mike Featherstone (London: SAGE, 1997), 111, 112, 114.

32 Susan Chandler and Jill B. Jones, *Casino Women: Courage in Unexpected Places* (Ithaca, NY: Cornell University Press, 2011).

33 Robert Futrell, Christie Batson, Barb Brents, Andrea Dassopoulos, Christine Nicholas, Mark Salvaggio, and Candace Griffith, "Las Vegas Metropolitan Area Social Survey 2010 Highlights" (University of Nevada, Las Vegas, Urban Sustainability Initiative, 2010).

34 Jean Baudrillard, *America* (London: Verso, 1988); George Ritzer and Todd Stillman, "The Modern Las Vegas Casino-Hotel: The Paradigmatic New Means of Consumption," *M@n@gement* 4 (2001): 83–99; Bégout, *Zeropolis*; Leslie Sklair, "Iconic Architecture and the Culture-Ideology of Consumerism," *Theory, Culture & Society* 27 (2010): 135–59; Simon Gottschalk and Marko Salvaggio, "Stuck Inside of Mobile: Ethnography in Non-places," *Journal of Contemporary Ethnography* 44 (2015): 3–33; and Stacy M. Jameson, Karen Klugman, Jane Kuenz, and Susan Willis, *Strip Cultures: Finding America in Las Vegas* (Durham, NC: Duke University Press, 2015).

35 David R. Dickens, "Is Las Vegas a 'Real City'?," *UNLV Gaming Research & Review Journal* 15 (2012): 119.

36 Hal Rothman, "Las Vegas and the American Psyche, Past and Present," *Pacific Historical Review* 70 (2001): 268.

37 Heather Jamerson, "Intoxicators, Educators, and Gatekeepers: The Enactment of Symbolic Boundaries in Napa Valley Wineries," *Poetics* 37 (2009): 232–98.

38 See Sheldon Stryker and Anne Statham Macke, "Status Inconsistency and Role Conflict," *Annual Review of Sociology* 4 (1978): 57–90.

39 For example, see Sharon Zukin and Laura Braslow, "The Life Cycle of New York's Creative Districts: Reflections on the Unanticipated Consequences of Unplanned Cultural Zones," *City, Culture, and Society* 2 (2011): 131–40.

40 Gottdiener, Collins, and Dickens, *Las Vegas*, 196.

41 I chose to focus on Michael Shetler because his experiences, in many respects, mirror the movement of craft beer in Las Vegas. His roles and experiences

highlight how both personal initiative and, even more importantly, a strong "support personnel"—to use Howard Becker's terminology about art worlds—can create aesthetic changes within a city. Without Clyde Burney's purchasing acumen, Shetler couldn't have served the brews he wanted his customers to savor. Clyde was honored by Big Dog's Brewing in early 2015 when they made a pale ale brewed with Nelson hops from Clyde's native New Zealand. They bottled it with his picture on the label and made it available at a few select craft beer bars around the valley. When Big Dog's announced this celebratory beer, they noted on social media that Clyde is "a man who has truly been a pioneer in growing the beer scene in Nevada. If you like to drink beer in Southern Nevada, odds are he has played a role in getting it here!"

42 Josée Johnston and Shyon Baumann, *Foodies: Democracy and Distinction in the Gourmet Foodscape* (New York: Routledge, 2014), 170.

43 Ocejo refers to this type of practice as "service teaching." Ocejo, *Masters of Craft*, chap. 7.

44 In 2015, the iconic Lagunitas IPA label, printed with its serif font, slimmed-down spacing between the "I," the "P," and the "A," and "slightly aged or weathered look," became a point of contention and litigation when Sierra Nevada used a similar design for their newly brewed Hop Hunter IPA. Due in large part to a storm of social media outrage, Tony Magee of Lagunitas dropped the lawsuit only a day after he filed it in US District Court in San Francisco in part because it seemed to violate the craft beer community's image of itself as a congenial band of brewers and drinkers. A decade ago, Russian River Brewing and Avery Brewing avoided a similar lawsuit by jointly producing a beer they called Collaboration Not Litigation Ale.

45 Steve Hindy, *The Craft Beer Revolution: How a Band of Microbrewers Is Transforming the World's Favorite Drink* (New York: Palgrave Macmillan, 2014), 128.

46 See Alexandra Rosenmann, "4 Reasons Never to Drink Budweiser Again," *Salon*, March 14, 2016, www.salon.com.

47 Tripp Mickle, "Craft Brewers Take Issue with AB InBev Distribution Plan," *Wall Street Journal*, December 7, 2015.

48 Journalist Josh Noel offers important insights into AB InBev and their relationship to craft beer, with a specific focus on his hometown Chicago's Goose Island. Josh Noel, *Barrel-Aged Stout and Selling Out: Goose Island, Anheuser-Busch, and How Craft Beer Became Big Business* (Chicago: Chicago Review Press, 2018).

CHAPTER 2: NOT-SO-NEON TERROIR

1 Elijah Anderson, "The White Space," *Sociology of Race and Ethnicity* 1 (2015): 18–19. Las Vegas seems to be on trend with the most recent statistics from the Brewers Association that show that the demographics of craft beer drinkers are diversifying across race, ethnicity, and gender. Bart Watson, "The Demographics of Craft Beer Lovers" (presentation at the Great American Beer Festival, Denver, October 3, 2014).

2 This is the tradition most closely associated with sociologist Pierre Bourdieu's analyses of links between taste preference and social calls. See Pierre Bourdieu, *Distinction: A Social Critique of the Judgement of Taste* (Cambridge, MA: Harvard University Press, 1984).
3 Marcel Mauss, *The Gift: The Form and Reason for Exchange in Archaic Societies* (New York: Routledge, 1990), 7.
4 Will Straw, "Scenes and Sensibilities," *Public* 22/23 (2001): 248.
5 Ibid., 249.
6 Pepper G. Glass, "Doing Scene: Identity, Space, and the Interactional Accomplishment of Youth Culture," *Journal of Contemporary Ethnography* 41 (2012): 696.
7 The infamous, at least to craft beer enthusiasts, Budweiser commercial aired during the 2015 Super Bowl. Both the commercial and reactions to it are discussed in chapter 5.
8 Antoine Hennion, "Those Things That Hold Us Together: Taste and Sociology," *Cultural Sociology* 1 (2007): 105–6.
9 Michael P. Farrell, *Collaborative Circles: Friendship Dynamics and Creative Work* (Chicago: University of Chicago Press, 2001), 12, 19.
10 Michael Ian Borer, "The Location of Culture: The Urban Culturalist Perspective," *City & Community* 5 (2006): 181.
11 Joseph A. Kotarba, *Baby Boomer Rock 'n' Roll Fans: The Music Never Ends* (Lanham, MD: Scarecrow Press, 2013), 95.
12 John Irwin, *Scenes* (Beverly Hills, CA: SAGE, 1977), 31.
13 See Steven M. Schnell and Joseph F. Reese, "Microbreweries as Tools of Local Identity," *Journal of Cultural Geography* 21 (2003): 45–69; Vanessa Mathews and Roger M. Picton, "Intoxifying Gentrification: Brew Pubs and the Geography of Post-Industrial Heritage," *Urban Geography* 35 (2014): 337–56; Alison E. Feeney, "Cultural Heritage, Sustainable Development, and the Impacts of Craft Breweries in Pennsylvania," *City, Culture and Society* 9 (2017): 21–30; and Daina Harvey and Ellis Jones, "Ethical Brews: New England, Networked Ecologies, and a New Craft Beer Movement," in *Untapped: Exploring the Cultural Dimensions of the Craft Beer Revolution*, ed. Nathaniel G. Chapman, J. Slade Lellock, and Cameron D. Lippard (Morgantown: University of West Virginia Press, 2017).
14 Daniel J. Monti, *The American City: A Social and Cultural History* (Malden, MA: Blackwell, 1999), 105–6.
15 Herbert Blumer, *Symbolic Interactionism: Perspective and Method* (Berkeley: University of California Press, 1986), 70–72.
16 Erving Goffman, *Interaction Ritual: Essays in Face to Face Behavior* (New York: Pantheon Books, 1967).
17 See Anselm L. Strauss, *Negotiations: Varieties, Contexts, Processes, and Social Order* (San Francisco: Jossey-Bass, 1978), and Gary Alan Fine, "The Sociology of the Local: Action and Its Publics," *Sociological Theory* 28 (2010): 355–76.

18 Andrew Deener, "Commerce as the Structure and Symbol of Neighborhood Life: Reshaping the Meaning of Community in Venice, California," *City & Community* 6 (2007): 293, 311–12.
19 Gary Alan Fine and Ugo Corte, "Group Pleasures: Collaborative Commitments, Shared Narrative, and the Sociology of Fun," *Sociological Theory* 35 (2017): 64–86.
20 Alan Blum, *The Imaginative Structure of the City* (Kingston: McGill-Queen's University Press, 2003), 165.
21 Borer, "Location of Culture," 175.
22 Thomas F. Gieryn, "A Space for Place in Sociology," *Annual Review of Sociology* 26 (2000): 465.
23 Irwin, *Scenes*, 135.
24 Tia DeNora, *Music-in-Action: Selected Essays in Sonic Ecology* (Farnham, UK: Ashgate, 2011), xi.
25 Richard Lloyd, "Neo-Bohemia: Art and Neighborhood Redevelopment in Chicago," *Journal of Urban Affairs* 24 (2002): 518.
26 Robert Lang and Paul K. Knox, "The New Metropolis: Rethinking Megalopolis," *Regional Studies* 43 (2009): 794–97.
27 Jonathan R. Wynn, *Music/City: American Festivals and Placemaking in Austin, Nashville, and Newport* (Chicago: University of Chicago Press, 2015), 220–22.
28 See Robert E. Stebbins, *Serious Leisure: A Perspective for Our Time* (New Brunswick, NJ: Transaction, 2015).
29 Mark Gottdiener, Claudia Collins, and David R. Dickens, *Las Vegas: The Social Production of an All-American City* (Oxford: Blackwell, 1999), chap. 7.
30 Hennion, "Those Things That Hold Us Together," 101.
31 Roger Haden, "Taste in an Age of Convenience: From Frozen Food to Meals in the 'Matrix,'" in *The Taste Culture Reader: Experiencing Food and Drink*, ed. Carolyn Korsmeyer (Oxford: Berg, 2005), 349.
32 See Amy B. Trubek, *The Taste of Place: A Cultural Journey into Terroir* (Berkeley: University of California Press, 2008).
33 Joy Santlofer, "Asphalt Terroir," in *Gastropolis: Food and New York City*, ed. Annie Hauck-Lawson and Jonathan Deutsch (New York: Columbia University Press, 2009); and John T. Lang, "Sound and the City," *Food, Culture & Society* 17 (2014): 571–89.
34 Howard S. Becker, *Art Worlds* (Berkeley: University of California Press, 1982), 57.
35 Ibid., 33.
36 In fall 2015, Tom took over the role as brewmaster at Downtown's Triple 7 Brewery in Main Street Station. Though Triple 7 had been brewing its own local craft beer for over a decade, it had mostly gone unnoticed by locals until Tom arrived and immediately started producing his Carlsbad IPA (a West Coast IPA he originally brewed as a one-off for Big Dog's that found a devoted local consumer base).
37 Of note, a portion of the profits of Las Vegas Lager supports the Keep Memory Alive foundation and the Lou Ruvo Center for Brain Health in Downtown Las Vegas.

38 Gary Alan Fine, *Kitchens: The Culture of Restaurant Work* (Berkeley: University of California Press, 1996), 183.

39 Lee Breslouer, "America's Best Craft Breweries: State-by-State Breakdown" (2013), www.thrillist.com. Though it is not the official state motto, despite its appearance on the Nevada's flag, many Nevadans refer to their home state as "Battle Born" because it became part of the Union during the Civil War.

40 Pascual left Chicago Brewing for Big Dog's in late 2015 and brought home a Great American Beer Festival (GABF) bronze medal for Tripel Dog Dare, another Belgian-style brew.

41 Matt Lynch, Andy Kryza, and Zach Mack, "The Best Craft Brewery in Every State" (2015), www.thrillist.com.

42 Jan Hogan, "Big Business Beer: Tenaya Creek Relocating Downtown," *Las Vegas Review Journal*, August 25, 2015.

43 Michael Ian Borer, "Re-sensing Las Vegas: Aesthetic Entrepreneurship and Local Urban Culture," *Journal of Urbanism: International Research on Placemaking and Urban Sustainability* 10 (2017): 115.

44 Earnest N. Bracey, *The Moulin Rouge and Black Rights in Las Vegas: A History of the First Racially Integrated Hotel-Casino* (Jefferson, NC: McFarland, 2008).

45 Krista E. Paulsen and Hayley E. Tuller, "Crafting Place: Craft Beer and Authenticity in Jacksonville, Florida," in Chapman, Lellock, and Lippard, *Untapped*.

46 Mathews and Picton, "Intoxifying Gentrification," 338.

47 Melinda J. Milligan, "Interactional Past and Potential: The Social Construction of Place Attachment," *Symbolic Interaction* 21 (1998): 22.

48 Ibid., 16.

49 Robert J. McKee, *Community Action against Racism in West Las Vegas: The F Street Wall and the Women Who Brought It Down* (Lanham, MD: Lexington Books, 2014).

50 In a strange twist of fate or act of the gods of craft, Ballast Point Brewing renamed their Calico Amber shortly after they were bought for one billion dollars by Big Beer conglomerate Constellation Brands.

51 In 2011, after they held their first public tasting at local stalwart and nationally recognized cocktail bar Herbs 'n' Rye, local food and beverage reporter Xania Woodman wrote a celebratory profile of the homebrewer-turned-pro "Banger Gang." Due to legislative loopholes, they wouldn't open until 2014. Xania Woodman, "The Banger Gang," *Vegas Seven*, September 8, 2011.

52 William A. Douglass and Pauliina Raento, "The Tradition of Invention: Conceiving Las Vegas," *Annals of Tourism Research* 31 (2004): 17.

53 In November 2012, Tony Hsieh, CEO of Zappos (an internet-based footwear distributer owned by Amazon), announced that his company's headquarters would move from an office park in suburban Henderson to the old Las Vegas City Hall in the heart of Downtown. As part of the move, Hsieh instituted the

Downtown Project as a means for "revitalizing" the Downtown area for his almost two thousand employees, who would work, live, and play in the area. The organization invested about $350 million in everything from real estate to restaurants to tech startups. Hsieh quickly became a local media darling—he was dubbed the "Crown Prince of the City" by a Las Vegas–based weekly magazine—because of his efforts to "deliver happiness" (the title of Hsieh's best-selling book) by redeveloping a much maligned part of the city. The project has yielded mixed results due to a number of issues, including Hsieh's management style as well as the presumed onslaught of corporate-driven gentrification. See Aimee Groth, *The Kingdom of Happiness: Inside Tony Hsieh's Zapponian Utopia* (New York: Touchstone, 2017).

54 Bad Beat Brewing opened two months before CraftHaus in the same industrial park, but wouldn't have been able to do so if Dave and Wyndee hadn't worked with the city on creating a new license for breweries and taprooms.

55 A firkin is a small wooden or metal keg that holds about eleven gallons of beer. It usually sits at room temperature on its side and is opened by hammering a tap into it. This was the traditional way that beer was served before the advent of sophisticated modern tap systems. They have become a popular way to test innovative infusions for craft breweries like CraftHaus and their patrons.

56 Monti, *American City*, 248–49.

57 Of note, Kyle brewed an imperial smoked porter with cacao nibs that won a GABF gold medal for the Chocolate Beer category in 2017.

58 At Aces' seventh Stone Domination event in 2016, accompanied by hard-to-find kegs and bottles, Stone cofounder and CEO Greg Koch raffled off an all-expenses-paid trip to their new brewery in Berlin.

59 Derek Stonebarger was also a minority owner but had to sell his share to pay for cancer-related surgery. He has, however, contributed to the local craft beer scene by opening two craft-centric bars in Downtown Las Vegas: ReBar, an antique store with a bar that serves mostly local craft beers and sausages, and the Nevada Taste Site, a bar devoted to local craft beer that, like the Atomic, pays homage to local history.

60 The Atomic has the seventh liquor license in all of Las Vegas. The previous six all went to casinos.

61 It is the setting for the scene where Joe Pesci's character uses a pen to kill a man. In the *Hangover*, the "wolf pack" crash their car outside the bar. And the Atomic Liquors sign makes appearances in an episode of the Twilight Zone as well as Clint Eastwood's 1977 *The Gauntlet*.

62 Clint Lanier and Derek Hembree, "Atomic Liquors Las Vegas: A 'BLAST' from the Past," *HuffPost: The Blog*, August 1, 2013, www.huffingtonpost.com.

63 Both breweries and retailers can enter local markets on a temporary basis through distributors. Doing so requires signatures from all parties involved. Despite being a formalized and often bureaucratic nightmare, it can pay off as a means for

breweries to test certain markets and, especially in the case of local Las Vegas beer festivals, give local beer drinkers a chance to try new brews they wouldn't otherwise be able to without leaving the city or state.

64 Jester King Brewery is located outside of Austin, Texas, on a farm that provides many of the ingredients they use in their experimental wild ales. They produce popular sought-after brews and have been vocal about the cultural and economic problems that result from craft breweries losing their independence to Big Beer.

65 See George Herbert Mead, *Mind, Self, and Society: From the Standpoint of a Social Behaviorist* (Chicago: University of Chicago Press, 1934).

66 Isabelle Nilsson, Neil Reid, and Matthew Lehnert, "Geographic Patterns of Craft Breweries at the Intraurban Scale," *Professional Geographer* 70 (2018): 114–25.

CHAPTER 3: THINK GLOBALLY, DRINK LOCALLY

1 Victor Turner, *The Ritual Process: Structure and Antistructure* (London: Routledge and Kegan Paul, 1969), 96–97.

2 For a brief yet informative interpretation of experiencing live music, see Emily M. Boyd, "Seeing Live Music," in *Popular Culture as Everyday Life*, ed. Dennis D. Waskul and Phillip Vannini (New York: Routledge, 2015).

3 Antoine Hennion, "Those Things That Hold Us Together: Taste and Sociology," *Cultural Sociology* 1 (2007): 105.

4 Erving Goffman, *Encounters: Two Studies in the Sociology of Interaction* (Indianapolis: Bobbs-Merrill, 1961), 65.

5 The first thing you notice when you walk into Cascade isn't the sign that declares that you've entered the "House of Sours." It's the barrels jutting out of the wall behind the bar. Some of those barrels have been hammered open by those lucky enough to be at the helm during Tap It Tuesdays, a ritual that leaves participants splattered with sour beer. All of those barrels are filled with beer that has been brewed and blended not far behind where you stand waiting to order. Blending is a historic practice that can be traced to the invention of the roasty porter in nineteenth-century London and the wild blended lambic gueuzes in Brussels of the same period. The goal is to create a beer that is greater than the sum of its parts, a collage of flavors derived from varying times spent against oak or on top of fruit or inoculated with bacteria.

6 Gary Alan Fine and Ugo Corte, "Group Pleasures: Collaborative Commitments, Shared Narrative, and the Sociology of Fun," *Sociological Theory* 35 (2017): 73–75.

7 Pepper G. Glass, "Doing Scene: Identity, Space, and the Interactional Accomplishment of Youth Culture," *Journal of Contemporary Ethnography* 41 (2012): 698–716.

8 Chris Rojek, *Celebrity* (Chicago: Reaktion Books, 2001), 62.

9 Kerry O. Ferris, "The Next Big Thing: Local Celebrity," *Society* 47 (2010): 392–95.

10 In one of the first analyses of fame and celebrity in the modern era, historian Daniel J. Boorstin defined "celebrity" in this purposely self-referential and superficial way. Daniel J. Boorstin, *The Image: A Guide to Pseudo-events in America* (New York: Atheneum, 1961).
11 "The artist's interest in form or style is the scientist's interest in structure or type. . . . The problems, insights, ideas, and forms which come to the artist and to the scientist seem to come as often from the unconscious as the conscious mind, from wide, eclectic, and unorganized reading, observing, and experiencing, from musing, browsing, and dreaming, from buried experiences, as from anything immediately and consciously in view." Robert Nisbet, *Sociology as an Art Form* (New Brunswick, NJ: Transaction, 2002), 10, 19.
12 See Sam Calagione, *Extreme Brewing: An Enthusiast's Guide to Brewing Craft Beer at Home* (Beverly, MA: Quarry Books, 2012).
13 Colin Campbell, "The Craft Consumer: Culture, Craft, and Consumption in a Postmodern Society," *Journal of Consumer Culture* 5 (2005): 39.
14 Ibid., 27.
15 Ibid., 39.
16 Wes Flack, "American Microbreweries and Neolocalism: 'Ale-Ing' for a Sense of Place," *Journal of Cultural Geography* 16 (1997): 44.
17 Ibid., 38.
18 Ross Haenfler, Brett Johnson, and Ellis Jones, "Lifestyle Movements: Exploring the Intersection of Lifestyle and Social Movements," *Social Movement Studies* 11 (2012): 1–20.
19 Though he focuses mostly on the environmental complications of industrialization on food production and the "taste of place," anthropologist Brad Weiss shows how local pigs are valued by various groups with similar interests for sometimes different or even conflicting reasons. See Brad Weiss, "Making Pigs Local: Discerning the Sensory Character of Place," *Cultural Anthropology* 26 (2011): 438–61.
20 For a discussion of the "romantic discourse" surrounding the notion of local, see Jeff Pratt, "Food Values: The Local and the Authentic," *Critique of Anthropology* 27 (2007): 285–300.
21 Sociologists Jason Kaufman and Orlando Patterson provide a useful discussion of the complexities of "global diffusion" of cricket from its origins across the British Empire and then outward to other countries with varied degrees of success. Jason Kaufman and Orlando Patterson, "Cross-National Cultural Diffusion: The Global Spread of Cricket," *American Sociological Review* 70 (2005): 82–110.
22 Clifford Geertz, *The Interpretation of Cultures* (New York: Basic Books, 1973), 90.
23 Stanford M. Lyman and Marvin B. Scott, "Territoriality: A Neglected Sociological Dimension," *Social Problems* 15 (1967): 238.
24 Krista E. Paulsen, "Making Character Concrete: Empirical Strategies for Studying Place Distinction," *City & Community* 3 (2004): 243–62.

25 The Lawson's Finest booth at GABF in 2015 was one of the few that I received pours from multiple times. The maple-barrel-aged Fayston Maple Imperial Stout was in my top five favorite beers of the festival, but as any beer geek will be bound to tell you, their Sip of Sunshine IPA is among the top IPAs produced in the United States. *BeerAdvocate* gives it a "world class" rating of a hundred out of a hundred. As for Citizen Cider, in the interest of full disclosure, the cidery was founded by one of my longest and greatest friends, Kris Nelson. Kris and two of his good friends, Brian Holmes and Justin Heilenbach, have been a part of and are regarded as leaders of the craft hard cider movement, revolution, and scene. They worked closely with Vermont senator Pat Leahy on redefining cider, and the taxation on it, to create the Cider Act of 2015.

26 See Peter Chua, "Orientalism as Cultural Practices and the Production of Sociological Knowledge," *Sociology Compass* 2 (2008): 1179–91.

27 Robert K. Merton, *Social Theory and Social Structure* (New York: Free Press, 1957), 441–46.

28 Sociologist Lyn Lofland notes that the term "cosmopolitanism" is defined and used in varying and contradictory ways often to signify some form of tolerance for difference. She argues that we can see these contradictions most clearly "by drawing a distinction between two types of tolerance: negative and positive." Lyn H. Lofland, *The Public Realm: Exploring the City's Quintessential Social Territory* (New York: Aldine de Gruyter, 1998), 237–40.

29 Benedict Anderson, *Imagined Communities: Reflections on the Origin and Spread of Nationalism* (New York: Verso, 1983).

30 This is a purposeful riff on Georg Simmel's definition of the "stranger." Georg Simmel, "The Stranger," in *On Individuality and Social Forms*, ed. Donald Levine (Chicago: University of Chicago Press, 1971). For more on the roles of strangers and their relevance for local urban cultures, see Lyn H. Lofland, *A World of Strangers: Order and Action in Urban Public Space* (Prospect Hills, IL: Waveland Press, 1973), and Daniel J. Monti, *Engaging Strangers: Civil Rites, Civic Capitalism, and Public Order in Boston* (Lanham, MD: Rowman & Littlefield, 2013).

31 Richard A. Peterson and Andy Bennett, "Introducing Music Scenes," in *Music Scenes: Local, Translocal, and Virtual*, ed. Andy Bennett and Richard A. Peterson (Nashville: Vanderbilt University Press, 2004), 9.

32 Here, I am extending sociologist Margarethe Kusenbach's work on intraurban hierarchies of neighborhoods to interurban hierarchies across cities. See Margarethe Kusenbach, "A Hierarchy of Urban Communities: Observations on the Nested Character of Place," *City & Community* 7 (2008): 225–49.

33 Starting in 2014, the journey to Anaheim might require two stops. In 2013, five different beers "didn't go as planned," as the company put it on its blog, mainly due to rogue yeast strains from open fermentation invading bottles and causing unintended souring over time. The key word is "unintended," because the Bruery is hailed as one of the top American brewers of purposely soured beers. Instead of

pretending that the accidentally infected beers were planned, something that other breweries have been accused of doing, they ponied up and offered refunds for the bad beer and devised a more permanent solution the following year by founding Bruery Terreux, a completely separate label and brewing facility focused on wild ales and brettanomyces-yeast-infused sour beers.

34 Of note, wine distributors not beholden to Big Beer, like Vin Sauvage, have provided alternative routes for distributing nonlocal craft beer by creating and expanding their craft beer portfolios.

35 See Christie D. Batson and Shannon M. Monnat, "Distress in the Desert: Neighborhood Disorder, Resident Satisfaction, and Quality of Life during the Las Vegas Foreclosure Crisis," *Urban Affairs Review* 51 (2015): 205–38.

36 The word "nostalgia" was coined by Swiss medical student Johannes Hofer in 1688 to describe a condition endured by soldiers who had traveled to foreign lands. It was considered to be a curable disease that opium, leeches, and a trip to the Swiss Alps could treat.

37 Melinda J. Milligan, "Displacement and Identity Discontinuity: The Role of Nostalgia in Establishing New Identity Categories," *Symbolic Interaction* 26 (2003): 381–403.

38 Dennis D. Waskul, Phillip Vannini, and Janelle Wilson, "The Aroma of Recollection: Olfaction, Nostalgia, and the Shaping of the Sensuous Self," *The Senses and Society* 4 (2009): 5–22.

39 Svetlana Boym, *The Future of Nostalgia* (New York: Basic Books, 2001), xvi.

40 Founders Brewing, "Announcing Northern California and Nevada Distribution" (September 16, 2015), http://foundersbrewing.com.

41 Both Avery and Paradox entered the Las Vegas market in limited capacities in 2017 and 2018, respectively. Funkwerks came to Las Vegas in late summer 2018. And Great Divide is rumored to be entering the market in the next year or two.

42 Timothy J. Dowd, Kathleen Liddle, and Jenna Nelson, "Music Festivals as Scenes: Examples from Serious Music, Womyn's Music, and Skatepunk," in *Music Scenes: Local, Translocal and Virtual*, ed. Andy Bennett and Richard A. Peterson (Nashville: Vanderbilt University Press, 2004), 149.

43 Jennifer E. Porter, "To Boldly Go: Star Trek Convention Attendance as Pilgrimage," in *Star Trek and Sacred Ground: Explorations of Star Trek, Religion, and American Culture*, ed. Jennifer E. Porter and Darcee L. McLaren (Albany: State University of New York Press, 1999), 252.

44 Ibid., 267.

45 For a detailed discussion of the transformation of ordinary places in "festival spaces," see Bruce Willems-Braun, "Situating Cultural Politics: Fringe Festivals and the Production of Spaces of Intersubjectivity," *Environment and Planning D: Society and Space* 12 (1994): 75–104.

46 Victor Turner, *From Ritual to Theater: The Human Seriousness of Play* (New York: Performing Arts Journal Publications, 1982).

47 Turner, *Ritual Process*.
48 Phillip Vannini, Guppy Ahluwalia-Lopez, Dennis Waskul, and Simon Gottschalk, "Performing Taste at Wine Festivals: A Somatic Layered Account of Material Culture," *Qualitative Inquiry* 16 (2010): 386–87, emphasis added.
49 Sociologist Claudio Benzecry makes a similar point about learning "passionate etiquette" and other so-called rules of engagement with opera. Claudio E. Benzecry, *The Opera Fanatic: Ethnography of an Obsession* (Chicago: University of Chicago Press, 2011), 93–96.
50 Mikhail Bakhtin, *Rabelais and His World* (Bloomington: Indiana University Press, 1984), 7–8.
51 The first GABF took place in 1982 with twenty-four breweries, forty-seven beers, and eight hundred attendees.
52 For detailed analysis of craft beer's role in LoDo, see Stephan Weiler, "Pioneers and Settlers in Lo-Do Denver: Private Risk and Public Benefits in Urban Redevelopment," *Urban Studies* 37 (2000): 167–79.
53 Sociologist Erving Goffman coined the term "civil inattention" to describe "the slightest of interpersonal rituals" whereby strangers notice others but, not out of fear or hostility, choose not to engage with one another. Erving Goffman, *Behavior in Public Places: Notes on the Social Organization of Gatherings* (New York: Free Press, 1963), 84. Also see Lofland, *Public Realm*, 28–34.
54 Hennion, "Those Things That Hold Us Together," 101.
55 See B. Joseph Pine and James H. Gilmore, "Welcome to the Experience Economy," *Harvard Business Review* 76 (1998): 97–105.
56 Anne Lorentzen, "Cities in the Experience Economy," *European Planning Studies* 17 (2009): 840, emphasis added.
57 Jonathan R. Wynn, *Music/City: American Festivals and Placemaking in Austin, Nashville, and Newport* (Chicago: University of Chicago Press, 2015), 16.
58 Andy Bennett, Ian Woodward, and Jodie Taylor, "Introduction," in *The Festivalization of Culture*, ed. Andy Bennett, Ian Woodward, and Jodie Taylor (New York: Routledge, 2016), 1.
59 Gary Alan Fine, "The Sociology of the Local: Action and Its Publics," *Sociological Theory* 28 (2010): 366.
60 Big Dog's Brewing holds seasonal festivals each year in the parking lot of their brewery. They have dealt with the problems associated with "all you can drink with the price of admission" festivals by instituting a token system. Admission is free but attendees who want to sample beers must buy tokens. The tokens are then used to purchase varying size pours of the available beers. How many tokens are necessary for a particular pour of a particular beer is often correlated with the ABV of the beer as well as some other factors that determine the price of the keg. I've noticed that this helps curb the need that many feel to get the most bang for their buck by trying to drink as much as they can in a predefined amount of time.

61 Ann Swidler, "Culture in Action: Symbols and Strategies," *American Sociological Review* 51 (1986): 277.

62 Alan Snel, "Nevadan at Work: West Point Grad Finds Passion in Craft Beer," *Las Vegas Review Journal*, March 8, 2014.

63 Due to threats of rain and high winds, the 2017 festival was moved indoors at the World Market Center.

64 Michael Schudson, "How Culture Works: Perspectives from Media Studies on the Efficacy of Symbols," *Theory & Society* 18 (1989): 164–66.

65 Motley Brews press release, December 13, 2014.

CHAPTER 4: FUSSING OVER STATUS

1 I used this term, "artifactual witness," in my book about Boston's Fenway Park to make the claim that historical places can provide windows into the past. Michael Ian Borer, *Faithful to Fenway: Believing in Boston, Baseball, and America's Most Beloved Ballpark* (New York: New York University Press, 2008).

2 This neighborhood meets the definition of a "food desert," even more so since White Cross closed in mid-December 2015. See Yuki Kato and Cate Irvin, "Flow of Food and People across the City: An Examination of Local Food Access in a New Orleans Food Desert," *Spaces & Flows* 3 (2013): 45–56.

3 See Kurt Borchard, *The Word on the Street: Homeless Men in Las Vegas* (Reno: University of Nevada Press, 2005), and Kurt Borchard, *Homeless in Las Vegas: Stories from the Street* (Reno: University of Nevada Press, 2011).

4 See Mark Greif, Kathleen Ross, and Dayna Tortorici, *What Was the Hipster? A Sociological Investigation* (New York: n+1 Foundation, 2010); Janna Michael, "It's Really Not Hip to Be a Hipster: Negotiating Trends and Authenticity in the Cultural Field," *Journal of Consumer Culture* 15 (2015): 163–82; and Ico Maly and Piia Varis, "The 21st-Century Hipster: On Micro-Populations in Times of Superdiversity," *European Journal of Cultural Studies* 19 (2016): 637–53. Of note, sociologist Richard Lloyd was one of the first to notice and systematically analyze some of the attributes pegged to so-called hipsters, though he used the term "neo-bohemians," and their valuing of "authenticity" and "urban grit." Most importantly, he showed how such desires can impact the cultural landscapes of urban culture. Richard Lloyd, *Neo-Bohemia: Art and Commerce in the Postindustrial City* (New York: Routledge, 2005).

5 Josh Noel, "Craft Brewery Co-founder Not Happy with Super Bowl Ad Snark," *Chicago Tribune*, February 2, 2015.

6 See Erving Goffman, *Stigma: Notes on the Management of Spoiled Identity* (New York: Simon & Schuster, 1963).

7 Pepper G. Glass, "Doing Scene: Identity, Space, and the Interactional Accomplishment of Youth Culture," *Journal of Contemporary Ethnography* 41 (2012): 698.

8 Christena E. Nippert-Eng, *Home and Work: Negotiating Boundaries through Everyday Life* (Chicago: University of Chicago Press, 1996), 7–8.

9 Kathryn Joan Fox, “Real Punks and Pretenders: The Social Organization of a Counterculture,” *Journal of Contemporary Ethnography* 16 (1987): 344–70. For a more recent analysis that further examines the role of punk style as a form of status, see William Ryan Force, “Consumption Styles and the Fluid Complexity of Punk Authenticity,” *Symbolic Interaction* 32 (2009): 289–309.

10 Joshua Gamson, “Messages of Exclusion: Gender, Movements, and Symbolic Boundaries,” *Gender & Society* 11 (1997): 179–80.

11 Omar Lizardo and Sara Skiles, “Cultural Consumption in the Fine and Popular Arts Realms,” *Sociology Compass* 2 (2008): 498.

12 Josée Johnston and Shyon Baumann, “Democracy versus Distinction: A Study of Omnivorousness in Gourmet Food Writing,” *American Journal of Sociology* 113 (2007): 172.

13 Ibid., 173.

14 Thorstein Veblen, *The Theory of the Leisure Class* (New York: Penguin, 1994). As distinctions between social classes were becoming more visual evident, Veblen coined the term “conspicuous consumption” to highlight the ways that luxurious goods and services, with little to no functional utility, were used to show off one’s social status and position at the turn of the twentieth century.

15 A similar argument can be made about other defining social attributes like race, ethnicity, and sexuality.

16 Alan Warde and Lydia Martens, “The Prawn Cocktail Ritual,” in *Consuming Passions: Food in the Age of Anxiety*, ed. Sian Griffiths and Jennifer Wallace (London: Mandolin, 1998), 120.

17 It is worth noting that in April 2018 the Brewers Association announced their first “Diversity Ambassador,” J. Nikol Jackson-Beckham. She wrote her dissertation on craft beer and has run a blog titled “The Unbearable Whiteness of Brewing” since 2012. If they amount to more than simple PR moves, the creation of the position and appointment of Jackson-Beckham seem like steps in the right direction toward greater gender, sexuality, and racial inclusivity.

18 The title of this section is a whimsical and metaphorical nod to Candace West and Don Zimmerman’s seminal article “Doing Gender.” They show “gender” differences are not natural or essential categories but are, rather, socially constructed and performed during interactions. As such, gender is an accomplishment rather than a given and is therefore malleable across and between social contexts. Such an understanding of gender is important for recognizing the ways that scene participants actively either enact or dismantle stereotypical notions and ideals of masculinity and femininity. Candace West and Don H. Zimmerman, “Doing Gender,” *Gender & Society* 1 (1987): 125–51.

19 Josh Noel, “Does Craft Beer Have a Sexism Problem? Binny’s Rejects Happy Ending,” *Chicago Tribune*, March 26, 2015.

20 Helana Darwin, "Omnivorous Masculinity: Gender Capital and Cultural Legitimacy in Craft Beer Culture," *Social Currents* 5 (2018): 302.

21 Patrick E. McGovern, *Uncorking the Past: The Quest for Wine, Beer, and Other Alcoholic Beverages* (Berkeley: University of California Press, 2009), 69.

22 Despite perpetuating a heteronormative sexist culture that affects and infects both Las Vegas and craft beer in Las Vegas and beyond, Rich Johnson, the head brewer of Sin City Brewing, seems to call upon craft's democratic ideology in an op-ed he penned as guest writer for Robin Leach's regular column in the *Las Vegas Sun* in 2014: "I've been brewing beer for 25 years, since the first wave of the craft revolution. Craft beer in Las Vegas initially struggled to gain traction, as most restaurants and bars cared more about catering to the masses with a well-known brand label outside the bottle rather than the content inside. But as the public began to take notice of what craft beer had to offer through its variety of flavors and styles, so did the people selling it. . . . It's been thrilling to see all demographics begin to engage with beer and even more exciting for me to come up with five styles of Sin City beer (and that's not even counting our rotating seasonal brew) to accommodate these new audiences. One factor that really contributed to the craft beer boom in Las Vegas was the emergence of the city as a culinary destination thanks to celebrated chefs opening restaurants all across the Strip. Additionally, I credit the change in the environmentalism movement that's swept the nation and encouraged people to support local food and beverage businesses." Rich Johnson, "Las Vegas' Craft Beer Scene Is on the Rise," *Las Vegas Sun*, July 10, 2014.

23 "A Modest Proposal: No More Tarts, Devil Chicks, or Mermaids," *Pour Curator*, June 25, 2011, www.pourcurator.com.

24 As I was told by three of the core five members of Banger Brewing, Nick Fischella, Roberto Mendoza, and Eddie Quiogue, the name "Banger" is derived from head brewer Michael Beaman's nickname that was bestowed upon him when he worked in the kitchen of a high-end restaurant on the Strip; because of his large stature, he couldn't move throughout the close quarters without banging into the pots, pans, and food ready to be served.

25 Pink Boots is an acronym: Passion, Integrity & Inspiration, Networking, Knowledge, Beer & Brewing, Opportunity, Open Exchange of Ideas, Teach, Success.

26 Pierre Bourdieu, *Distinction: A Social Critique of the Judgement of Taste* (Cambridge, MA: Harvard University Press, 1984), 176–78.

27 Hunters actively seek out rare limited-release beers, often by traveling to breweries; mules are those who find out-of-market or rare beers and bring them back to their home territory; and traders exchange beers with others across geographical regions. All three social actors and their corresponding practices complicate, and paradoxically reinforce, the relationship between the local and translocal scenes.

28 Igor Kopytoff, "The Cultural Biography of Things: Commoditization as Process," in *The Social Life of Things: Commodities in Cultural Perspective*, ed. Arjun Appadurai (Cambridge: Cambridge University Press, 1988).
29 Frederick F. Wherry, "The Social Characterizations of Price: The Fool, the Faithful, the Frivolous, and the Frugal," *Sociological Theory* 26 (2008): 377.
30 In 2013, hoarding was listed as its own discrete disorder in the fifth edition of the *Diagnostic and Statistical Manual of Mental Disorders* (*DSM*-5).
31 Russell Belk, *Collecting in a Consumer Society* (New York: Routledge, 1995), 1.
32 Colin Jerolmack and Iddo Tavory, "Molds and Totems: Nonhumans and the Constitution of the Social Self," *Sociological Theory* 32 (2014): 74.
33 Colin Campbell, "The Craft Consumer: Culture, Craft, and Consumption in a Postmodern Society," *Journal of Consumer Culture* 5 (2005): 34.
34 Chris Colin, "Rate This Article: What's Wrong with the Culture of Critique," *Wired*, July 2011. The roles of critics as gatekeepers, cultural authorities, and tastemakers have been well documented. Less is known about the influence and effect of common evaluations of cultural products. Such evaluations have become a part of everyday life for the digitally aware looking for a place to eat, a movie to watch, or a lawn mower to buy. See Denise D. Bielby and William T. Bielby, "Audience Aesthetics and Popular Culture," in *Matters of Culture: Cultural Sociology in Practice*, ed. Roger Friedland and John Mohr (Cambridge: Cambridge University Press, 2004); Phillip Vannini, "The Meanings of a Star: Interpreting Music Fans' Reviews," *Symbolic Interaction* 27 (2004): 47–69; Nancy Weiss Hanrahan, "If the People Like It, It Must Be Good: Criticism, Democracy and the Culture of Consensus," *Cultural Sociology* 7 (2013): 73–85; and Marc Verboord, "The Impact of Peer-Produced Criticism on Cultural Evaluation: A Multilevel Analysis of Discourse Employment in Online and Offline Film Reviews," *New Media & Society* 16 (2014): 921–40.
35 Robert E. Stebbins, *Serious Leisure: A Perspective for Our Time* (New Brunswick, NJ: Transaction, 2015), 13.
36 Ibid., 18.
37 Georg Simmel, "The Concept and Tragedy of Culture," in *Simmel on Culture: Selected Writings*, ed. David Frisby and Mike Featherstone (London: SAGE, 1997), 57.

CHAPTER 5: #CRAFTBEER

1 In June 2018, there were one billion Instagram users, with about a quarter who use the app daily.
2 Nina Eliasoph and Paul Lichterman, "Culture in Interaction," *American Journal of Sociology* 108 (2003): 738.
3 John Irwin, *Scenes* (Beverly Hills, CA: SAGE, 1977), 31.
4 Ibid., 31.
5 Though the leap from the Protestant Reformation to the promotion of independent rock and punk music might seem like one of faith or desperation, but as

radical practices they share a similar form regardless of content or expansive effect. For what still stands as the greatest articulation of influence of the Protestant Reformation on the modern world, see Max Weber, *The Protestant Ethic and the Spirit of Capitalism* (New York: Scribner, 1958). For the influence of zines—specifically fan-generated self-published magazines—on music scenes and contemporary culture, see James A. Hodgkinson, "The Fanzine Discourse over Post Rock" and Kristin Schilt, "'Riot Grrrl Is . . .': Contestation over Meaning in a Music Scene," both in *Music Scenes: Local, Translocal, and Virtual*, ed. Andy Bennett and Richard A. Peterson (Nashville: Vanderbilt University Press, 2004); William Ryan Force, "Consumption Styles and the Fluid Complexity of Punk Authenticity," *Symbolic Interaction* 32 (2009): 289–309; and Janice Radway, "Girl Zine Networks, Underground Itineraries, and Riot Grrrl History: Making Sense of the Struggle for New Social Forms in the 1990s and Beyond," *Journal of American Studies* 50 (2016): 1–31.

6 See Manuel Castells, *Networks of Outrage and Hope: Social Movements in the Internet Age* (Malden, MA: Polity Press, 2012).

7 Angela Cora Garcia, Alecea I. Standlee, Jennifer Bechkoff, and Yan Cui, "Ethnographic Approaches to the Internet and Computer-Mediated Communication," *Journal of Contemporary Ethnography* 38 (2009): 38–39.

8 Erving Goffman, *Interaction Ritual: Essays in Face to Face Behavior* (New York: Pantheon Books, 1967), 11–12.

9 Erving Goffman, *Gender Advertisements* (New York: Harper & Row, 1979), 10.

10 See Susan Murray, "Digital Images, Photo-Sharing, and Our Shifting Notions of Everyday Aesthetics," *Journal of Visual Culture* 7 (2008): 147–63.

11 Irwin, *Scenes*, 199.

12 Carrie Cummings, "Craft Beer Drinkers Consult Their Phones before Opening Their Wallets," *AdWeek*, June 19, 2016, www.adweek.com.

13 In 2017, longtime craft beer gourmand and Brooklyn Brewery brewmaster Garrett Oliver controversially quipped that New England–style hazy IPAs are "the first beer style based around Instagram culture and social media."

14 Detlev Zwick, Samuel K. Bonsu, and Aron Darmody, "Putting Consumers to Work: Co-creation and New Marketing Govern-Mentality," *Journal of Consumer Culture* 8 (2008): 163–96.

15 The fledgling record store owned and operated by passionate fans is a stark and ubiquitous example of this. Nick Hornby's *High Fidelity* and the John Cusack–starring movie based on it provide a peek inside a fictitious example. For an example of a real-life record store in Ybor City, Florida, see Timothy A. Simpson, "Streets, Sidewalks, Stores, and Stories: Narrative and Uses of Urban Space," *Journal of Contemporary Ethnography* 29 (2000): 692–716.

16 See Megan Halpern and Lee Humphreys, "Iphoneography as an Emergent Art World," *New Media & Society* 18 (2016): 62–81.

17 See Holly Kruse, "Local Identity and Independent Music Scenes, Online and Off," *Popular Music and Society* 33 (2010): 625–39.

18 Christine Harold, *Ourspace: Resisting the Corporate Control of Culture* (Minneapolis: University of Minnesota Press, 2007), 34–40.

19 Marjorie D. Kibby, "Home on the Page: A Virtual Place of Music Community," *Popular Music* 19 (2000): 95.

20 @louiebaton is an American Instagrammer who warns his over thirty-four thousand followers that "by tapping Follow/Like you acknowledge that Lego and Beer pictures paired with hastily written summaries are the cut of your jib." His account is packed with crude jokes and obnoxious puns, and he has paired over three thousand craft beers with Lego figures, using the figures and various Lego props to enact the name, visual, or style of the beer and its label.

21 Paul E. Willis, *Common Culture: Symbolic Work at Play in the Everyday Cultures of the Young* (Buckingham, UK: Open University Press, 1990), 12.

22 Ibid., 22.

23 Of note, Budweiser's behemoth parent company AB InBev bought a minority share of ratebeer.com in June 2017. Within a few days Dogfish Head and Sixpoint breweries asked ratebeer.com to remove any ratings of their beer from the site. A number of other craft breweries, including Belgium's world-renowned Cantillon, followed suit soon after.

24 Loïc Wacquant, "For a Sociology of Flesh and Blood," *Qualitative Sociology* 38 (2015): 2, 4.

25 Sarah Pink and Larissa Hjorth, "Emplaced Cartographies: Reconceptualising Camera Phone Practices in an Age of Locative Media," *Media International Australia* 145 (2012): 147.

26 Sherry Turkle, *Life on the Screen: Identity in the Age of the Internet* (New York: Simon & Schuster, 1995).

27 Sociologist Jeffrey Kidder comes to a similar conclusion about the "emplacement of virtual worlds" in his study of parkour practitioners' use of both physical places and virtual spaces. Jeffrey L. Kidder, "Parkour, the Affective Appropriation of Urban Space, and the Real/Virtual Dialectic," *City & Community* 11 (2012): 229–53. Sociologist Christine Hine takes these notions further to show how they have important methodological implications and offers ethnographic strategies for studying virtual field sites. Christine Hine, *Ethnography for the Internet: Embedded, Embodied, and Everyday* (London: Bloomsbury, 2015).

28 Anselm L. Strauss, *Negotiations: Varieties, Contexts, Processes, and Social Order* (San Francisco: Jossey-Bass, 1978); David R. Maines, "In Search of Mesostructure: Studies in the Negotiated Order," *Urban Life* 11 (1982): 267–79; Gary Alan Fine, "The Sociology of the Local: Action and Its Publics," *Sociological Theory* 28 (2010): 355–76.

29 Lyn H. Lofland, *The Public Realm: Exploring the City's Quintessential Social Territory* (New York: Aldine de Gruyter, 1998), 10.

30 See Lee Humphreys, "Mobile Social Networks and Urban Public Space," *New Media & Society* 12 (2010): 763–78.

31 Wicked Weed's sour ales, as well as their IPAs and "dessert" stouts, were once highly coveted but lost their luster, and trade value, after AB InBev bought the brewery in May 2017. After a quick four-year run to the top of the craft beer food chain, Wicked Weed's reputation plummeted. Many Instagrammers posted pics of pouring Wicked Weed beers into their sinks (#drainpour) or justifying drinking their beers they acquired pre-"sellout." Bars and taprooms showed similar pics. And the vast majority of craft breweries quickly pulled out of Wicked Weed's upcoming festival.

32 Antoine Hennion, "Those Things That Hold Us Together: Taste and Sociology," *Cultural Sociology* 1 (2007): 105.

33 Donileen R. Loseke, "The Study of Identity as Cultural, Institutional, Organizational, and Personal Narratives: Theoretical and Empirical Integrations," *Sociological Quarterly* 48 (2007): 673.

34 Georg Simmel, "The Philosophy of Fashion," in *Simmel on Culture: Selected Writings*, ed. David Frisby and Mike Featherstone (London: SAGE, 1997), 188.

35 Ibid., 188.

36 Sociologist Erving Goffman writes that "the general notion that people make a presentation of themselves to others is hardly novel; what ought to be stressed . . . is that the very structure of the self can be seen in terms of how people arrange for such performances." The idea can easily be extended beyond individuals to organizations or groups (like a brewery) and from face-to-face interactions to virtual performances. Erving Goffman, *The Presentation of Self in Everyday Life* (Garden City, NY: Doubleday, 1959), 252.

37 Richard Chalfen, "Snapshots 'R' Us: The Evidentiary Problematic of Home Media," *Visual Studies* 17 (2002): 147.

38 W. J. T. Mitchell, *What Do Pictures Want? The Lives and Loves of Images* (Chicago: University of Chicago Press, 2005), 9.

39 As stereotypical as the connection between bearded men and craft beer might be, it gains empirical support with the vast number of Instagram accounts that playfully fuse the terms together, such as @beerdbrewing, @beerdedbeing, or even @jenniferthebeerdedlady. For those who can't get enough of craft beer and facial hair, see the "well-groomed collection of craft beer labels featuring beards, sideburns, and moustaches" in *The Book of Craft Beerds* by Fred Abercrombie, with photography and design by Tyler Warrender and David Hodges (Petaluma, CA: Abercrombie + Alchemy, 2012).

40 Chris's "brand" has grown so much through social media that he's collaborated with a few breweries on "limited release" beers and, in 2017, curated his first Beer Zombies Festival in Las Vegas consisting of locally brewed, locally available, and out-of-market beers.

41 Phillip Vannini, Dennis Waskul, and Simon Gottschalk, *The Senses in Self, Society, and Culture: A Sociology of the Senses* (New York: Routledge, 2014), 162.

42 Antoine Hennion, "The Pragmatics of Taste," in *The Blackwell Companion to the Sociology of Culture*, ed. Mark D. Jacobs and Nancy Weiss Hanrahan (Malden, MA: Blackwell, 2005), 137.
43 Eva Illouz, "Emotions, Imagination and Consumption: A New Research Agenda," *Journal of Consumer Culture* 9 (2009): 394–97.
44 Jeffrey C. Alexander, "Iconic Consciousness: The Material Feeling of Meaning," *Thesis Eleven* 103 (2010): 11.

CHAPTER 6: BEAUTY IN THE EYES OF THE BEER HOLDER

1 See Christian Smith, *Moral, Believing Animals: Human Personhood and Culture* (Oxford: Oxford University Press, 2003).
2 Lucia Ruggerone and Neil Jenkings, "Talking about Beauty: A Study of Everyday Aesthetics among Low Income Citizens of Milan," *Symbolic Interaction* 38 (2015): 394.
3 Lyn H. Lofland, *The Public Realm: Exploring the City's Quintessential Social Territory* (New York: Aldine de Gruyter, 1998), 66.
4 Mead's seminal analytical construction of a dualistic self that consists of an active and individualized "I" and a more passive and socialized "me" remains a key heuristic for understanding how individuals interpret the world instead of merely just reacting to it. George Herbert Mead, *Mind, Self, and Society: From the Standpoint of a Social Behaviorist* (Chicago: University of Chicago Press, 1934).
5 Michael Ian Borer and Tyler S. Schafer, "Culture War Confessionals: Conflicting Accounts of Christianity, Violence, and Mixed Martial Arts," *Journal of Media and Religion* 10 (2011): 168.
6 The move to pay attention to the foreground over the background was initiated by sociologist Jack Katz in his study of the seductive elements of crimes. See Jack Katz, *Seductions of Crime: Moral and Sensual Attractions in Doing Evil* (New York: Basic Books, 2008).
7 Claudio E. Benzecry, "Becoming a Fan: On the Seductions of Opera," *Qualitative Sociology* 32 (2009): 137n9.
8 Turning-point moments in people's lives are often connected to objects they choose to purchase and, as sociologist Ian Woodward found, display in their homes. And people often use objects as part of the narratives they tell about themselves and those pivotal moments. This was indeed the case with many craft beer drinkers who openly acknowledged the roles specific craft beer played in changing their respective aesthetic dispositions. Moreover, Woodward notes that the "investigation of consumption processes at the level of the object—notably the 'epiphany object'—has the advantage of directing attention to the meaning and consequence of the thing being consumed, rather than a preoccupation with theoretical, ideological questions concerning the viability and authenticity of consumer practices." As such, we can then focus on how meaning is constructed

rather than merely given. Ian Woodward, "Domestic Objects and the Taste Epiphany: A Resource for Consumption Methodology," *Journal of Material Culture* 6 (2001): 115–36.

9 Antoine Hennion, "Those Things That Hold Us Together: Taste and Sociology," *Cultural Sociology* 1 (2007): 101.

10 Iddo Tavory and Daniel Winchester, "Experiential Careers: The Routinization and De-routinization of Religious Life," *Theory and Society* 41 (2012): 369. I support their claim that "reducing 'experience' to 'talk about experience' ignores the enculturation of the body and circumscribes ethnography to the analysis of situational talk." Trying to get as close as possible to the point or moment of experience is a difficult yet worthwhile task for ethnographers interested in the ways that people internalize and live through various social worlds and scenes.

11 Though his insights about scenes as pathways to re-enchantment are invaluable, Irwin nevertheless spends the majority of his pages discussing the, perhaps inevitable, downfall of various scenes at the time of his writing in the late 1970s. John Irwin, *Scenes* (Beverly Hills, CA: SAGE, 1977).

12 Hennion, "Those Things That Hold Us Together," 109.

13 Barry Shank, *Dissonant Identities: The Rock 'N' Roll Scene in Austin, Texas* (Hanover, NH: Wesleyan University Press, 1994), 131.

14 Hennion, "Those Things That Hold Us Together," 108.

15 Antoine Hennion, "The Pragmatics of Taste," in *The Blackwell Companion to the Sociology of Culture*, ed. Mark D. Jacobs and Nancy Weiss Hanrahan (Malden, MA: Blackwell, 2005), 138.

16 See Dennis D. Waskul and Phillip Vannini, "Smell, Odor, and Somatic Work: Sense-Making and Sensory Management," *Social Psychology Quarterly* 71 (2008): 53–71.

17 See Lyn H. Lofland, *A World of Strangers: Order and Action in Urban Public Space* (Prospect Hills, IL: Waveland Press, 1973), chap. 5.

18 Howard S. Becker, "Becoming a Marihuana User," *American Journal of Sociology* 59 (1953): 235.

19 Claudio E. Benzecry, *The Opera Fanatic: Ethnography of an Obsession* (Chicago: University of Chicago Press, 2011), 66.

20 Thomas DeGloma, *Seeing the Light: The Social Logic of Personal Discovery* (Chicago: University of Chicago Press, 2014), 29.

21 Herbert J. Gans, *Popular Culture & High Culture: An Analysis and Evaluation of Taste* (New York: Basic Books, 1999), 4.

22 DeGloma, *Seeing the Light*, 9.

23 Ibid., 13–14.

24 Antoine Hennion, "Music Lovers: Taste as Performance," *Theory, Culture & Society* 18 (2001): 3.

25 DeGloma, *Seeing the Light*, 28–29.

26 Hennion, "Those Things That Hold Us Together," 103.

27 Bruno Latour, *Reassembling the Social: An Introduction to Actor-Network-Theory* (Oxford: Oxford University Press, 2005), 72.
28 Steven M. Schnell, "Deliberate Identities: Becoming Local in America in a Global Age," *Journal of Cultural Geography* 30 (2013): 57–60.
29 Erving Goffman, *Frame Analysis: An Essay on the Organization of Experience* (Cambridge, MA: Harvard University Press, 1974), 504.
30 Rex J. Rowley, "Religion in Sin City," *Geographical Review* 102 (2012): 76–92.
31 William Bostwick, *The Brewer's Tale: A History of the World according to Beer* (New York: Norton, 2014). A beer writer by trade, Bostwick not only tells the history of brewing but also shows it by interviewing contemporary brewers to help him figure out how to brew beers from each distinctive historical period, ranging from Babylonian honey ales to machine-produced macro lagers.
32 See David Wright, *Understanding Cultural Taste: Sensation, Skill, and Sensibility* (New York: Palgrave Macmillan, 2015).
33 As sociologist Meredith McGuire notes in her discussion of gardening and dancing, "Bodies matter because humans are not disembodied spirits." Meredith McGuire, "Embodied Practices: Negotiation and Resistance," in *Everyday Religion: Observing Modern Religious Lives*, ed. Nancy T. Ammerman (Oxford: Oxford University Press, 2007), 198.
34 Josée Johnston and Shyon Baumann, *Foodies: Democracy and Distinction in the Gourmet Foodscape* (New York: Routledge, 2014), 206.
35 Ibid., 207.
36 Maurice Merleau-Ponty, *Phenomenology of Perception* (London: Routledge, 1962), 213.
37 Hennion, "Music Lovers," 1.
38 Ibid., 12.
39 Hennion, "Those Things That Hold Us Together," 105.
40 Johnston and Baumann, *Foodies*, 52. Of note, their claims about snobbery and pretentiousness become a bit more muted when they move from analyzing gourmet food magazines to sitting with and interviewing self-described foodies.
41 See Stan Hieronymus, "How Craft Became Craft," *All About Beer*, March 1, 2015, http://allaboutbeer.com.
42 Like many of the counter workers at in-store butcheries, cocktail bartenders, and neo-traditional barbers that sociologist Richard Ocejo studied, Steve engages in "service teaching." Ocejo notes that "service teaching" is about providing information and, in turn, democratically spreading omnivorous tastes. Richard E. Ocejo, *Masters of Craft: Old Jobs in the New Urban Economy* (Princeton, NJ: Princeton University Press, 2017), 193, 202.
43 Erving Goffman, *Encounters: Two Studies in the Sociology of Interaction* (Indianapolis: Bobbs-Merrill, 1961), 7.
44 Ibid., 18.
45 Ibid., 10–11.

46 See Gary Alan Fine, "Group Culture and the Interaction Order: Local Sociology on the Meso-Level," *Annual Review of Sociology* 38 (2012): 159–79.
47 Merleau-Ponty, *Phenomenology of Perception*, 144.
48 Heather Paxson, "The 'Art' and 'Science' of Handcrafting Cheese in the United States," *Endeavour* 35 (2011): 116–24; Erin O'Connor, "Embodied Knowledge: The Experience of Meaning and the Struggle towards Proficiency in Glassblowing," *Ethnography* 6 (2005): 183–204; and Richard E. Ocejo, "At Your Service: The Meanings and Practices of Contemporary Bartenders," *European Journal of Cultural Studies* 15 (2012): 642–58.
49 It's worth noting that over the course of human existence, over vast time periods and locations, the commodification of beer is a relatively recent phenomenon. Before the industrial era, all beer was, in today's terms, homebrewed.
50 Nearly all craft breweries trace their roots to homebrewing, which has in turn created market demand and aesthetic desire for locally brewed elixirs. Glenn R. Carroll and Anand Swaminathan, "Why the Microbrewery Movement? Organizational Dynamics of Resource Partitioning in the U.S. Brewing Industry," *American Journal of Sociology* 106 (2000): 731.
51 See Diane M. Rodgers and Ryan Taves, "The Epistemic Culture of Homebrewers and Microbrewers," *Sociological Spectrum* 37 (2017): 127–48.
52 Sociologist Robert Stebbins notes that even when hobbies turn into professional careers, they at some point must enter through the realm of "serious leisure." Robert E. Stebbins, *Serious Leisure: A Perspective for Our Time* (New Brunswick, NJ: Transaction, 2015), 39.
53 Charlie Papazian, *The Complete Joy of Homebrewing*, 4th ed. (New York: William Morrow, 2014).
54 Sarah Feldberg, "Calling All Vegas Homebrewers: Craft Beer Community Is Catching Up Thanks to One Local Shop," *Las Vegas Weekly*, October 25, 2012.
55 Former U Bottle It employee Grant Heuer worked as an assistant brewer at local Big Dog's then left Las Vegas to take a brewing position at Refuge in Temecula, California, and then at Indian Joe in Vista, California, as the head brewer. Another U Bottle It employee who brewed some of the first sour beers in the valley moved to Michigan to take a position with the well-regarded sour and wild beer brewery Jolly Pumpkin Artisan Ales.
56 For extended discussions of the connections between the craft ethos and local economies, see Richard Lloyd, *Neo-Bohemia: Art and Commerce in the Postindustrial City* (New York: Routledge, 2005); Charles Heying, ed., *Brew to Bikes: Portland's Artisan Economy* (Portland, OR: Ooligan Press, 2010); Susan Luckman, *Craft and the Creative Economy* (New York: Palgrave Macmillan, 2015); and Ocejo, *Masters of Craft*.
57 Colin Campbell, "The Craft Consumer: Culture, Craft, and Consumption in a Postmodern Society," *Journal of Consumer Culture* 5 (2005): 39.

58 Pierre Bourdieu introduced the term "cultural intermediaries" to define a new class of "occupations involving presentation and representation (sales, marketing, advertising, public relations, fashion, decoration, and so forth) and in all the institutions providing symbolic goods and services." Pierre Bourdieu, *Distinction: A Social Critique of the Judgement of Taste* (Cambridge, MA: Harvard University Press, 1984), 359.

59 Heather Jamerson, "Intoxicators, Educators, and Gatekeepers: The Enactment of Symbolic Boundaries in Napa Valley Wineries," *Poetics* 37 (2009): 90.

60 Randy Mosher, *Tasting Beer: An Insider's Guide to the World's Greatest Drink* (North Adams, MA: Storey, 2009).

61 Waskul and Vannini, "Smell, Odor, and Somatic Work," 55.

62 See Latour, *Reassembling the Social* as well as Ignacio Farías and Thomas Bender, eds., *Urban Assemblages: How Actor-Network Theory Changes Urban Studies* (New York: Routledge, 2012).

63 Joseph A. Schumpeter, *The Theory of Economic Development* (Cambridge, MA: Harvard University Press, 1934).

64 Entrepreneurialism, however, can take other forms. Researchers have tried to delineate conventional, institutional, social, and cultural entrepreneurship in order to understand their distinct qualities, missions, visions, and organizational structures and tensions. See Peter A. Dacin, M. Tina Dacin, and Margaret Matear, "Social Entrepreneurship: Why We Don't Need a New Theory and How We Move Forward from Here," *Academy of Management Perspectives* 24 (2010): 37–57.

65 Paul DiMaggio, "Cultural Entrepreneurship in Nineteenth-Century Boston: The Creation of an Organizational Base for High Culture in America," *Media, Culture & Society* 4 (1982): 33–50; Victoria Johnson, "What Is Organizational Imprinting? Cultural Entrepreneurship in the Founding of the Paris Opera," *American Journal of Sociology* 113 (2007): 97–127; and Kerry Dobransky and Gary Alan Fine, "The Native in the Garden: Floral Politics and Cultural Entrepreneurs," *Sociological Forum* 21 (2006): 559–85.

66 See Sharon Zukin, *Naked City: The Death and Life of Authentic Urban Places* (Oxford: Oxford University Press, 2009), and Jerome Krase, *Seeing Cities Change: Local Culture and Class* (Aldershot, UK: Ashgate, 2012).

67 Of note, Grazian prefers the term "cultural producers," but those involved in many facets of "staging" nightlife activities clearly engage in entrepreneurship. David Grazian, *On the Make: The Hustle of Urban Nightlife* (Chicago: University of Chicago Press, 2008), 30.

68 Richard Swedberg, "The Cultural Entrepreneur and the Creative Industries: Beginning in Vienna," *Journal of Cultural Economics* 30 (2006): 260, emphasis added.

69 Anthropologist Sarah Pink explicitly connects the senses, and thereby aesthetics, to "place-making," Sarah Pink, "An Urban Tour: The Sensory Sociality of Ethnographic Place-Making," *Ethnography* 9 (2008): 175–96. For other takes on

"place-making" as a significant cultural practice for local urban cultures, see Krista E. Paulsen, "Making Character Concrete: Empirical Strategies for Studying Place Distinction," *City & Community* 3 (2004): 243–62, and Jonathan R. Wynn, *Music/City: American Festivals and Placemaking in Austin, Nashville, and Newport* (Chicago: University of Chicago Press, 2015).

70 Alison E. Feeney, "Cultural Heritage, Sustainable Development, and the Impacts of Craft Breweries in Pennsylvania," *City, Culture and Society* 9 (2017): 21–30.

71 Richard Sennett, *The Craftsman* (New Haven, CT: Yale University Press, 2008), 117.

72 Lofland, *Public Realm*, 78.

73 Paul E. Willis, *Common Culture: Symbolic Work at Play in the Everyday Cultures of the Young* (Buckingham, UK: Open University Press, 1990).

74 Daniel Aaron Silver and Terry Nichols Clark, *Scenescapes: How Qualities of Place Shape Social Life* (Chicago: University of Chicago Press, 2016), 31.

CONCLUSION

1 For a useful discussion of collective memory and trauma, see the last section of Jeffrey K. Olick, "Collective Memory: The Two Cultures," *Sociological Theory* 17 (1999): 343–45.

2 Kai Erikson, "Notes on Trauma and Community," *American Imago* 48 (1991): 460.

3 In an "out-of-the-ashes"-type moment that seems too coincidental to be real, the National Hockey League's Vegas Golden Knights played their first home game a little over a week after the shooting. The start of the city's first professional sports team's inaugural season couldn't have come at a better time—a city in need of healing.

4 See Colin Jerolmack and Iddo Tavory, "Molds and Totems: Nonhumans and the Constitution of the Social Self," *Sociological Theory* 32 (2014): 64–77.

5 In this way, the object, the people who made it, the people who made the ingredients needed to make it, the people who served it, and the people who consumed it create a "double bind" whereby humans depend "on things that depend on humans." Ian Hodder, "The Entanglement of Humans and Things: A Long-Term View," *New Literary History* 45 (2014): 20. For a further in-depth exploration and discussion of the entanglements of people, places, and things, see Tim Ingold, "Bindings against Boundaries: Entanglements of Life in an Open World," *Environment and Planning A* 40 (2008): 1796–810.

6 Lyn H. Lofland, *The Public Realm: Exploring the City's Quintessential Social Territory* (New York: Aldine de Gruyter, 1998).

7 See Allison Hayes-Conroy and Jessica Hayes-Conroy, "Taking Back Taste: Feminism, Food, and Visceral Politics," *Gender, Place & Culture* 15 (2008): 461–73.

8 In her thorough explication of the "social construction of social problems" approach, sociologist Donileen Loseke notes that "a claim is any verbal, visual, or behavioral statement that seeks to persuade audience members to define a

condition as a social problem." I have tried to extend that argument beyond the realm of social problems toward the realms of culture and aesthetics whereby claims aren't only *reactive* but can also be *affirmative* of beliefs, preferences, and social conditions. Donileen Loseke, *Thinking about Social Problems: An Introduction to Constructionist Perspectives* (New Brunswick, NJ: Transaction, 2003), 26.

9 Examining the crafted realms of bartending, small-batch distilling, whole-animal butchery, and revitalized men's barbershops, sociologist Richard Ocejo found a devotion to an "ethos of craft" that sustained many of those engaged in these occupations. Consumers of their work have at least a minimal connection to such an ethos, and sometimes a considerable connection it, as I've uncovered here. See Richard E. Ocejo, *Masters of Craft: Old Jobs in the New Urban Economy* (Princeton, NJ: Princeton University Press, 2017).

10 Sociologist Amanda Koontz notes that authentication—a process by which people make claims about what is and is not authentic—is a means for "otherizing" competitors as well as a means for "traditionalizing" modes of production and connections to nostalgic histories. See Amanda Koontz, "Constructing Authenticity: A Review of Trends and Influences in the Process of Authentication in Consumption," *Sociology Compass* 4 (2010): 977–88. Perhaps because cities are inevitably *built* (i.e., unnatural) environments, authenticity has emerged as a popular subject of inquiry. Urban sociologists interested in the lived experiences and cultures of cities have provided analyses of claims about authenticity and their consequences (from collective sentimentality to manipulative hip desires) across multiple geographical areas and scenes. See, for example, Michael Ian Borer, *Faithful to Fenway: Believing in Boston, Baseball, and America's Most Beloved Ballpark* (New York: New York University Press, 2008); Japonica Brown-Saracino, *A Neighborhood That Never Changes: Gentrification, Social Preservation, and the Search for Authenticity* (Chicago: University of Chicago Press, 2010); Kevin Fox Gotham, *Authentic New Orleans: Tourism, Culture, and Race in the Big Easy* (New York: New York University Press, 2007); David Grazian, *Blue Chicago: The Search for Authenticity in Urban Blues Clubs* (Chicago: University of Chicago Press, 2003); David Grazian, *On the Make: The Hustle of Urban Nightlife* (Chicago: University of Chicago Press, 2008); Richard Lloyd, *Neo-Bohemia: Art and Commerce in the Postindustrial City* (New York: Routledge, 2005); Ocejo, *Masters of Craft*; and Sharon Zukin, *Naked City: The Death and Life of Authentic Urban Places* (Oxford: Oxford University Press, 2009).

11 Michele Hardy, "Feminism, Crafts, and Knowledge," in *Objects and Meaning: New Perspectives on Art and Craft*, ed. M. Anna Fariello and Paula Owen (Oxford: Scarecrow Press, 2005), 180.

12 Steven M. Schnell and Joseph F. Reese, "Microbreweries as Tools of Local Identity," *Journal of Cultural Geography* 21 (2003): 46.

13 Gary Alan Fine and Ugo Corte, "Group Pleasures: Collaborative Commitments, Shared Narrative, and the Sociology of Fun," *Sociological Theory* 35 (2017): 67–68.
14 Michel Maffesoli, *The Time of the Tribes: The Decline of Individualism in Mass Society* (London: SAGE, 1996), 86–88.
15 On the concept of "group style"—which is useful for small groups but has yet to be fully examined for larger and more amorphous collectivities—see Nina Eliasoph and Paul Lichterman, "Culture in Interaction," *American Journal of Sociology* 108 (2003): 735–94.
16 John A. Hall and Charles Lindholm, *Is America Breaking Apart?* (Princeton, NJ: Princeton University Press, 2001), 96–97.
17 Sociologist Gary Alan Fine has been the most ardent and prolific supporter of group-level analyses for the past several decades. For good reason, a slew of scholars have followed his lead by studying groups at the meso level of analysis between faceless social structures and individualized interactions. Focusing on scenes, however, provides a means for showing how those small groups are connected to other groups either in close proximity or not, adding an extra layer of complexity to the study of group life and urging analyses to be context dependent. For a good overview of group-level research, see Gary Alan Fine, "Group Culture and the Interaction Order: Local Sociology on the Meso-Level," *Annual Review of Sociology* 38 (2012): 159–79. Though my ideas about the importance of scenes for understanding city life have much in common with those of sociologists Daniel Aaron Silver and Terry Nichols Clark, especially the connections between scenes and cultural amenities, they are more interested in comparative studies across city scenes than in understanding the processes that construct, maintain, and reconstruct local cultures. Daniel Aaron Silver and Terry Nichols Clark, *Scenescapes: How Qualities of Place Shape Social Life* (Chicago: University of Chicago Press, 2016).
18 Michael Schudson, "How Culture Works: Perspectives from Media Studies on the Efficacy of Symbols," *Theory & Society* 18 (1989): 160–64.
19 Will Straw, "Some Things a Scene Might Be," *Cultural Studies* 29 (2015): 83.
20 Michael Ian Borer, "The Location of Culture: The Urban Culturalist Perspective," *City & Community* 5 (2006): 186–87.
21 John Irwin, *Scenes* (Beverly Hills, CA: SAGE, 1977), 194.
22 Émile Durkheim, *The Elementary Forms of Religious Life* (New York: Free Press, 1965), 476.

INDEX

ABOUT THE AUTHOR

Michael Ian Borer is Associate Professor of Sociology at the University of Nevada, Las Vegas, and the author of *Faithful to Fenway: Believing in Boston, Baseball, and America's Most Beloved Ballpark* and co-author of *Urban People and Places: The Sociology of Cities, Suburbs, and Towns.*